Finding Intentional Community

Finding Intentional Community

Your Journey Home

James Werning

RESOURCE *Publications* • Eugene, Oregon

FINDING INTENTIONAL COMMUNITY
Your Journey Home

Copyright © 2017 James Werning. All rights reserved. Except for brief quotations in critical publications or reviews, no part of this book may be reproduced in any manner without prior written permission from the publisher. Write: Permissions, Wipf and Stock Publishers, 199 W. 8th Ave., Suite 3, Eugene, OR 97401.

Resource Publications
An Imprint of Wipf and Stock Publishers
199 W. 8th Ave., Suite 3
Eugene, OR 97401

www.wipfandstock.com

PAPERBACK ISBN: 978-1-5326-1226-8
HARDCOVER ISBN: 978-1-5326-1228-2
EBOOK ISBN: 978-1-5326-1227-5

Manufactured in the U.S.A.   JULY 18, 2017

Scriptures taken from the Holy Bible, New International Version®, NIV®. Copyright © 1973, 1978, 1984, 2011 by Biblica, Inc.™ Used by permission of Zondervan. All rights reserved worldwide. www.zondervan.com. The "NIV" and "New International Version" are trademarks registered in the United States Patent and Trademark Office by Biblica, Inc.™

Scriptures marked KJV are taken from the Holy Bible, King James Version. Public Domain.

Scriptures marked God's Word translation taken from GOD'S WORD®, © 1995 God's Word to the Nations. Used by permission of Baker Publishing Group.

Scriptures marked NLT are taken from the Holy Bible, New Living Translation, copyright © 1996, 2004, 2015 by Tyndale House Foundation. Used by permission of Tyndale House Publishers Inc., Carol Stream, Illinois 60188. All rights reserved.

As I completed the last sentence of the last chapter of this book, I stopped and prayed for someone who needed to read this surprising conclusion.

(*Don't look ahead at that chapter. Let it unfold. It surprised even me!*)

Immediately, I saw a picture (in my mind's eye) of a man-made lake in a desert. This reservoir represents someone who is blessed, but feels isolated and alone. These final words in the book are like a small but explosive force that demolishes the dam. I saw the water gushing out of the reservoir, mingling with dozens of other streams and rivulets, turning the desert into a lush, green landscape. In the beautiful gardens that formed there, I saw friends and family working side by side, and children laughing and playing.

If you see yourself in this picture, then I dedicate this book to you. And as you turn each page . . . *prepare to demolish the dam!*

Contents

Chapter 1   The Journey Begins Here | 1

Chapter 2   A Brief Introduction to Community | 8

Chapter 3   Taking the Long Way Home | 12

Chapter 4   Background Information | 30

Chapter 5   Featured Communities | 34

    Alleluia Community | 37

    Bethany International | 46

    Brothers and Sisters of Charity | 56

    Church of the Sojourners | 67

    Dathouse | 76

    Good Works, Inc. | 88

    Hillside Fellowship | 98

    The Julian Project | 109

    Koinonia Farm | 119

    Life Mission Fellowship | 127

    Lotus House | 139

    Reba Place Fellowship | 147

    Riverbend Commons | 155

    Rutba House | 164

    The Simple Way | 173

    Susanna Wesley House | 182

    The Word of God | 195

Contents

Chapter 6   Surprising Discoveries about Intentional Communities | 205

Chapter 7   Down in the Dirt | 226

Postscript | 237

Appendix 1: Intentional Christian Community Associations | *243*

Appendix 2: Community Covenants | *247*

Intentional Christian Community Resources | *251*

Chapter 1

The Journey Begins Here

Hey.

I know you.

Weren't you on that hike the other day?

No, that wasn't it . . .

Oh, I remember now!

We used to go to church together. You know, back in . . .

Yeah, that's it . . .

Wow . . . What a flashback. It's great to see you again . . .

It *has* been a long time. What have you been up to? . . .

We had some great times back then. Remember hanging out with . . . Yeah, how could I forget? Do you still hear from . . . ?

Not me. I lost touch with all of them. So what brought you here? . . .

Me? I've been all over the map. But I feel like I'm settling in now. How about you? Do you plan to stay here awhile? . . .

Well, I'll be honest. I'm tired of moving. I'm sick of leaving friends behind. I miss some of those guys who I don't talk to anymore. Do you know what I mean? . . .

Then you might understand some of the *deeper* things I've been thinking about lately. I'd dump it on you, but you probably don't want to hear about . . .

Really? Well, okay then. This is going to sound like a fish saying, "I just discovered water," but let me begin by saying that I finally got *cars* figured out.

That's right: *automobiles.*

Stick with me, now.

Obviously, I always understood the great part about cars. When Henry Ford cranked up his assembly line, the world became much smaller. People began driving to jobs and places they couldn't walk to before. But "automobility," as they call it, made it possible for spouses, parents, and children to drive right out of their family's lives. It made it possible for the "Haves" to leave the "Have-Nots" in ghettos, rather than sticking around and trying to make the neighborhood a better place for everybody. It became easy for friends to leave friends behind . . . for people to run away from things they'd be better off facing.

And think about the church we used to go to. Remember how people would drive a half hour to church, work forty minutes in another direction, and take the kids to school and shop in totally different directions? Everybody was so busy driving all over the place.

People can't build decent friendships while spending so much time on the road. Not healthy friendships, in my opinion. That's one reason why I moved, because my friends didn't have much time for me. And of course, I didn't have much time for them either.

Besides, I was always drawn to the adventure of the open highway. After graduating from high school, that was my great escape. I tore up the West on my motorcycle. Of course, I was also running from the ghosts of my childhood.

I remember being at a laundromat way out in western Nebraska when a tall, red-faced, John Wayne-type character walked in. I secretly called him "Big Red." He was a talkative dude, and he told me about working in just about every state in the union. He was presently headed for Detroit.

"Is that your hometown?" I asked.

"No," Big Red said. Then turning his face to the horizon, he said in his big, deep voice, "I live where I lay my hat."

I chuckled, wondering what he was running from. But in all honesty, I wasn't much different from Big Red. I went out the door that day humming, "On the Road Again."

Until recently, I even took *pride* in my ability to pull up roots so easily. Doesn't the culture say that only losers stay put? You have to jump fast and far to grab the best opportunities, whether you're reaching for school, career, property, or fortune. You gotta keep moving. Don't get me going, or I'll start singing about how I plan to escape from this dead-end town called Troubleville.[1]

Now, I'm not saying that automobility is all bad. And it's obviously not the only factor contributing to cultural dysfunction.

But imagine our great-grandparents living within walking distance of their closest friends and family . . . for all of their lives. That lifestyle must have held a lot of challenges *and* blessings.

My ears perk up when people talk about living with long-term relationships, just like they did in the old days. I meet people who have lived in one house for decades, and it seems like I'm talking to someone from a black and white TV show.

"What's it like to live in the same place for so long?" I ask.

To them, of course, it's nothing special.

If they're surrounded by healthy relationships, I see the benefits they receive from being in a stable network of friends and family.

My spirit tells me that something about that permanence is good and true.

And I want it.

I feel as if connectedness and stability are forgotten treasures needing to be rediscovered today. But let's not get overly nostalgic about it. Lots of people in your great-grandparent's neighborhood felt trapped. If you had been there, I could definitely see you ducking behind your grandma's house to avoid some of the quirky characters.

Moreover, if you were to visit a tight-knit community today, haloed saints will not greet you and angels will not sing "hallelujah." Eventually, you'll discover real humans there with real human traits.

Just think about that church we used to attend. What if we had never moved away? I'm not mentioning any names, but I had issues with some of the people there. You did too, as I recall. What if we'd stayed put? What if we had been forced to work through those issues, rather than jumping ship and sailing out of their lives? What if we had achieved what it says in Psalm

---

1. Thanks to my good friend Nate Spencer! "Maybe someday I'll put my boots on and walk away from Troubleville." Search online for Nate Spencer's "All the Honey Sweet" album.

133, "How good and pleasant it is when brothers and sisters live together in harmony"?

This may sound pompous, but I'm gonna say it anyway: Some of my friends in that town would have been better off today if I'd stayed and not allowed our relationships to die. And I would have been better off as well, because of their positive influence on me. The best relationships take time, and a lot of it. They take the weathering of all kinds of storms. Deep, abiding friendships aren't possible for people who spend all their time commuting, changing churches and clubs, or moving from place to place.

What's more, I now understand that relationships are the only way for spiritual gifts to mature in each one of us. We don't obtain love, joy, peace, and all the fruits of the spirit by sitting alone in our rooms or by visiting sacred places. These fruits are crafted in community, as our roots and branches intertwine with others.

The way I see it, life is a journey, and that journey is shared with others. I have always believed that the journey is not over until we reach our final resting place. But until recently, I never knew that God designed a resting place for his people right here on earth . . . a foreshadow of the final resting place in heaven.

This place of rest is actually the House of God, a community of people whose glory exceeds that of any building made by human hands.

While we journey on *earth*, we can truly have a home base with a deep sense of permanence and connectedness . . . *on earth*. This connectedness is shared with other people, and especially with followers of Christ who join us in the journey, because the Bible says that his Spirit ties us together, soul to soul. There is continuity in this connectedness and this resting place. It extends from these finite days on earth into the infinite future. It is a sense of permanence with the people in my community. These people with whom I laugh, cry, work, struggle, play, and pray will be my cosmic companions from one world into the next, beginning with the kingdom of God on earth . . . and extending into his kingdom in heaven.

So in one sense, heaven begins right here and now, within my Christian community.

You might ask, *How in the world can we expect to discover relationships that foreshadow heaven? That honestly sounds unattainable.*

It's a good question. Still, when I think of my wife, my kids, and the handful of brothers and sisters who might have died for me, I begin to believe that these kinds of heavenly relationships are actually possible.

All those deep thoughts about connectedness and stability led me to the next step, which was to look seriously into intentional Christian communities . . . and what I discovered gave me pause to think. I observed some fascinating experiments in tribal living in a post-modern culture.

I have to admire people who truly and absolutely love living in an economically deprived neighborhood—or on a farm—solely because they are sharing life with people to whom they have committed themselves. I can't wait to share their stories with you! These people value friendships more than house and possessions. They bear one another's burdens. Sure, they struggle just like anyone else. Nobody said these folks are perfect, but they are keeping their commitments to each other, and that's rare these days. They are living out what I've previously only read about in the Bible. I want to have relationships like that in my life! But that's only possible if you are intentionally committed to each other on a daily basis.

It might be helpful to pause here momentarily, to establish a clear definition of intentional Christian communities, in case that term is new to you.

David Janzen of Reba Place Fellowship community writes, "Our working definition of intentional Christian community is a group of people deliberately sharing life in order to follow more closely the teachings and practices of Jesus and his disciples. The more essential dimensions of life that are shared—such as daily prayer and worship, possessions, life-decisions, living in proximity, friendships, common work or ministry, meals, care for children and elderly—the more intentional is the community."[2]

So you don't get spooked, it's not like you move onto a compound where people tell you, "Think this. Drink this. Lose your mind to our control." That kind of cultic control is usually found in communes with a strong leader who lacks accountability . . . which is antithetical to the leadership styles of the communities that I explored.

---

2. Janzen, *The Intentional Community Handbook*, 12.

Moreover, you don't actually lose anything by moving from independence to healthy interdependence. You actually gain a lot. And there are all different levels of commitment. Each community is as unique as people. Some you will love, and others you might not care for. That's the beauty: these communities have a wide diversity of thinking and practice, suitable for all different kinds of people.

For example, some communities all worship together and expect members to have similar religious beliefs. Other communities encourage members to attend whatever church they prefer outside the community.

Some communities share part or all of their finances. Others simply require monthly dues, like a homeowners association. A few don't require any financial commitment at all.

Some are urban, some are suburban, and others are rural.

Some work together in businesses or on farms, while others expect you to find your own work.

Some communities own apartments or houses for the use of members. In other communities, members are responsible to build, buy, or rent their own housing.

Most communities are governed by democratic consensus, while some have a leadership team.

You could move across the continent to join a community, or you might choose to develop one right where you are at, never leaving your home, church, job, and neighborhood.

Communities are as diverse as the people who inhabit them.

If this sounds interesting to you, stick with me. I would love to help point you in the direction of a community that interests you. I'll even help you plan a visit, since that's the best way to personally check a community out.

Alternately, you might hear what I have to say and then consider developing your own intentional community, right where you're at. I will point you to some excellent resources that can help you do that. I will also tell you about some umbrella organizations for intentional communities. These associations shepherd the communities, providing them with the support they need to thrive. If you do decide to start a community, you may want to get plugged into one of these associations.

The Journey Begins Here

That's enough of my pontifications and perambulations.

I haven't heard *your* story yet.

What do you find intriguing about intentional communities?

Perhaps, like me, you yearn for authentic and abiding relationships.

Maybe you believe you'll find these more authentic relationships in community.

But you're not sure, and you need to know more.

If you feel as if it's time to end a chapter of independence or instability, then possibly your perfect home is described in the coming pages.

This may be the end of a long journey.

It may be the beginning of a new season of rootedness.

Your dream of cultivating deep roots may be coming true.

Be forewarned, though: It won't be all fun and games. You'll find sweat and tears, in addition to laughter and joy.

But I suspect that at the end of your seeking, you'll wake up one day and say, "This is the best family and friends I could ever ask for."

Is this journey for you?

Is it time for you to get plugged into community?

Is it time to make that final move?

Well, keep turning pages, and together we'll learn the answers to these questions and more.

Now enjoy the ride, because there's nothing quite so satisfying as a long-awaited journey home.[3]

---

3. This opening scenario is a fictitious conglomerate of factual events in my life journey. And yes, I did meet Big Red when I was seventeen, while bicycling coast to coast with my friends David and Steve Schmidt.

Chapter 2

A Brief Introduction to Community

As a place to start, I'd like to introduce you to a few of the amazing people I've met in the last year. These folks are living in community and loving it, and they have some terrific perspectives on community life.

Melissa Turkett lives in the Susanna Wesley House in Waco, Texas, with four other adults and two children. These people's lives overlap significantly as they share the responsibilities of managing a house of hospitality and a small urban farm. Here are some of Melissa's thoughts:

> I live in intentional Christian community because I think it gets us back to the church in the book of Acts. We've lost the heart of that in so much of Christendom today. We've made it complicated when it's so simple. It's really about living with people. It's loving God and loving others. It's loving our neighbors. Living in community reminds me that my neighbor lives with me in my house. They can also literally be my next door neighbor. And how do I love them well? The more that I learn to love them well, the more I learn how to love God well. So that's what my heart beats for. That's why I think living in a Christian community is so important, and why living with people who are on the same journey with me is so important—living with those who can hold me accountable and call me to confession. It's such a beautiful way to do life and this thing called Christianity.

A Brief Introduction to Community

Maril and Gregg Parker live in a large community house called the Julian Project in Julian, California. Here's what Maril has to say about her personal path toward community:

> I first learned about community in college at Summit Adventure, a Christian outdoor ministry. We lived in community at our base camp, and I loved it. Then I lived for six months in Christian community overseas, at a youth hostel called The Shelter in the red light district of Amsterdam. I grew up as a Christian in a traditional church, and when I experienced these communities I thought, "Wow. This is a lot different from box church and all the programming that comes with it." This community life showed me a whole different kind of existence than the typical American dream with your house and property, your fence, your 2.5 kids, and your dog, where nobody crosses your property line unless they make an appointment. And I thought, "That life is boring. Nobody gets to know you and you never get close to anyone." So we started blowing off the boundaries of the American dream and living the life we're still living today. This idea looked so much bigger and more synergistic and creative and pliable and counter-cultural and cross-cutting than the typical Christian ideal that I was used to. So we've moved through seasons of growth in that direction. It can be clumsy at times. When you're living in community, it's all out there, the good, the bad, and the ugly. It definitely forces you to grow up. But it's fun. I like it. Yeah, it's fun! With our ministry of hospitality, we have these wonderful people walking through our front door who would never have met us if we said, "That's my fence. Don't come without calling me first." How tragic that would be!

Maril's husband Gregg Parker agrees:

> When you talk about the synergy of many gifts functioning together in a body, it sounds great in theory, but try putting it into practice. We see that in the context of offering an array of ministries and services to people not individually, but as a team. It gets exciting when you see the very real and tangible reality of the many parts and gifts all working together. It's instantly beyond theoretical. Putting these gifts into practice is an incredibly powerful, enjoyable, and freeing experience.

What Maril said about box church and blowing off the boundaries reminded me of our family's experience with homeschooling. When Joan and I decided to homeschool our kids, we stepped off of the "normal" path and forged ahead into territory that was entirely foreign to us. We invested a lot of time, energy, research, and expense in this adventure. It was very countercultural, and plenty of people thought we had gone off the deep end. And yet in the final analysis, our kids exceeded academic standards, made wonderful friends in the homeschool community, and it brought the family together in a beautifully organic and communal educational experience. Plus, it was a lot of fun for Joan and me, even with the high level of commitment this choice required from us.

I wish I had a dime for everyone who ever told Joan or me that what we were doing with our kids was risky, weird, backwards, antisocial, or downright dangerous. And yet homeschooled children (in general) are doing quite well, thank you, as they have for hundreds of years.

Similarly, you might encounter some opposition against living in community. It's a bit countercultural. People don't really understand how community works, so they might be skeptical about it. Some of these communities consider themselves to be churches, and that won't sit right with a lot of traditional church people. The "more experienced" religious opinion of the twenty-first century asserts that modern church-going is the industry standard.

"It's too weird," some people will say. "You might end up in a cult. What's wrong with going to a regular church?"

Well, you *can* still go to a "regular church" in many of these communities. You will read about that in the coming pages.

I should pause here to explain that this book will include a significant discussion about church, which in ways is synonymous with intentional Christian community. People in most of these communities use the word "church" *not* to mean a neighborhood building, but to mean people. While you may be accustomed to phrases like "going to church," that particular wording does not make sense if you are living within a church organism. You cannot "go to church" when you "are church." Moreover, these people have learned how to build "church practices" like prayer, study, and spiritual growth into the natural rhythms of life.

These communities have problems to work through, just like any other church. They disagree at times and butt heads. They say they are sorry. These communities, in general, do a very good job of cross-pollination and involvement with other believers who meet in church buildings outside their communities. They recognize that they are subsets of the larger, universal Church.

A Brief Introduction to Community

Now as we move ahead in this journey, maybe you, like me, can look back in time and be grateful for the loving and nurturing Christian people who have brought you to this place today. But maybe you find yourself in a spot where you need some room to grow. Your branches yearn to develop rich fruit, but the box in which you are planted is limiting your roots and branches.

If that describes your experience, then now might be a good time to get rooted into intentional Christian community. Thankfully, we can learn how to do that by listening to the stories of those who have walked this path before us.

But first, I would like to share some painful choices that you will definitely *not* want to make, and I am sorry to say that the bloke who made these blunders looks a lot like me.

Argh!!!

Chapter 3

Taking the Long Way Home

MY CROOKED PATH TO COMMUNITY

If foolish choices and brokenness have been your traveling companions, then you and I have a lot in common. We have crossed forsaken desert wastes to discover that our desires and dreams have been mirages. We have rejoiced at pictures, tastes, and promises of family, only to watch these visions fade away.

My journey—perhaps like yours—began alone, with confusion and tears.

Today I sit in the coffee shop where they know my name and won't let me pay for refills. I put my ear buds in and turn up the music. I take a deep breath and look back in time.

I close my eyes.

I see a small boy standing all alone in front of the bathroom mirror.

Tears are streaming down his face

He cannot understand why the kids on the playground hate him so much. "Fat lips," they call him.

Why am I so ugly? he cries out. *I wish I'd never been born.*

I see a fifth-grader who feels a great void, understanding from the pain that something is missing, but not even knowing what.

I breathe deep, watching as a teen shuts himself into his room, angry and alone. The battlefield just outside his door is strewn with the shrapnel of bitter strife and hateful words.

I see a young man running, seeking, busy, never at rest, always looking "out there" for God knows what. I see him achieving big things, seeking fulfillment in his accomplishments. He is unhappy, not knowing love. I see him acting tough, playing the part of the Lone Ranger, but always doing things the hard way, running in circles without the help of mentors and friends. I see him frustrated, anxious, and alone.

I feel the crashing impact of flesh and bone against glass and pavement . . . of stubborn will against harsh authority.

Enough!

I will not walk down that road today.

I allow the rich aroma of coffee to fill my lungs. My hands cradle the comforting cup. Rich sunlight washes into my quiet sanctuary.

My attention turns inward again, to an unforgettable moment that rises high above that barren wasteland.

This pinnacle—this supernatural encounter—atones for every moment of abandonment.

A shiver stirs my spine.

A quiet, present voice says, *I was there. I met you. I held you. I carried you.*

Yes, I breathe in response. *You were there.*

I close my eyes again, remembering the warm embrace on that hot summer night in high school. The water that floods my eyes is not for pain or regret, but out of gratefulness . . . thankfulness to the Father who tenderly counted each tear.

I whisper my thanks to the One who has never left me. He has walked with me ever since that day, although I can't say the journey has been easy. Still, it's made all the difference to know that I'm not alone.

Although that experience was, in reality, my deepest encounter with divine Community, I learned that it wasn't enough. A big piece was still missing.

But I'll be damned if I could figure out what it was . . .

HIPPIE COMMUNES AND CULTIC CASSEROLES

Brokenness is the gateway to wholeness, and loneliness leads straight to community. My past instilled in me a magnetic attraction to communes, monasteries, intentional communities, and big family gatherings with mountains of fried chicken and hot apple pie.

Finding Intentional Community

I first experienced Jesus community on wheels in the late 1970s, traveling for two years like the Partridge Family in a hippie school bus, sharing God-vibrations in churches, schools, and parks from coast to coast. One highlight was hosting musician Keith Green and his communal Last Days Ministries retinue at our band's huge, Victorian house in Milwaukee, Wisconsin.

In the 1980s, I was almost obsessed with drive-by sightings of communities past and present. I made pilgrimages to Jesus People USA in Chicago, Francis Schaeffer's L'Abri community in Switzerland, and millennia-old monastic epicenters like Iona, Meteora, Cappadocia, and the island of Lindesfarne.

My wife and I were beached at a service station while hitchhiking from London to Scotland, when hordes of men, women, and children dressed in military khakis with "Jesus Army" logos tumbled out of buses. Some carried crosses in their hands. Others wore big crucifixes like dog tags. We accepted their hospitality and I will never forget our time spent at their Jesus Army commune.

In later years, I shared dumpster-mined food with pacifist protesters who lived in tree houses in Scotland. Back on the Santa Monica pier in California, I accepted an invitation to dine on cultic casserole at a nearby Moonie compound . . . but not without calling a friend and pleading to be rescued if I failed to reappear by morning.

Joan and I took our four kids like gypsy missionaries on a fantastic eighteen-month journey through the United Kingdom and the Philippines, immersed in our tight-knit Youth with a Mission community. Stateside, we accepted the hospitality of Benedictine monks on the Pecos River in New Mexico, enjoying their unforgettable beef steak, natural honey, fresh bread, and home-brewed beer. The pinnacle of our family dreams was to establish the Fox and Fiddle bed and breakfast and organic farm in the Appalachian Mountains of North Carolina, where we shared countless potluck meals and bluegrass jams with friends and family. It was community done right, y'all . . . southern style.

I have always been drawn to community . . . but unfortunately, I rarely stopped moving long enough to truly benefit from it. I was continually abandoning old friendships, stale churches, boring neighborhoods, and deeper commitments. I kept looking for that rush of a new experience in a different city, state, or country.

And until recently, I never even stopped to wonder if something might be wrong with that picture.

PLATE TECTONICS AND PEOPLE IN MOTION

I always took it for granted that people should keep moving, just like the continents under our feet. I drew inspiration and justification from the culture, as well as from Bible missionaries like Paul.

Wanderlust runs in the family. My father's job took him all across the map, and my siblings and I continued the trend. After high school, I breezed through multiple addresses in Wisconsin, Nebraska, Wyoming, and California. While working in Yellowstone National Park at the age of twenty, I determined that I would never marry, never have children, and live the life of a mountain man in the wilderness.

Thankfully, a beautiful young woman named Joan persuaded me to crawl out of the woods and shave. (She's now a beautiful bride of more than thirty-five years.) Joan and our four children fulfilled my greatest desires for family, desires I never even knew I had. Even with frequent moves, we always created our own safe home base which included tree forts, crafts, story time, and games, wherever we found ourselves.

For me, this was an indescribably beautiful and redemptive part of my journey. It took me back to the very beginning, allowing me to experience the innocence of childhood for the first time as I courageously ventured into Pooh's Hundred Acre Woods in search of Heffalumps with a toddler in my lap. Together we discovered the incredible blessings of family. Experiencing our own child-rearing challenges certainly gave me a greater appreciation for my loving parents, and our past broken relationships were restored at this time.

We made some terrific friendships outside of our family during those days, although it was always a battle with the culture to approach the depth of authenticity that we desired. Spontaneous invitations for meals with friends were rarely accepted, as other busy parents juggled their schedules to squeeze us in between soccer practice and home improvement projects . . . three or more weeks in advance.

I've never been the sharpest tool in the shed, and I just couldn't understand why we had so much trouble forming deep and lasting relationships. Meanwhile, we kept pulling up roots and moving to new places.

AN EPIPHANY

Joan and I experienced a huge epiphany not long after moving from California to Colorado. We were on vacation back in Southern California, visiting friends who still lived in the same neighborhood where we had once lived.

In the years since we had moved away, our friends had helped to establish a new Antiochian Orthodox Church. We were intrigued to learn that most of their church members had bought homes in the same neighborhood to make it easier for them to attend daily services together. Since we had nearly birthed one of our children in our car on a jammed Southern California freeway, we were easily convinced of the wisdom of doing anything possible to avoid L.A. traffic.

"We have so much more time for each other," our friend Doug explained. "We're not spending all our time in cars."

Our friends suggested that we take a walk through the neighborhood. We did, and in the first few blocks we said "Hello" to two families from their church. At the third family's house, we were invited inside for a tour.

"This is my painting room," the woman explained, showing us a set of elegant icons she was creating. Then we were taken into the backyard to meet the chickens.

A block or two further down the street, we accepted an invitation for dinner at another friend's house, bringing to the table extra kids and garden produce that we had picked up along the way.

This is different, I thought. *The boundaries between people and property are looking a little blurry here. I don't even know whose children these are.*

About ten families from this small church had intentionally sold their houses in the vast inland empire of Southern California. They had intentionally moved into the same neighborhood. In all my days, I could not think of anyone I knew who valued church and friends this highly. I was nearly speechless, watching in amazement as meals, children, time, lawnmowers, and garden produce were shared lovingly among friends.

And *BOOM!*

I finally got it.

I was seeing community as God intended for it to be.

I was experiencing the same fragrance that caused observers in the early days of the church to say, "I don't know what these people have . . . but I want it."

This imperfect but beautiful community gave me reason to begin questioning some of my fundamental assumptions, which included the so-called "American Dream" of prosperity. I wondered what my life might be like if I truly valued people more than place or things.

> If a trial comes upon you in the place where you live, do not leave that place when the trial comes. Wherever you go, you will find that what you are running from is ahead of you. So stay until the trial is over.
>
> —Anonymous wisdom of the monastic desert tradition (Wilson-Hartgrove, *The Wisdom of Stability*, 149.)

STRIKING IT RICH IN THE PHILIPPINES

I might have done a clumsy job of fathering four children, but I sure had a lot of fun. Our little community of six did everything together, no matter where we found ourselves. Meanwhile, we sent out at least ten change-of-address letters, with home bases that included California, Colorado, Scotland, England, and North Carolina.

Outside of my family, I still felt broken in terms of deep and abiding relationships. Ironically, my yearning for community caused me to jettison the best relationships I had formed, moving to new places in hopes of finding . . . uh, better relationships. You probably know this by now, but I've never been the brightest light in the harbor.

The summer that our family spent in the Philippines with Youth with a Mission opened my eyes to our own national curses of isolation and loneliness. While there, we were nearly always surrounded by small people with large smiles. We spent a lot of time helping people in need, and that's when we discovered that some of the poorest folks were also some of the happiest. They always had time to talk or offer us something to eat. Wherever we went, we had instant community. Children, food, and dogs flowed freely from house to house. Friendships sprouted quickly, and leaving was seldom easy.

I remember a woman pointing to one light bulb that dangled on bare wires from her ceiling. "I'm sorry we are so poor," she said. "Our homes are not like yours."

She was so ashamed of her poverty, and yet she had welcomed us with lavish hospitality.

"You have no idea how rich you are," I later told some Filipinos. "You are rich in friends and family, which brings so much more joy than money. We have lived in neighborhoods in America where people have the nicest homes you can imagine, but they don't even know their neighbors."

Some of the Filipinos laughed.

"They think you are kidding," one of the Filipino leaders explained. "They can't imagine people not knowing their neighbors."

I was aghast!

"I'm not kidding," I explained. "In America, people with big homes also have tall fences and strong walls. Their homes and yards are not open like yours. These people come home from work, they drive their cars into the garage, they shut and lock all the doors, and then they eat dinner alone while watching a big screen television. Many of these people never talk to their neighbors. You might think they are rich because their houses are much bigger than yours, but they are very poor. These people are starving for love and friendship. Pray for us, because in the things that matter most, we are poor and you are rich."

Returning to America meant not only leaving these beautiful Filipinos, but also leaving a rich community of fellow YWAM missionaries with whom we had traveled and lived in close proximity for a year and a half.

BRIGHT PEOPLE—DARK AGE

Looking back through the centuries, I am impressed by the parallels between the medieval times and our culture today. For about a thousand years, the Middle Ages of Western Civilization were dominated by an uneducated, superstitious, warring people who lived fearful, sick, and short lives. This "Dark Age" was book-ended by the collapse of Roman infrastructures in the fifth century and the Renaissance ("rebirth") of culture beginning in the fourteenth century.

The deterioration of culture in the Middle Ages is contrasted by pockets of people who preserved ancient Greek, Roman, and Middle Eastern treasures of art, medicine, mathematics, science, law, and politics. There would never have been an Italian Renaissance if the walled city and Eastern Roman Empire of Constantinople had not preserved priceless pieces of culture from the past.

In *How the Irish Saved Civilization*, Thomas Cahill shows how monks like Saint Columba of Iona "single-handedly refounded European civilization throughout the continent."[1] Similarly, hundreds of monastic enclaves throughout Europe, Asia, and Africa fanned the coals of civilization within their cloister walls.

Intrigue for history was one of the reasons why I chose to pursue graduate studies in Edinburgh, Scotland. We had ample opportunities to comb through monastic ruins across Europe and parts of Asia, from cave churches in Cappadocia to Celtic monasteries off the rocky coast of Scotland. I visualized the inhabitants of these places as light-bearers . . . lovers of light in a dark, dark age.

In all fairness, these people were also freaks, out of step with the mainstream culture of their day. Many of them took drastic measures to swim against the tide of culture.

How does that apply to us today?

Well, in case you haven't noticed, we are living in another Dark Age. Which makes me wonder, who will preserve civilization today? Who are the monks and freaks today?

Jonathan Wilson-Hartgrove, an author and leader in the intentional community movement, wrote a book called *New Monasticism* in which he describes Christians who are bringing radical monastic ideals with fresh expression and relevance to the postmodern world. New Monasticism has

---

1. Cahill, *How the Irish Saved Civilization*, 4.

diverse manifestations among married and single people, in both urban and rural settings, but what all these expressions hold in common is their commitment to community, compassion, justice, and righteousness. Like the monks of old, these people strive to obey God's call to stand apart from the corrosive powers of the world.

The Bible says that Christians are peculiar people. God asks us to be "holy," which means "set apart." We are counter-cultural, and that's an especially good thing when the culture is self-combusting. When the mainstream values are defined by TV commercials, I personally would rather not be floating in the mainstream. Could someone please throw me a rope?

THE DESIRE OF NATIONS

Before our last move, I prayed fervently for spiritual guidance about how and where next to put down roots. To my astonishment, I was repeatedly pointed to the story of the rebuilding of the Jewish temple as described in the book of Ezra.

My favorite part of that story is when the Israelites got their land back after the Babylonian captivity, and all their needs were lavishly financed by a foreign king.

Surely, I thought, *God wants to give me and my family huge tracts of land with all expenses generously paid.*

But, no. God kept leading me to one specific part of that story, which was the *rebuilding of the temple*.

I would ask God for counsel about our next home or neighborhood, and his consistent answer was, "Rebuild the house of God." It didn't make much sense to me, but the word nevertheless came in direct answer to my prayers. I may be slow, but since the scenario kept happening over and over again, I couldn't ignore it.

One brick to my thick head came when I received this prophetic word:

> Then the word of the Lord came through the prophet Haggai: "Is it a time for you yourselves to be living in your paneled houses, while this house remains a ruin? . . . Give careful thought to your ways. Go up into the mountains and bring down timber and build my house, so that I may take pleasure in it and be honored," says the Lord.
>
> —Haggai 1:3, 7–8

Okay, I thought. *I get that. I live in a comfortable, paneled house, and now I'm looking to buy another comfortable house. Yes, I will put God's house first. But how?*

I didn't have a clear picture of how to build the temple of God today, and I barely saw its relevance to our moving. We weren't about to sell our house, buy land, and build a church for us to live in.

We did, in fact, go ahead and sell our bed and breakfast and farm, downsizing significantly to a modest home in an older part of the same town. Meanwhile, I kept seeking counsel about the house of God.

The next huge breakthrough in my understanding came when I happened upon a sermon called "The Desire of Nations" by nineteenth century evangelist Charles Spurgeon. It especially caught my attention when I saw that it was—like the previous revelation—based on the book of Haggai, which was becoming so redundant in my moments of spiritual awakening.

Charles Spurgeon preached on these verses from the second chapter of Haggai:

> "I will shake all nations, and the desire of all nations shall come: and I will fill this house with glory," says the Lord of hosts. "The silver is mine, and the gold is mine," says the Lord of hosts. "The glory of this latter house shall be greater than of the former," says the Lord of hosts, "and in this place will I give peace."
>
> —Haggai 2:7–9 (KJV)

I was fascinated by Spurgeon's take on this passage about the rebuilt temple, which Haggai called the "latter house." Concerning the coming "desire of all nations," most Bible commentators claim that this is a reference to Jesus. Jesus did, in fact, come to this temple that was prophesied by Haggai. However, Spurgeon chose to differ with the popular interpretation of this verse. Spurgeon said that to claim that Jesus is the desire of nations "is a rendering scarcely to be sustained by the original."[2] In other words, he believed it is not the correct interpretation.

Why did Spurgeon not believe this phrase referred to Jesus? He explained that the Greek phrase for "desire of all nations" is in the plural tense. Translated literally, it says, "the desire of nations, *they* will come."

---

2. Spurgeon, Charles. "The Desire of Nations," Public Domain, accessed June 2017, www.spurgeon.org/sermons/3442.php.

Spurgeon goes on to explain that *we*, the *church*, are the desire of nations.

> Reading it thus, "I will shake all nations," and the desire—the desirable persons, the best part, or as the Septuagint reads it, the elect of all nations—shall come. They shall come—the true temple of God, and they shall be the living stones that shall compose it; or, as others read it, "The desirable things of all nations shall come," which is, no doubt, the meaning . . . The choice men, the pick, the best of all men shall come and constitute the true temple of God."

Wow! I was finally getting some clarity!

The message of Haggai, therefore, is that we, the church, are the desire of all nations, the choice men, and the best of all people. Our glory is supposed to exceed the glory of the first temple!

I had never thought of us—my Christian friends and me—in such elevated terms. I felt promoted. I felt ashamed. It made me want to live up to my high inheritance as a part of God's glorious Temple.

My limited outlook was truly being shaken, especially as I put these two revelations from the book of Haggai together in the context of my own instability and buying a new house.

*I finally understood what God had been trying to tell me, that **building and strengthening Christian community around me was more important and far more satisfying than moving to the perfect home.***

A LIVING, BREATHING HOUSE

That revelation from Haggai about rebuilding Christian community literally made me feel as if I'd just woken up, and about thirty years too late. I needed to know more about this house of God in the latter days. So I scoured the pages of Scripture and discovered these facts about the "house of God," which I clearly understood to be *me* and *others*, not a building or physical temple:

- The house of God is spiritual, not physical (1 Peter 2:5)
- God does not dwell in physical buildings (Acts 7:48)
- There is no more need for a physical temple, since Jesus died and the temple curtain was torn in two (Matthew 27:51)
- God dwells among his people in this living house of God (Ephesians 2:22; Hebrews 3:6)

- Jesus is the cornerstone of the house of God (1 Peter 2:6–8; Ephesians 2:20)
- Jesus deserves more praise than the house of God, "in the same way that the builder of a house is praised more than the house" (Hebrews 3:3)
- The apostles and prophets are the foundation of the house of God (Ephesians 2:20)
- We believers are all living stones in the house of God (1 Peter 2:5)
- We are "chosen people, a royal priesthood, a holy nation, people who belong to God . . . chosen to tell about the excellent qualities of God, who called [us] out of darkness into his marvelous light" (1 Peter 2:9)
- God's house will be holy with no false gods (2 Corinthians 6:16)
- God's house is comprised of diverse people who all bring complementary gifts; the stones are not all of one color or size; these diverse children of God "fit together and grow into a holy temple in the Lord" (Ephesians 2:22)
- The house of God actually completes Christ, like a bride completes the groom; we are his fullness, as he fills us (Ephesians 1:23)
- Every member fits together and edifies each other in love (Ephesians 4:16)

I learned that the spiritual House of God today has a critical purpose in the world, much like the Jewish temples of old. Whether we meet in church buildings, streets, barns, or homes, our purpose is the same:

- To worship, pray, and share sacraments
- To celebrate holidays, feasts, and personal milestones
- To offer spiritual, emotional, and practical help, support, and encouragement
- To preserve truth
- To educate and equip
- To connect with friends and family
- To administer justice and compassion
- To share God's love with each other and the world

Today, I read many Scriptures and prophecies differently than I did before I understood that we are the house of God. For example, Psalm 122 says:

> I was glad when they said unto me, "Let us go into the house of the Lord."
>
> —Psalm 122:1

This verse certainly describes the joy of going to worship in a physical building. But on another level, it also says, "I was very excited at the suggestion of moving into deeper friendship with the people of God." I have found great encouragement reading Scriptures about the temple and the house of God in this way.[3]

REBUILDING THE THIRD TEMPLE

There's a lot of speculation today about the rebuilding of the third temple in Jerusalem. I've heard that a coalition of Jews is prepared at a moment's notice to quickly restore the temple building and Jewish rites, should the Muslim Dome of the Rock ever fall.

Hold your breath, because here's a newsflash: The third temple is already built. Jesus said (speaking about the second temple as a metaphor for his own body), "Destroy this temple, and I will raise it again in three days" (John 2:19). Jesus's resurrection was the inception of the third temple, rebuilt on Easter morning. This third temple became fully manifest when he breathed upon his disciples and gave them the Holy Spirit.

As we have seen, the Scriptures are very clear that *we* are now the holy temple, the desire of all nations, the house of God.

Unfortunately, as in the days of Haggai, the temple lies in ruins in many places today, due to divisions and neglect. As you have seen from my story, I repeatedly neglected the ruins of the house of God. Beyond my immediate family, I scarcely strengthened its walls. My stone did not stop rolling until God placed some significant obstacles in my path that shouted, "Forget about your little house. Repair my temple by connecting with my people!"

---

3. Here's another example: The anti-Christ ("the abomination of desolation" in the temple; Daniel 9:27) will likely arise from the church—the living temple—rather than from a rebuilt Jewish temple.

Look what happened in the book of Acts when God's people were completely dedicated to the living temple of God:

> They devoted themselves to the apostles' teaching and to fellowship, to the breaking of bread and to prayer. Everyone was filled with awe at the many wonders and signs performed by the apostles. All the believers were together and had everything in common. They sold property and possessions to give to anyone who had need. Every day they continued to meet together in the temple courts. They broke bread in their homes and ate together with glad and sincere hearts, praising God and enjoying the favor of all the people. And the Lord added to their number daily those who were being saved.
>
> —Acts 2:42-47

These people were crazy about God, and they showed it by truly caring for each other. They were the "desire of all nations," and people from the world were falling over each other to get into this church. And why should the nations of the world NOT desire to be part of such a truly loving community?

Their love and good works produced such a fragrance that spectators who had no understanding of the Kingdom of God would stop and say, "I don't understand what these people have, but it's so contrary to the spirit of the world. Whatever it is, I want it too!"

The desire for that fragrance is a great motivation for people like us to move into deeper commitment with each other today.

CULTIVATING MY GARDEN

As I write, it's springtime. The weather has been ideal, so Joan and I are spending a lot of time in the garden this week, hauling manure and planting fruit trees, flowers, and vegetables. I tended the bee hives, rebuilt the chicken coop, and added some fence to keep the varmints out. I'm on the verge of starting the little shaded fire pit project that I've been putting off for a year.

As I sit here nursing my sore muscles and back, this Scripture comes to mind:

Finding Intentional Community

> This is what the Lord Almighty, the God of Israel, says to all those I carried into exile from Jerusalem to Babylon: "Build houses and settle down; plant gardens and eat what they produce. Marry and have sons and daughters; find wives for your sons and give your daughters in marriage, so that they too may have sons and daughters. Increase in number there; do not decrease. Also, seek the peace and prosperity of the city to which I have carried you into exile. Pray to the Lord for it, because if it prospers, you too will prosper."
>
> This is what the Lord says: "When seventy years are completed for Babylon, I will come to you and fulfill my good promise to bring you back to this place. For I know the plans I have for you," declares the Lord, "plans to prosper you and not to harm you, plans to give you hope and a future."
>
> —JEREMIAH 29:4–7, 10–11

While the Jews in Babylon were still lamenting the destruction of the temple in Jerusalem, God encouraged them to seek prosperity and contentment. In a similar way today, many of us lament the ruined house of God. We desire a greater experience of community and Christian fellowship. Be encouraged. Like it says in Jeremiah, work in the garden, haul manure, repair fences, get married, and have babies. Invite people over and host potlucks. Get to know your neighbors. Nurture life right here in Babylon.

After all my wanderings in life, I am finally learning stability. I have run away from too many things in life, only to discover that my problems have preceded me to my new location. I am learning contentment. We are building community around us, right here and now.

A tree can't bear mature fruit if it is constantly transplanted.

Is it ever appropriate to move?

Sure, but I cannot tell you when that is. That's your call.

> Just as any young tree, if constantly transplanted or often disturbed by being torn up after having recently been planted in a particular place, will never be able to take root, and will rapidly wither and bring no fruit to perfection, similarly an unhappy monk, if he often moves from place to place at his own whim, or remaining in one place is frequently agitated by hatred of it, never achieves stability with roots of love, grows weary in the face of every useful exercise and does not grow rich in the fruitfulness of good works.
>
> —ANSELM OF CANTERBURY
> (WILSON-HARTGROVE, *THE WISDOM OF STABILITY*, 152.)

The ancient monastic orders all placed a high priority on rootedness and stability. The first vow of Benedictine monks is to promise stability and promise to remain in community. Obviously that makes prospective monks think twice before committing to monastic life.

The fourth century Coptic monk Saint Antony said, "In whatever place you find yourself, do not easily leave it."[4]

In *The Wisdom of Stability*, Jonathan Wilson-Hartgrove writes:

> I am convinced that the most important thing most of us can do to grow spiritually is to stay in the place where we are . . . [W]e are able to best discern the call of God in the company of friends when we are rooted in the life-giving wisdom of stability . . . Until we give ourselves to a place—until we care enough to learn the names of its flowers and its second cousins—stability's wisdom suggests we cannot know very much about the One who so loved the world that he gave his only begotten Son . . . The practice of stability, then, is an exercise in putting down roots. A good tree bears good fruit, we know, and the fruit of the Spirit begins with love.[5]

Deep abiding friendships are not discovered. They are built with sweat and forged in the fires of time. Good friends are the tools that God needs to complete his good work and bring us to maturity.

God's best plans for us require rootedness. He leans back in his lawn chair laughing with delight when your crazy Uncle Ned pulls that stupid practical joke on the kids. He sees the old guys and gals chatting over tea on the porch, the kids picking teams for the big game, while delicious aromas roll out of the kitchen. He's even happy for the conflicts you all have run into, pushed through, and overcome. None of the greatest blessings of community are available to you and me if we are not rooted to a place long enough to experience them. God has designed each one of us to bear much fruit, but that requires rootedness.

THE BEST NEIGHBORHOOD YOU'LL EVER FIND

So now you know my crooked path to community. I took the long way home. Hopefully your path will be more direct.

The main points I treasure in this journey are these:

First, we as believers are the living temple and house of God.

---

4. Wilson-Hartgrove, *Wisdom of Stability*, 148.
5. Wilson-Hartgrove, *Wisdom of Stability*, 1,5,83–84.

Second, the deeper our love and commitment is to each other, the greater our blessings, and the more we will be a blessing to the world.

Third, we must embrace stability, because a rolling stone can never be built into a temple. Our lives cannot develop mature fruit apart from stable, healthy, godly relationships.

Fourth, our immediate families are designed to be the stable inner core of community, so we ought to protect our marriages and families first.

Finally, we reject the national curses of loneliness and isolation. Alone in this hostile world, we are strangers struggling to stay afloat against a powerful tide.

Fish survive in schools, bees in hives, and believers in community. In the words of the Apostle Paul:

> Consequently, you are no longer foreigners and strangers, but fellow citizens with God's people and also members of his household, built on the foundation of the apostles and prophets, with Christ Jesus himself as the chief cornerstone. In him the whole building is joined together and rises to become a holy temple in the Lord. And in him you too are being built together to become a dwelling in which God lives by his Spirit.
>
> —Ephesians 2:19–22

This is our house.

This is the place where broken building blocks like you and I fit together. The Spirit binds us together like mortar. We take pride in our cornerstone, Jesus. This is where wonderful, miraculous, and redemptive things happen. The connectedness that we share is God's tool for crafting the fruits of the Spirit in each one of us.

This temple is the greatest move of God in these dark, latter days. You and I are his Number One Plan for bringing life to each other and light to the nations. There is no Plan B! He is counting on us to rebuild his temple and show his glory to each other and to the world.

Perhaps God is calling you to work out this beautiful plan by moving into an already-established intentional community. If so, then I trust that this book will be helpful in your journey. Or perhaps you can better accomplish God's purposes by developing community right where you are, and if so, the stories here will be very helpful indeed.

Mainly, let us never forget that our high calling happens *together*. We are the desire of nations, the house of God, the most amazing temple the world will ever see. Let us nurture this priceless gift, as our intertwined roots grow deep into the rich soil of community.

Be blessed as you come home to a neighborhood where, like our friends in Southern California that I told you about, you can live within walking distance of your closest friends today, tomorrow, and throughout all eternity.

Now, enjoy your journey home!

Chapter 4

Background Information

W E ARE ON THE brink of hearing some wonderful stories from people who are living in community.

I can hardly wait to tell you about these communities!

But first . . . I have a few things to share that will answer some of your questions and prepare you for the coming pages.

HOW WERE THESE SEVENTEEN COMMUNITIES CHOSEN?

These are the criteria I used for selecting the communities featured in this book. Each community:

- Is located in the United States with English as the primary language
- Subscribes to an orthodox, biblical Christian theology
- Is stable and has been around for more than a few years
- Has a visible, public presence, and is happy to be featured in this book (*not all communities want media exposure, which is understandable when you consider that the community is their private home and sanctuary*)
- Is prepared to receive visitors and inquiries from people reading this book
- Has long-term commitments (*e.g., I did not include mission organizations or college communities where people only commit to six months or a year of living together*)

Background Information

I tried to include communities with geographical proximity, where members could walk to each other's homes, but this wasn't always possible. I also strove for diversity in my selections, assuming that you probably did not want to read about a dozen communities that are all alike.

These are some of the areas of diversity I sought:

- Diversity of size, structure, leadership, theology, location, and practice
- Diversity of property ownership and financial arrangements
- Diversity of community-owned apartments and houses, cohousing neighborhoods (privately-owned houses that often share a common building, kitchen, or outdoor space), and privately-owned homes in conventional neighborhoods
- Diversity of location in North America, although there are large areas where I could not find communities that wanted to be included here
- Communities in urban, rural, suburban, and mixed settings

You should know that there are many more terrific communities that are not featured in this book. I only had room for so many! See the "Appendix" and "Bibliography" sections for ways to connect with additional communities.

WHAT IS NOT INCLUDED IN THIS BOOK

I do not cover some of the most well-recognized, sect-based intentional Christian communities. For example, I did not interview historic Amish, Hutterite, Mennonite, Catholic Worker, Catholic monastic orders, or Bruderhof communities. My rationale is that if someone already has an attraction to one of these communities, there are more than enough resources available to guide them toward their destination. The communities featured here generally do not have that kind of broad, denominational, or organizational support and affiliation. I *did* write about the Brothers and Sisters of Charity, a monastic community, because it is more unique and not directly affiliated with any one of the major Roman Catholic orders.

Finally, I do not cover all the things you need to know about living in community. That information is available from others who are much more experienced and knowledgeable in community than me. I am a storyteller, and the gems of this book are to be discovered in the stories. I'm following the lead of Jesus, of whom it is said, "He did not speak anything to them without using a parable" (Mark 4:34).

See the Appendix for a good resource list about intentional Christian communities. Additionally, you will find information about community associations and covenants in the Appendix.

THINGS TO KNOW BEFORE VISITING A COMMUNITY

Suppose you are intrigued by one of these communities and you want to plan a visit. Most communities welcome guests, but please don't show up on their doorstep unannounced, or surprise them with a call saying, "I'm an hour away. Can I join you for dinner?"

Don't be pushy or in a hurry. Introduce yourself with a courteous call or email. This isn't like contacting a car mechanic. You are approaching a *personal home*, not a business. Work with their schedule, and offer to stay at a nearby hotel or campground.

Many communities have spare rooms that they offer to overnight guests. Most are offered free of charge, but some communities charge a fee. Still, it's polite to leave a nice gift or offer to take your hosts out to dinner. Not every community can accommodate overnight guests. If you stay overnight, you won't have to bring towels or sheets. Children are likely welcome, but ask. If at all possible, leave the pets at home. You may be invited to join members for meals. Some of the larger communities may charge for meals. Parking is an issue at some of the big city communities, so ask about that in advance. We took public transportation into San Francisco at the advice of our hosts.

Most communities have a special meal, worship service, or tour that is especially suitable for guests. Try to plan your visit around these events. Tours may take you into many areas of community life, but you may not be invited into some spaces like private apartments. Ask before taking photos, respecting that you are a guest in their home.

Approach communities with a childlike curiosity, seeking to receive and discover.

Caz Tod-Pearson of The Simple Way community says, "When people read about you, they sort of romanticize what life in community is like. Then when they come to visit, there's kind of a disappointment. We've let people down because we're not everything that they imagined we would be."

Background Information

When you visit a community, you might easily observe all the exciting things about living in community, but don't stop there. Ask about life's most dreary, mundane, or discouraging moments. Ask them to give you some words of advice or caution about moving into intentional community. Do your best to receive a full and realistic picture of life there.

Inquire about the community membership process. Many communities have a three or more year internship or apprenticeship program. You don't want to rush things. The first year is definitely the honeymoon period. It takes time for everybody to get to know each other and determine if newbies will fit well into community.

Finally, pray sincerely that God will lead you to the right community, or that he will open your eyes to the community possibilities that already surround you. Pray for wisdom and divine appointments to guide you. Don't be discouraged, because this search could take some time. Be encouraged that God is working for you, not against you. Jesus has already been praying for you, that you would connect with others in meaningful community.

That's true!

Jesus prays for you and your Christian friends, that you may be one (John 17:21).

Moreover, he prays for you *in community with the Father and the Spirit*, and I can think of no prayer team more powerful than that.

Chapter 5

Featured Communities

My wife Joan and I felt like love bus hippies when we jumped in our retro Green Machine camper and went road-tripping from North Carolina to California. We visited a number of intentional Christian communities, and I also interviewed some by phone. The goldmine of research we uncovered along the way led to the seventeen communities that are featured in the following pages.

Featured Communities

I'd like to add that in all our research of intentional Christian communities, we did not find a single community that we didn't like. In fact, we liked each one *a lot*.

The communities featured in this section are:

- Alleluia Community, Augusta, Georgia
- Bethany Fellowship, Bloomington, Minnesota
- Brothers and Sisters of Charity, Berryville, Arkansas
- Church of the Sojourner, San Francisco, California
- Dathouse, Indianapolis, Indiana
- Good Works, Inc., Athens, Ohio
- Hillside Fellowship, Fort Wayne, Indiana
- The Julian Project, Julian, California
- Koinonia Farm, Americus, Georgia
- Life Mission Fellowship, Hammonton, New Jersey
- Lotus House, St. Louis, Missouri
- Reba Place Fellowship, Evanston, Illinois
- Riverbend Commons, Corona, California
- Rutba House, Durham, North Carolina
- The Simple Way, Philadelphia, Pennsylvania
- Susanna Wesley House, Waco, Texas
- The Word of God, Ann Arbor, Texas

Note that the communities featured here are only a small sampling of the many excellent intentional Christian communities. See the resource list in the Appendix for books and websites that will lead you to other communities, or help you connect with people who desire a greater depth of community.

FINDING INTENTIONAL COMMUNITY

MAP OF COMMUNITIES FEATURED IN THIS BOOK

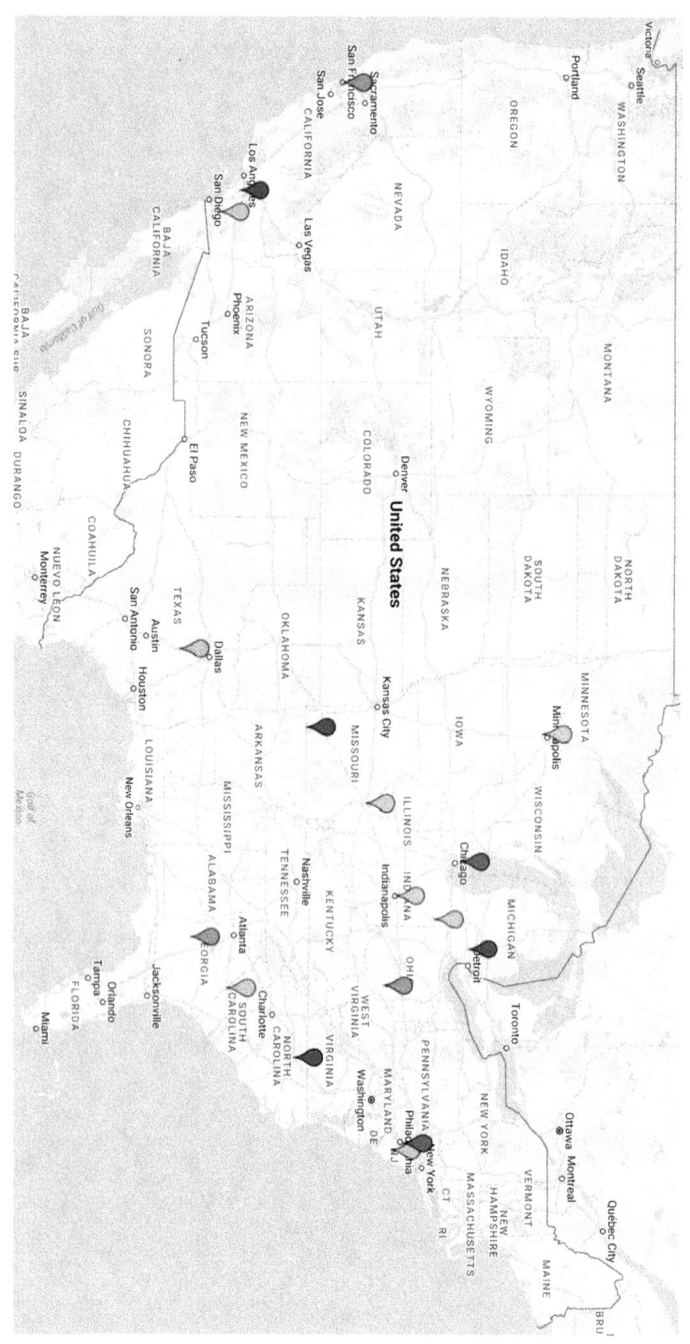

ALLELUIA COMMUNITY

Address	2819 Peach Orchard Rd. Augusta, Georgia 30906
Phone	800-937-5673
Email	office@yeslord.com
Website(s)	www.yeslord.com/
Type of Housing	About two hundred private homes with school and community buildings
Urban/Rural/Suburban	Urban
Founded	1973
# of Core Members	About seven hundred
# of Residents	About seven hundred
Property and Financials	Private property and financials; 5 to 10 percent of income for dues, plus 3 to 6 percent for the school
Community Businesses	None, but members help each other find work
Common Meals	Small groups and households regularly eat together
Other Shared Activities	Thursday evening worship; bi-annual community celebrations; monthly work days
Leadership and Decision-making	About six elders make decisions with community input
Outreach Ministries	Low-income apartments for poor; urban renewal; pro-life events and outreach; individual local and international outreach
Christian Affiliation	Charismatic ecumenical, although most members are charismatic Catholic
ICC Association Membership	Catholic Fraternity of Charismatic Covenant Communities
Non-Profit Org.	Yes
Key Values	Baptism in the Holy Spirit; unity; ecumenism; sanctification in community

On the surface, Alleluia Community in Augusta, Georgia, might look like any other neighborhood in the United States. People own their own homes. They go to work or school each day. They get together with friends.

Finding Intentional Community

If anything is strange about this neighborhood, it's the fact that neighbors get along with each other unusually well.

All things considered, a person's introduction into intentional Christian community at Alleluia Community will most likely be a seamless and smooth transition.

Why is that?

- Experience. This stable and mature community has been working out the kinks since 1973.
- You will get plugged into an instant "extended family."
- You may choose from three different levels of involvement—Associate, Underway, or Full Covenant—according to your own comfort level.
- The emphasis here is upon smaller cell groups and household clusters within the larger context of a stable, seven-hundred person community.
- Houses are comfortable, affordable, and privately owned . . . which means you can accrue equity in your home.
- You can choose the level you prefer for sharing things like finances, chores, or resources.
- Children of Underway and Full Covenant members can attend the safe and competent Alleluia Community School.
- You will discover ample opportunities to be involved in Christian missions and outreach.
- You can experience significant discipleship, spiritual growth, and abiding, lifelong relationships.
- You will be around the kinds of miracles you've read about in the book of Acts.

If that sounds like everything you've ever wanted, you might pause a moment and consider the cost before packing your bags and heading south. The preeminent word to consider when evaluating any Christian intentional community is "compromise." The best relationships thrive on compromise, and that involves some level of personal surrender.

These are some of the costs of living in Alleluia Community:

Featured Communities: Alleluia Community

- You will undergo a two-to four-year probationary ("Underway") period to determine if Alleluia Community is a good fit for you.
- Alleluia expects you to subscribe to conservative Christian, biblical doctrine, and to submit to their pastoral leadership.
- You will need to be comfortable with the fact that Alleluia Community is about 85 percent Roman Catholic, although they are truly ecumenical (meaning people from all different denominations are welcome).
- You must be open to charismatic gifts and the fullness of the Holy Spirit.
- The community is safe, but surrounded by neighborhoods that are not.
- There are no financial commitments at the Associate level, but Underway members give 5 percent of their gross income to support the community, and 3 percent to support the community school. This financial commitment doubles when one makes a lifetime, Full Covenant commitment.
- Members are expected to attend occasional meetings and weekly prayer and worship gatherings.

Dan Almeter, one of the Elders of Alleluia Community, was more than happy to chat at length with me about Alleluia Community, which has been his home for forty years. The community is governed by a half-dozen elders whose style is more pastoral than authoritarian. When neighbors come to odds over barking dogs or differing opinions, these elders don't rush in with rules and fines. Their primary objective is to equip members with the biblical tools they need to grow in maturity and act in love.

"What if Jesus lived in one house," Dan Almeter said, "and the Father lived in another? What if the Holy Spirit lived next to them? What would the Lord do about a barking dog? I suspect that they would bend over backwards to care for one another, making sure that the other person was not put out."

I mentioned to Dan that the transition into Alleluia appeared to be smooth because of the reasons mentioned earlier, and he agreed.

"Community is based on commitment and common vision. However, each family or single finds their own level of participation. Yes, we expect people to attend the Thursday night gathering each week in the Alleluia Community School gymnasium, for prayer and worship. We take our commitments seriously. But we give new people a lot of space to find their way. We assign a pastor to help them adjust, because there's always an adjustment."

Dan is a champion of intentional community.

"When I moved here in 1977," he says, "I couldn't believe that any place like this existed on earth. Of course, that was the honeymoon period. It's different for everybody. For people who are outgoing, they think they've hit pay dirt here. There are so many opportunities to relate to people, it's just non-stop. But it's a little harder for people who are introverted. They might expect to move in and have people rush over to their homes, show up at their doorstep, and reach out to them. It doesn't always happen that way. People will assume that you want some space. Life is extremely active and busy here, but you have to choose to enter into the lives of others. It's your choice to invite people over to your home. Some people can actually live in the middle of this community and still be isolated, so you have to make a decision to reach out and build relationships."

Unlike the typical American scenario, you don't have to drive thirty minutes across town once or twice a week to find good friends. Community is right outside your door here, whenever you want it. On our visit to Alleluia, Joan and I absolutely loved sharing meals with our hosts and their neighbors. They made us feel extremely welcome in their homes. The greatest hazard we might have encountered traveling to a dinner invitation next door might have been getting hit by a pecan nut plummeting from the Georgian sky.

It's not difficult to get connected with others who share your common interests here. Try having a baby, and you'll be inundated with offers of food, clothing, childcare, and parenting resources. Activities like gardening or home improvement projects are often shared with neighbors, as are lawnmowers and cars (not mandatory, but according to personal preference). Birthdays and anniversaries are significant events. Everybody loves the block parties and July fourth festivities. Community-wide celebrations are exciting, but they are far less common than shared meals and get-togethers that are arranged around small clusters of homes or families. Community work days are shared once a month on Saturday mornings.

Alleluia is, perhaps, more like a multi-cellular creature than a single-celled organism. Most of the action happens in smaller cell groups. Personal connections are more frequently made at the street level, among groups of ten or twenty, rather than in gatherings of seven hundred.

Perhaps Alleluia learned this habit from Jesus, who spent more time with twelve than he did with hundreds.

Not everyone who joins Alleluia comes from a charismatic church background, but all are expected to be open and supportive of the gifts of the Spirit. Alleluia Community proclaims that miraculous signs and wonders are not a closed chapter of history. In fact, Alleluia is a testimony to how the book of Acts continues today. The gifts of the Spirit are alive and well here in Augusta, Georgia.

Dan Almeter explains, "If people coming to join our community haven't come from a charismatic background, we ask if they are open to the baptism of the Spirit. They have to be open to charismatic gifts like prophecy, speaking in tongues, words of knowledge, or healings, because we use them all the time. This is part of our DNA. It's a significant part of our lives."

Dan and two other community members had finished speaking in a local church when a woman with a walker came forward.

"She could hardly get to the front of the church," said Dan. "Her ankle was broken in three places. She had had several surgeries, but they were not successful. She was in great pain, and she asked if we could pray for her. So we started praying. When we finished, I said, 'Okay, now you're going to have to trust us. You can stand up now.' She was afraid to do that, but as she stood up and put a little weight on her ankle, she said it was feeling better."

"So I said, 'Would you be willing to let go of your walker and hold my hand? We'll just take a few steps together.' She said that would be okay, and the next thing I knew, she was running around the room, just crying and weeping! She had been totally healed! I actually have that on video tape."

Dan and his friends have lots more stories where that one came from. They view these miracles as more than simply a blessing for those who are healed, but also as a means for bringing people into the body of Christ.

"That's a way we evangelize," said Dan, "by using the charismatic gifts. When someone experiences healing, it opens their heart to the love of God in a way that words can't do. Many people are tired of talk. They want to see a demonstration of God's power. We have a sizeable team of people who are active in these charismatic gifts. We've seen a lot of people touched by God in this way."

Another tool that Dan and his colleagues use is what they call "treasure hunting."

"You pray and ask the Lord to give you places to go, people's names, what article of clothing they might be wearing, and something they might need prayer for. Then you go out and trust that God has somebody there to bless. We have so many stories of how God has used this. We've seen strangers just blown away when one of us goes up to them in a place like the mall and says, 'This is gonna sound strange, but I'm on a treasure hunt. I've been praying, and the Lord told me that if I came to this store, I'd find somebody to pray for who has red hair, green shorts, a tattoo on their right arm, whose name is John.' Then we pray for them and whatever their need is. They're totally blown away because they realize that God knows their needs and he loves them enough to send a stranger to pray for them. We have seen people literally throw away their crutches or just start weeping on the spot because we identified the need that they had."

Again, not everybody is required to practice these gifts, but everyone is expected to be open to them.

Generosity is another quality that Alleluia has learned from Jesus and the book of Acts.

Dan says, "I know one family who is giving four hundred dollars to another family each month because the man lost his job. That might not happen in a regular church because most people wouldn't even know that the need is there. That's the kind of commitment people have here. Some of the people who have been living this life for some years ought to be canonized when they die because they have grown so deeply in their holiness and love of God. They are living saints. They are so close to Jesus that they don't have a bad bone in their body. On the other end, we have new people who are just coming out of the world. They have one foot in the world and one in the Kingdom of God. And we have everything in the middle. It's a composite here. We're different people, all on a journey together."

Stagnation is difficult at Alleluia Community, where the prevailing current takes people in a direction that they definitely *do* want to go.

For over thirty-five years, an onsite intercessory prayer team has been praying 24/7 for requests from the Alleluia Community. In the context of daily life and small cell groups, people have the opportunity to truly *know* each other in non-superficial ways. But again, the depth of spiritual intimacy depends upon the personal investment.

The same is true with the sharing of time and treasures. Alleluia leadership encourages generous sharing, and many people are reaping the benefits of giving and receiving at a deep and rewarding level.

Alleluia Community is mostly comprised of families, although it has a significant number of singles, including some who were born and raised here. Singles sometimes rent rooms in married people's homes.

"A lot of our singles are attached to family households and share meals with them," says Dan. "They look out for each other. They help those who are sick. There's always someone to watch out for your kids. We try to support the family, not replace the family. You can think of us as a family supplement. Our community is like a large, extended family."

People are born into Alleluia Community, and people also die here. Alleluia even has its own cemetery for those who want their bodies to remain among friends when their lifetime commitment expires.

Many people are attracted to Alleluia Community because of its affordable housing. A nice two-to three-bedroom home might cost under sixty thousand dollars. That's almost ridiculous, considering the priceless relationships that come with each home at no additional cost.

But there's a reason why these homes are so reasonably priced, and in realty language it's simply *location, location, location.*

"Our community neighborhood is quite nice," says Dan, "but outside of our neighborhood, it's not. We're in a high-crime area. But this is a safe neighborhood. I feel safe walking around at night. People watch out for each other. They watch out for the kids."

Alleluia even has a team of members who patrol and pray through the neighborhood all hours of the night—I know because I was privileged to join them for an hour while we were there. What a great experience it was, seeing the alleys, streets, homes, apartments, and school by headlight and streetlight, in fellowship with my new Alleluia Community brothers. They really do watch out for each other!

Being surrounded by depressed neighborhoods has put Alleluia in a good position for urban renewal and ministry opportunities. They own apartment buildings which they offer as affordable housing for their poorer neighbors. Individuals and small groups within Alleluia Community have a long-standing tradition of helping people in need in Augusta. Community members have been responsible for establishing a city soup kitchen and a large food bank, and they are involved in ongoing efforts to help poor and homeless people in Augusta. They organize a city-wide, monthly prayer breakfast with a primary focus on racial reconciliation. They are active in helping women find positive alternatives to abortion. They are involved in urban renewal and partnership housing through Habitat for Humanity.

Alleluia Community has earned a great amount of respect from city government and the local media, who thought they were a cult in the early years. These days, they get nothing but positive coverage in the press, which has been witness to their signs and wonders. A public figure was instantly healed of cancer when prayed for by community members—a miracle that was validated by medical tests—and the story of this healing was broadcast on the evening news. As Dan said, miracles are a wonderful evangelistic tool.

In addition to the gifts of the Spirit, Alleluia's key values include unity, discipleship, ecumenism, and caring for one another. As with most communities, "one another" Scriptures are very important to Alleluia.

Employment is a personal choice for Alleluia Community members, and there are no community businesses apart from the Alleluia Community School. Individuals do, however, sometimes offer jobs to other members through their personal businesses.

Dan Almeter stresses the rewards and challenges of being in sustained relationship with others, day after day and year after year. This, he says, is what it means "to grow holier and deeper in union with God." Thinking about the scenario of barking dogs and niggling neighbors, I asked Dan if it isn't easier to do it the "American way" and simply avoid your neighbors altogether. After all, they say that strong fences make good neighbors.

"That's exactly why most people don't want to join community," says Dan, "because it gets sticky. It's much easier to avoid relationships than have to deal with them. But you grow so much through acts of love. It's like the nuclear family. Think about how much time families spend together and the opportunity they have to grow in love. Now, if you multiply that by all the people that you rub up against here every day, the opportunities grow exponentially. You begin to understand how holy people can become when they make the right choices in community."

"Community is not for the faint of heart, but it is for the weak," says Dan. "It's for the weak who know they can't grow in holiness by themselves. You have to humble yourself to receive the greatest gifts you'll find here."

I certainly appreciate the picture of a humble home that was presented by Dan Almeter and the beautiful people we met on our visit to Alleluia Community in Augusta, Georgia.

BETHANY INTERNATIONAL

Address	6820 Auto Club Rd. Bloomington, Minnesota 55438
Phone	952-944-2121
Email	https://bethanyinternational.org/contact/
Website(s)	www.bethanyinternational.org/; https://bethanygu.edu
Type of Housing	Private homes; fifty-two community apartments and student dorms on sixty-two acres
Urban/Rural/Suburban	Suburban campus
Founded	1945
# of Core Members	~375
# of Residents	~375
Property and Financials	Private property and financials; paid staff
Community Businesses	School; office; missions staff; coffee shop; self-publishing business
Common Meals	Optional cafeteria
Other Shared Activities	Weekly worship; weekly staff meetings; seasonal celebrations
Leadership and Decision-making	Non-profit corporate structure with staff leadership and board of directors
Outreach Ministries	Global missions; personal involvement in local ministries
Christian Affiliation	Non-denominational
ICC Association Membership	None
Non-Profit Org.	Yes
Key Values	The Cross, Prayer, Evangelism, Commitment, Faith

The mission of Bethany International is concise and clearly stated. It seemed to jump right off the homepage when I first visited their website:

Taking the church to where it is not . . .

As I conducted interviews with Bethany community members, I found this theme to be quite popular, perhaps even redundant—which was definitely a positive thing.

Featured Communities: Bethany International

"Ask anyone here, 'What is the vision of Bethany?'" says Derek Brokke, "and they will respond, 'To take the church where it's not.' Everybody here knows how their role fits into that mission of getting the church where it's not."

Derek's father Dan Brokke sang the same refrain. "Our mission is taking the church where it's not. That's what you'll hear if you visit. That is the common theme."

Repetition denotes significance, right? Well, then I get it. This is a significant theme.

Dan deepened my understanding when he explained that community, for Bethany, is not an end in itself, "but it comes out of a desire in love for God to fulfill his purposes in the earth."

We can conclude, therefore, that the *primary purpose* of Bethany is *not* to form a club or create a Christian culture. It is not even to bear one another's burdens, help widows and orphans, or share resources. Like the early church in the book of Acts, the primary purpose of the Bethany community is to lift up the name of Jesus. And as Derek and Dan stressed, Bethany members are fully vested in this vision.

I discovered that this single-minded purpose has been Bethany's driving force since it was founded in 1945. Five Christian families sold their homes and bought a thirty-room house in Minneapolis. The name "Bethany" was chosen because that was a place where Jesus would go with his disciples for rest, prayer, and reflection. These believers shared finances, meals, and housing for practical reasons: living in community enabled them to channel more time and resources into the vision God had given them to send one hundred missionaries to the world. Nobody received a salary, but all income was pooled together and everyone's needs were met from a common fund. When Bethany outgrew its home in 1948, it moved to a sixty-two acre farm in nearby Bloomington, Minnesota. This is the setting for Bethany's campus today, although the intervening decades have transformed the surrounding countryside into suburbia.

Dan Brokke now serves as president of the organization he was born into in 1952. Though his parents lived their entire lives together at Bethany, Dan and his wife lived away from the community for thirty-some years.

Recalling those early days of Bethany International, Dan says, "We always knew we were part of Bethany for a reason. It wasn't just community for community's sake. The calling to missions—the training, sending, and supporting of one hundred missionaries—was part of everything we did.

We were part of something that was bigger than our individual family. I think that's why everyone was there in community. It was a way to advance the gospel efficiently and together, as the whole pursuit of life."

Of course, community life can be challenging at times for young people like Dan. "I had more mothers than any boy would want. You couldn't go anywhere without one of your moms watching you. I remember getting into trouble just for spitting on the sidewalk. Your life was always on display, although it really wasn't a problem. We shared an apartment with another dear family for eleven years. They had their own bedrooms and we shared a common living room. It was an enriching experience. I remember meeting people from other countries, whether African or Asian, Indonesian or Brazilian, or folks from the Caribbean Islands. I remember a missionary named Arthur Mouw talking about navigating up the remote rivers of Borneo, meeting a Dyak Indian man on the riverbank who had a dream about meeting a white man coming up the river. Dr. Mouw told us how God used that miraculous encounter to bring the whole village to Christ. To have these stories told into your life as a very young child was so rich. It showed me that the world was much bigger than this little rural spot in the southwest part of Minneapolis."

Like other mature communities, Bethany International has evolved considerably through the years. Members still work together, but they earn a salary now. They no longer share finances or homes. The community does not eat meals together, although everyone is welcome to eat in the Bethany cafeteria. Members who don't work together might only see each other once a week at the Wednesday chapel service in the Bethany Church on campus.

The community numbers about 375. A third of the members are staff and two thirds are students at Bethany Global University. Most staff find their own accommodations off-campus, and most students live in Bethany's dorms. Staff and students are equally considered to be community members, and all subscribe to Bethany's statement of faith and lifestyle commitments. After graduation, university students often continue their relationship with Bethany International by becoming staff or missionaries, although some do leave at that time. Bethany's one hundred missionaries in twenty-five countries are an extension of the Bloomington community. These men, women, and children have a place to come home to when they are on furlough or when transitioning out of the mission field. They keep in touch with each other through newsletters and correspondence.

As I spoke with Dan and Derek Brokke about Bethany, I had no trouble understanding the school and ministry aspects, which fit conventional non-profit, academic, and corporate models. Staff work together and get paid just like any other business. The organizational-chart is straightforward, with a hierarchy of managers and a board of directors at the top. The structure on the academic side is equally common. If you live in Bethany's dorms or apartments—and if your garbage disposal or heater is not working—you go to the apartment manager or maintenance team, just like any other facility.

I got that. I understood the business model. I understood the school, staff, and ministry tracks. What I *didn't* understand was the *intentional community*. It wasn't like the other communities I had seen.

So, where's the community in all this? I wondered.

"The same Bethany model does not exist today as it did when I was growing up," says Dan Brokke, "but the same spirit of community is present. We still talk about it being the Bethany community. My wife and I live a mile from campus, but my mother still lives on campus. Two of our sons live on campus. We have a number of folks who have lived here for decades. We're not so transient as other missions organizations that have short-term workers, although it does feel like a college campus with some students coming and going. But we have a very stable staff. It's not like thirty years ago when we had enough campus housing to hold all of our staff. We do have some transience, but a lot of folks live here for a good period of time and are fully engaged in the life of the community."

A short walking tour of the Bethany campus will lead you on tree-lined paths past grassy lawns, apartments, dorms, administrative buildings, Bethany Church, Bethany Global University, and a historic, red barn.

The roots of Bethany Global University go back to 1948, when Dan Brokke's father started teaching Bible classes in partnership with another teacher at the fledgling community. Today, Dan's son Derek Brokke carries on the family tradition as Dean of Men at BGU. The university has acquired a Work-Education College moniker, meaning students receive a tuition waver by working fifteen hours per week in different ministry departments. This apprenticeship alongside Bethany staff is an important part of their education. Students generally spend their last two years overseas serving in missions.

FINDING INTENTIONAL COMMUNITY

Bethany's outreach is obviously very pronounced overseas, but they are also active locally. In everything from street evangelism to helping people who are poor, members reach out to the broader community individually or through local churches and ministries that are not under the Bethany umbrella.

Community members find employment through Bethany Global University, Bethany Gateways (the missionary sending agency), and Publish4All (which helps indigenous people print resources on demand in their own languages). Some are employed by Bethany in property management and maintenance. For many years, Bethany was home to Bethany

House Publishers, a highly successful publishing company that was sold in 2003. Some members work at Mugshots, a community-owned coffee shop in Bloomington.

According to the Mugshots website, "Our goal is to provide the Bloomington community with a place for quality coffee and meaningful conversations. We want every customer who enters Mugshots to know that they are valued and cared for. Here at Mugshots, your mug matters!"[1]

Work is an important component of the Bethany community, but only as it relates to their calling and mission. President Dan Brokke explains:

"We have almost a fanatical commitment to global missions. That is so ingrained in our DNA, to train and send and support missionaries globally. After that, we have been good at creating industry to support our ministry, although that is not as strong today as it once was. Bethany has been known for its model of the community working in industry together to raise funds to support missions. That has been a unique component of Bethany that people have loved. It illustrates that community is never a thing of itself, but it comes out of a desire in love for God to fulfill his purposes in the earth. So community is in support of that. And giving our lives in service is not a means of gaining God's pleasure, but it is an expression of love. So we lay everything down in love, not out of a sense of duty or obligation. That has been one of the prime motivators throughout our entire history, that acknowledgement of our union with Christ and all that was won for us. Out of that flows our loving response to him."

It seems as if everything leads right back to their paramount mission, which (as you probably know by now) is:

Taking the church to where it is not . . .

When I asked Dan Brokke for memorable moments of living in community, perhaps I expected to hear some cute or clever stories. Instead, what he narrated left me with sorrow and a sense of loss for those who were removed from Bethany's family photo nearly fifty years ago.

"In August of 1969, our family was at Bethany's resort area when it was hit by a tornado," says Dan.

---

1. Mugshots Coffee Company, "Our Story & Work," accessed June 2017, https://mugshotscoffeeco.com/about/.

Members swiftly scattered as a thunderous roar and unstoppable destruction descended from black skies. Imagine the chaos and fear as Dan and his father lay on the ground behind a cabin. Suddenly, the cabin, which sheltered some of the community members, was picked up and hurled a hundred yards into the lake. Dan and his dad were spared, but the complete devastation surrounding them was unfathomable. The wind had barely died down when dazed survivors spread out to assess the damage, hoping to God that property was all that was lost. But it wasn't. Their worst fears were multiplied.

"At the funeral held in Bethany Church, seven caskets were lined up across the front . . . There was confusion. There were questions that, frankly, never get answered, and there was second guessing about decisions and personal choices."[2]

"It was tragic," says Dan. "I remember one mom who lost her nineteen-year-old daughter saying, 'I thought that if I served God, I wouldn't have to go through this kind of thing.' It shook everybody, but it also brought us together. A message of the hope we have in Christ was spoken powerfully into our local community. We strengthened each other. This event opened so many doors to share the gospel. Sometime later, my dad was ministering in prison when he actually met the guy who found my brother Paul in the bottom of the lake, and my dad was able to witness to him. Living in community, we didn't go through this alone. But being in community doesn't mean that you are exempt from the tragedies of life."

"On a different, lighthearted note," Dan continues, "I remember all the fun and silly times we had together growing up in community. Everybody has such different giftings, and that makes life fun. We did a lot of laughing together, and that continues to this day. We have staff and student appreciation times, crazy musicals, and skits. It's just fun, especially with people who normally seem to be a little too serious on the job. I think it's kind of cool that both staff and students will give themselves for each other in the community as a whole."

---

2. Bethany International, "The Tornado; Reflections from Dan Brokke," accessed June 2017, https://bethanyinternational.org/news/the-tornado/.

Featured Communities: Bethany International

The picture of Bethany International as an intentional Christian community crystalizes when you see its continuity through many years of joys and tragedies, feasts and famines.

"My goal is to see the spirit of community very strong," says Dan, "even if the model is not the same as it was twenty or thirty years ago, because you can actually have the model in place but not have the spirit. The needs of community change over time. There are actually seasons of distress around the whole area of community that require some change. So I continue to pray for unity of vision, unity of purpose, unity of respect, and an environment of honor. In John 17:21, Jesus prayed, 'that all of them may be one, Father, just as you are in me and I am in you.' That spirit or atmosphere of honor can be among people who are committed to each other and working for the same purpose. I pray that we will have a stronger community at that level than perhaps we had when we were all eating meals in the same dining room. We can experience the dynamic of that environment, even if the model is not the same as it was thirty years ago."

The Bethany community finds inspiration from many other Scriptures that illustrate the unity, respect, and honor that God intends for his people to share with each other. These are some of the Bible verses that are important to the Bethany family:

> I appeal to you, brothers and sisters, in the name of our Lord Jesus Christ, that all of you agree with one another in what you say and that there be no divisions among you, but that you be perfectly united in mind and thought.
>
> —1 Corinthians 1:10

> I planted the seed, Apollos watered it, but God has been making it grow. So neither the one who plants nor the one who waters is anything, but only God, who makes things grow. The one who plants and the one who waters have one purpose, and they will each be rewarded according to their own labor. For we are co-workers in God's service; you are God's field, God's building.
>
> —1 Corinthians 3:6–9

> Therefore if you have any encouragement from being united with Christ, if any comfort from his love, if any common sharing in the Spirit, if any tenderness and compassion, then make my joy

Finding Intentional Community

> complete by being like-minded, having the same love, being one in spirit and of one mind. Do nothing out of selfish ambition or vain conceit. Rather, in humility value others above yourselves, not looking to your own interests but each of you to the interests of the others. In your relationships with one another, have the same mindset as Christ Jesus: Who, being in very nature God, did not consider equality with God something to be used to his own advantage; rather, he made himself nothing by taking the very nature of a servant, being made in human likeness. And being found in appearance as a man, he humbled himself by becoming obedient to death, even death on a cross!
>
> —Philippians 2:1–8

"The thing that is so powerful in Philippians two is that the mind of Christ can only be experienced through community," Dan explains. "You can't experience the mind of Christ in isolation. So while Jesus did not count equality with God as something to be grasped, we do not count equality with someone next to us as something to be grasped. Don't be in competition with them. Take on the nature of a servant toward the person next to you."

> All of you, clothe yourselves with humility toward one another, because, "God opposes the proud but shows favor to the humble."
>
> —1 Peter 5:5

"The call to submission in 1 Peter 5 is actually a military term," says Dan. "It's the description of a soldier submitting to his commander. Then when it says, 'All of you,' it means mutual submission to each other. It's the idea of soldiers fighting back to back with each other, fighting for each other's welfare, for mutual protection. I love these kinds of pictures of the healthy attitudes that actually allow community to be a safe place, a productive place, and a life-giving place. Everyone at Bethany was brought together by the message of the cross. When Christ died, we died. That means being willing to lay down your life for your friend. This isn't just theology or a doctrine, but it has a very practical application in the community. Learning how to walk that out is a significant thing."

"I want Bethany to be a life-giving place for the next generation," says Dan. "One of the most exciting things has been to see this younger tier of friends come to be a part of this. I've heard some people from the younger generation say, 'Yeah, I think we ought to start that old model of community again, sharing resources and doing things in common.' It's exciting to see that desire in their heart. I don't think that's my calling, or that right now is the time. It could come back, though. The model could shift, but what's most important is that honor and respect is given to each other. I'm really excited to see that happen."

One thing is certain: If you ever come to Bethany, you can be sure that you will have a united army of spiritual warriors covering your back side, and they will all have the same vision and purpose in mind, which is . . . (*Yeah, you probably know by now . . .*)

BROTHERS AND SISTERS OF CHARITY

Address	350 CR 248, Berryville, Arkansas 72616
Phone	479-253-0253
Email	info@LittlePortion.org
Website(s)	https://littleportion.org/
Type of Housing	Shared men's and women's apartments; married couple's units; on 450 acres
Urban/Rural/Suburban	Rural monastery and smaller urban monastery
Founded	1980
# of Core Members	Fourteen
# of Residents	About twenty
Property and Financials	Shared finances; monastic property
Community Businesses	Little Portion Bakery; Troubadour for the Lord music and publishing
Common Meals	Once daily except Saturday
Other Shared Activities	Work, chores, prayers, meetings, recreation
Leadership and Decision-making	Ordained leadership and church structure
Outreach Ministries	Select local, national, and international ministry opportunities
Christian Affiliation	Roman Catholic
ICC Association Membership	None
Non-Profit Org.	Yes
Key Values	Poverty, chastity, obedience

It's the early sixth century. A dark-robed monk leads a donkey that is laden with packs of food, clothes, and goat-skin parchments down Wadi Qelt, not far from Jerusalem. A well-dressed man walks close behind, wiping beads of sweat from his brow. He has accepted the monk's offer of a simple meal, a place to rest for the night, and deeper knowledge of this Jesus whom some call the Messiah.

Featured Communities: Brothers and Sisters of Charity

The path follows a small stream lined with bushes, grapevines, and an occasional palm tree. The narrow, rocky walls of the deep gully are barren, rising steeply into a parched, cloudless sky. This is the road from Jerusalem to Jericho, where Jesus placed the parable of a man who was beaten and robbed by thieves, then cared for by a Good Samaritan. Wadi Qelt is no safer after five centuries. The monk prods his beast with a switch to hasten its pace.

The monk and donkey turn to cross a small, stone bridge, leading their guest up a steep, winding path. The guest pauses to catch his breath, tracing the cliff-like walls with his eyes. High above, he sees stone buildings and rugged walls that look as if they are hanging from the sky.

This is St. George's Monastery, which according to tradition was built over the cave where Elijah was fed by ravens. This monk is one of thousands who live in caves and monasteries in the region.

That was then.

Now jump forward fifteen hundred years.

I tap some numbers into my Android. A phone rings somewhere in the Ozark Mountains of northern Arkansas.

"John Michael Talbot Ministries and Little Portion Hermitage," the woman says.

I explain that I'm writing a book and would like to speak with John Michael Talbot.

"He's leading a tour to the Holy Land," she tells me.

We make arrangements to chat a few weeks later.

When we finally connect, John Michael tells me about the tremendous inspiration he has received on several trips to Israel, standing in places like the Mount of Olives with its breathtaking views of Jerusalem, the northern shore of the Sea of Galilee, and St. George's Monastery in Wadi Qelt. He describes the deep, spiritual connection that the Brothers and Sisters of Charity share not only with fellow Christians around the world today, but with God's Kingdom that stretches behind us and before us, throughout all eternity.

The Brothers and Sisters of Charity is an integrated monastic community of the Roman Catholic Church. They are guided by the teachings and traditions of a panoply of saints that include Francis and Clare of Assisi, Benedict and Scholastica, Antony and Pachomius, Augustine, Romuald, and Bruno. They seek to integrate Eastern and Western Christian teachings and traditions.

This community is thoroughly monastic, not for academic or historic reasons, but simply as a means of knowing and loving God better. They tap into the old to sanctify the new.

If you were to see a photo of the members of the Brothers and Sisters of Charity, you might *think* you're seeing about twelve faithful monks. However, if you close your eyes, then you will begin to see how vast this community really is.

John Michael, who is Founder, Spiritual Father, and Minister General of the Brothers and Sisters of Charity, explained to me the need for monastic communities today.

"I personally think, brother, that we live in a time of crisis in the West. Our culture is unraveling very, very quickly. The Western expression of the church is certainly in decline. One of the things we seem to have lost in the West is the monastic heart of the church. For the first sixteen hundred years of Christianity, monasticism was always viewed as the mystical, beating heart of the church. In the West particularly, we have lost a lot of that. So one of the things we're saying is that we want to keep that monastic heart of the church beating in the West."

"God gave me a vision of this community in 1971," says John Michael. "I call it a painting. It's an image I saw. In the foreground, men and women were sitting in prayer. Behind them, children were kicking a ball around and having fun. It was a beautiful place. Crops were being grown and people were living off the fruit of their labor. There was complete harmony with God, complete harmony with creation and the earth. That was the vision, and I had no idea what it meant or how to make it happen. I said, 'Lord, what do I do? I don't know any communities like this that have all these states of life and live together in peace.' And he said, 'Stay in music and I will open and shut the doors.' So that's what I did."

At that time, John Michael was playing in the band Mason Proffit. He soon transitioned into a community of Franciscan friars in Indianapolis. Then in 1980, God did indeed open doors for the Little Portion Hermitage to be established on a beautiful tract of land in Arkansas. The growing community embraced not only celibate brothers and sisters, but also singles and families, drawing inspiration from St. John Chrysostom who said, "The

Holy Scriptures do not know any distinctions. They enjoin that all lead the life of monks even if they are married."[3] John Michael, in fact, received the counsel of St. Chrysostom joyfully when he married Viola Pratka in 1989, with the blessing and support of the Roman Catholic Church. He continued to tour and write music and books under his Troubadour for the Lord label.

If you ever visit the monastery, you will think that 450 acres of heaven tumbled down into Eureka Springs, Arkansas. The tenderly cared-for grounds are adorned with flowers, gardens, forest, ponds, pergola, hills, and trails.

3. Brothers and Sisters of Charity, "Monastic Expressions," accessed June 2017, littleportion.org/index.cfm?load=page&page=157.

The church, chapel, and hermitages are tucked into this idyllic setting with as much artistic skill as St. George's Monastery in the cliffs of Wadi Qelt.

The typical day of an Ozark Mountain monk begins at six or seven in the morning with chanted prayers, followed by a silent breakfast. Brothers and sisters work until late morning, then gather for noontime prayer and a reading of the Gospel. Community lunch includes a sacred reading and freeform discussion. After cleaning up, monks spend the afternoon in prayer and work. Vesper prayers are at 5:30, sung and solemn. People disperse into small groups or singles for dinner. Time is set aside each week for meetings, cleaning assignments, recreation, and private meditation. Sunday is more relaxed, with mass, a community dinner, and planning for the week ahead.

The Little Portion Bakery employs brothers and sisters in the production of Viola's Granola, St. Anthony's Hermit Bars, and St. Clare's Heavenly Breakfast Cookies, in both regular and gluten-free recipes.

"Ten out of ten hermits agree," says the website. "Our bars will be the best molasses bars you have eaten!" "Put a little heavenly spring in your step each morning with this wholesome, lightly sweet but totally delicious granola." "We think this bakery leads us to Jesus, the Bread of Life, through an integration of holy simplicity and godly quality. It is truly Good News!"[4]

The monastery used to have a flourishing poultry farm, until the monks with chicken-giftings were called away to other pastures. Farming is too labor-intensive for the current community, although people with agrarian interests are more than welcome to apply.

According to John Michael, "The challenge in America is that although people love to dream about being farmers, it's not so easy to leave the technological immediacy and comfort of the Smart Phone world, come out here, and dig in the dirt. Taking care of chickens is a lot more fun on the Internet."

The Brothers and Sisters of Charity receive about six hundred inquiries a year from people wanting to know more about joining, although very few prospects end up pursuing the monastic life. Periodically, they hold Vocation Workshops to share information and answer questions about life at the Little Portion Hermitage. It takes several years to become fully initiated into monastic life. Along this journey, novitiates will relinquish their personal property to the monastery, keeping little more than the clothes

---

4. Brothers and Sisters of Charity, "Little Portion Bakery," accessed June 2017, little-portion.org/bakery.

they wear. Many people experience a new freedom as they live more like the birds of the air and flowers of the field that they read about in Christ's Sermon on the Mount.

As a Christian monastery under Roman Catholic leadership, this community traces its lineage all the way back to the early church. Their greatest law is God's love, guided by the authority and traditions of the church.

"We are Roman Catholic-based, with an ecumenical participation and ministry. We are bringing ancient integrations into a modern setting," says John Michael. "We integrate all religions from a Christian base. We integrate all Christian expressions from a Catholic base. We integrate all monastic expressions from a Franciscan base, but we're not a Franciscan community. We are a unique and new community. We love our mother which is Franciscan, but we're not our mother. We integrate the solitude of the hermitage with community life, and contemplative community with apostolic ministry. We integrate the contemplative with the charismatic, and the liturgical with spontaneous. We are something new, but we're also something old."

In other words, the packaging is new, but the classic content is ancient.

The Brothers and Sisters of Charity integrate more than monastic traditions. They are somewhat unique in how they integrate married couples, celibate singles, and singles who are living chaste lives but may still marry someday. All members commit to vows of poverty, chastity, and obedience. Poverty means simple living. Chastity applies not only to singles: for married couples, the vow of chastity means remaining faithful to matrimonial covenants. Members pledge obedience to Christ, to monastic leadership, and to church teaching.

As I researched the Brothers and Sisters of Charity, I learned that they integrate Franciscan, Augustine, and Benedictine monastic traditions. They also integrate hermitic practices (where monks live in seclusion) and cenobitic practices (where monks live in community), by utilizing scattered hermit cells and cottages around a traditional monastic common building.

I'm not from a Catholic background, so as I continued my research, I encountered more and more vocabulary that was new to me. Don't feel bad if you, like me, need to keep your dictionary close at hand for words like "cenobitic," "charism," "monos," "diocese," "oblate," "canonical," "patristics," "andules," and "horarium."

Don't sweat the lexicology. If this is your road to walk, these good folks will help you understand everything you need to know.

Besides, it's really not that difficult. To thrive here, you only need to know one thing: how to grow a green bean.

Huh?!?

Stick with me. You'll see what I mean.

The Brothers and Sisters of Charity have a daughter house on two acres in Houston, Texas. St. Clare Monastery is an urban monastic residence that currently houses two members. They host chapel services, prayer, cell groups, and a small number of overnight guests.

Another unique extension of the Brothers and Sisters of Charity is what they call the Domestic Expression, which are members who live in their own homes and neighborhoods while following the order's rules and way of life. The strongest Domestic community is in a suburb of Chicago, although there are members spread across the states and even in other countries. The optimum Domestic cell group has about a dozen members who worship, teach, intercede, and build community together. They have festivals of praise. They come to the Little Portion Hermitage once a year for a combined annual celebration. The Domestic Expression is suitable for someone who is attracted to the Brothers and Sisters of Charity way of life, but who cannot at this time make the more significant commitment of moving into community.

Monks who live on the 450 acre Little Portion Hermitage get to know each other quite well, spending many hours together in work, meals, and prayer. They also have a lot of fun together, and they like to laugh. Their spiritual father and mother, John Michael and Viola, set a pretty good example in these regards. I had to chuckle when I saw the title to one of John Michael's recent books: *Monk Dynasty* (perhaps a canonical version of *Duck Dynasty*?).

The core community is small, as was mentioned earlier. "But we've been big," says John Michael. "We've had as many as fifty monks. People tend to come and go. That's the challenge of doing community in America. Marriages and friendships come and go. That's the nature of our civilization. A life commitment like this is very, very difficult for people. They want to make a commitment, but it's hard for them to keep it. Whenever people leave, we say, 'Okay. What could we have done better?' But the fact is, if we

Featured Communities: Brothers and Sisters of Charity

were doing the very best that anybody could possibly do, people would still come and go because this is the United States. We don't see their departure as a failure, because they leave as better Christians, and we're all better for the time we've shared together."

I asked John Michael to name the biggest challenge for new members of the community.

"Authority," he said without hesitation. "The authority of being 'authored' by the essence of monastic life to the very core of your being through a changed life in Christ and the empowerment of the Holy Spirit. Most people can do the poverty thing easily, which means simplicity. Most people can do chastity. It might take a few starts and stops, but they get it. The tough one is obedience. They translate obedience into compliance: doing the thing externally, while fighting it and having the wrong attitude about it. This doesn't often happen in the big things of community, but in the little things. You ask someone to mow the grass in the morning, but they want to do it in the afternoon. You say, 'We need to get it done this way.' And they say, 'That's not the way my mommy and daddy taught me to do it.' This is where people run into problems. This is where the rubber meets the road in most communitarian expressions of Gospel-living in the United States today. Americans will submit to authority for money. That's just a fact. If the boss says, 'Show up at 8:30 wearing a suit and tie,' you will do it. People will give up a lot for money, but they'll give up so little for God."

John Michael says, "It's not the big stuff that gets you, it's the little stuff. We say you need to learn how to grow a green bean for God."

The life of a monk can feel pretty busy at times, whether they are mowing, praying, or planting beans. It's worth noting that the Brothers and Sisters of Charity proclaim that their *number one work* is . . . *worship*.

Here's what I found at the monastery's website, on the page where applicants are invited to request more information about joining the Brothers and Sisters of Charity:

> Our primary founder is Jesus, our primary rule is Scripture, and love is our primary law, guided by divine truth. Our most important work is to worship God daily as a community during the monastic Liturgy of the Hours. Secondly, we create a spiritual oasis of

prayer in our monastic way of life that ministers to the hundreds of pilgrims who come to us.[5]

I asked John Michael to comment on their "most important work" which "is to worship God."

"Most of the original communities in the church were not focused on a particular external work. They were focused on their relationship with Christ. They were focused on their worship of God. There's nothing wrong with focusing on a particular work like teaching or healing. But we tend to stand with the more ancient tradition, and I personally think it's a healthier one. I don't focus my life on my ministry, which comes and goes. When my life is over, I probably won't be remembered much for the things I've accomplished. So I focus on my relationship with God. If my center is being a man of God, then the other things can come and go, rise and fall, and I'm okay. I'm alright as long as I'm in a healthy relationship with God. So that's the most valued work in our community."

Remember the painting that the tenderfoot, bearded, and long-haired John Michael Talbot saw way back in 1971? Well, I asked the mature, bearded, and long-haired John Michael to recount some of the times when he has seen that painting come to life.

"It happens for me a lot in annual gatherings, when the whole community is here. Or sometimes in a small setting, on a normal day that is just like any other. I look around and say, 'Yeah. This is it. Just like God wanted it to happen. This is it.' The best of life happens when you just stay with it and let the old self fall away. Each time you let the old self fall away, you find a new creation. You actually rediscover the real person God created you to be. We do this through the cross and resurrection of Jesus. Every time you say, 'Wow, Here it is,' that's a resurrection. And those resurrections are real. Most people experience one or two big, big deaths and resurrections in the early process of becoming monks, and they usually have more after that. But it doesn't happen quick. It doesn't happen overnight. I always tell people, 'If you're having a difficult time, don't worry. Relax. Stay with it for ten years and maybe you'll get the hang of it.' That's what you see in the classic teachings of the monks. It takes years, and it also takes patience. What

---

5. Brothers and Sisters of Charity, "Monastic Vocations Inquiry Form," accessed June 2017, littleportion.org/vocations-form.

you discover is that a new self begins to emerge, and if you do it right, that new self is a completely liberated self. You become childlike. There are no pretenses. You're not putting on a show. You're just living for Jesus. Everything becomes a prayer. You enter into natural contemplation, where you just see God coming to us in and through everything: in the light on the water, in the sound of the bird, while petting the dog, while mopping the floor, while writing a song, or saying a prayer. You see him in everything. God is just there. So you experience what evangelicals rightly call being born again. Except for Catholics and monastics, being born again is not a one-time experience. It happens every single day. Then life becomes a miracle and life becomes a prayer. Saint Francis was zealous in prayer, but even more than that, his life *was* a prayer.[6] And you get to be a prayer. So that's the reward. It does happen. The older you get in monastic life, the more you walk with a sense of being born again, and also you realize that you just don't *get it*. I have come to the point where I realize I don't actually know that much. I haven't achieved much, and that's fine. It's okay because God still loves me. Isn't that astounding? All of our achievements don't add up to much. When we stand before God, he's going to say, 'How well have you loved?' And that's all that matters."

As trivial as it might seem, John Michael's sagacious perspectives sent my random thoughts to coffee shops and burger joints that try to give customers a predictably satisfying experience at any of their chain stores all across the planet. I thought about the dozens of Disney resorts and parks in Europe, Asia, and North America that faithfully represent Walt Disney's original vision of storytelling and magical fantasy. It seems almost profane to compare these franchises with the Son of God, who commissioned his followers to replicate the church into all nations.

And yet I can't help but wonder, *Is the service offered by God's people up to the Founder's standards? Are God's people around the globe delivering the goods as Jesus requested?*

I'm no scholar, but it seems to me that monasteries like the Brothers and Sisters of Charity have locked into a solid system for doing their best to assure the fidelity and consistency of the Gospel message across continents and centuries, by minimizing innovation and cultural trends . . . and maximizing beliefs and practices that have worked for many people in many places, for many generations.

---

6. Thomas of Celano. *The Lives of St. Francis of Assisi*, Chapter LXI, #95 (London: Methuen & Company, 1908), 134.

In other words, the bean planted by a monk at St. George's Monastery in Wadi Qelt fifteen hundred years ago might look remarkably similar to a bean planted at the Simple Portion Hermitage today, if it's done with a worshipful attitude of love for God and man.

Ten out of ten monks agree that planting beans here is the best that life has to offer.

Just ask anyone from *Monk Dynasty*.

CHURCH OF THE SOJOURNERS

Address	1129 Florida St., San Francisco, California 94110
Phone	—
Email	info@churchofthesojourners.org
Website(s)	www.churchofthesojourners.org
Type of Housing	Four community-owned homes
Urban/Rural/Suburban	Urban
Founded	1988
# of Core Members	About twenty-five
# of Residents	About forty
Property and Financials	Shared property and financials; living allowance
Community Businesses	None
Common Meals	Household meals several times weekly; community meals twice a week
Other Shared Activities	Morning prayer; weekly worship, weekly meetings, and fun activities
Leadership and Decision-making	Consensus with a leadership team
Outreach Ministries	Prison ministry, adoption mediation, immigration and literacy support, peace and justice issues, street kids and homeless ministry
Christian Affiliation	Ecumenical, with Anabaptist roots
ICC Association Membership	Shalom Mission Communities
Non-Profit Org.	Yes
Key Values	Church; family; discipleship; hospitality; outreach; common life

Imagine taking everything in the suburbs—the traffic, the stores, the homes, the schools, the hospitals, the parks, the businesses—and compressing them into a fraction of the area. Squish everything together and suck out the empty space, and that's what you have in the Mission District of San Francisco, where Church of the Sojourners resides.

Where I'm from, people give you a good five-foot clearance on the sidewalks. Here, I'd step up to the crosswalk and the next folks would already be rubbing my shoulders. It's hard to get away from people in this city. The Sojourners folks we met during our four-day visit thrive in this vibrant, multicultural environment. Meanwhile, each of their four homes has a feeling of peaceful sanctuary. These people are very good at protecting their nests.

One member assured me that city life is nothing special, especially if that's all you know.

"My daughter is a city kid," this parent said. "She rides the buses alone and walks alone. Of course, I can't get her to go camping, because nature feels a lot scarier to her than the city. But there's a lot of value in the diversity of people and experiences here. You have to be vigilant, though. You can't say, 'Go out and play. Be back by noon.' You don't do that here."

As for me, I loved every minute of it . . . from the moment we stepped off the B.A.R.T. and got picked up at the Chinese Donut Shop by a Sojourners member, until three mornings later when we said goodbye. It's exciting to dive into the flood of people on the sidewalks, all lapping the shores of eateries, coffee shops, hair cutters, laundromats, and boutiques. Alluring spices and aromas tempt you to exchange your earnings for a tantalizing meal. Restaurants place chairs right on the sidewalk, like traps to tumble you into their patronage. Everything is so close. You feel as if you could reach right through the glass and tap the hair stylist on the shoulder.

All this is just three minutes away from your place of sanctuary at the Church of the Sojourners.

If you want to stretch your legs and "get away from it all," do what I did. Walk south about fifteen minutes, up ridiculously steep streets, past gorgeous old Victorian homes, to the summit of Bernal Heights with its panoramic views of the bay, downtown, and the distant Golden Gate Bridge. Enjoy watching people walk their dogs on the lush, green turf, if the wind doesn't blow you away. Pause to snap pictures for tourists from France or Japan. On your walk home, enjoy the bursts of flowers, palms, and succulents that dangle over the sidewalks. Admire the brilliantly painted Latino wall murals. If you're not paying attention, you might walk for blocks and blocks, not sure if you are lost or not. You might pass a few homeless camps on the sidewalks. Then you see an iron lattice railing with potted ferns at the top of a narrow stairway, and suddenly you realize that you are home.

This was my first morning at Church of the Sojourners. And it only got better.

Featured Communities: Church of the Sojourners

My favorite experience at Church of the Sojourners was caroling in the neighborhood after dark. Our visit came a week before Christmas, so about fifteen of us took up candles and songbooks and hit the streets. First, we knocked on doors and sang to a few delighted friends of the community. Then we engaged patrons and shop owners at tiendas and taquerias along busy Twenty-Fourth Street. Several drivers stopped to take photos, sing a few lines with us, and wish us a merry Christmas. Down the quieter side streets, we received bright smiles and toothless grins from street people and folks spending an otherwise dreary night at the lavanderia. Then we returned home for hot tea and warm conversation.

Finding Intentional Community

This experience was an unforgettable highlight of my holiday season.

Being in the city puts Church of the Sojourners shoulder-to-shoulder with many people in need. They have a long history of helping Spanish-speaking immigrants. Members teach classes in San Quentin Prison and work for open adoption among Latino families. They frequently participate in peaceful protests and prayer walks for victims of violence. They share food, clothes, and friendship with street people.

"Sometimes an outreach can become an in-reach," says Sojourner's member Zoe Mullery. "I came here in severe crisis twenty-one years ago. I needed someone to listen to me and tell me the truth about myself. I had met Debbie, one of the founding members, and I still had her phone number in my wallet. So I gave her a call and we met. For two full hours, I just spilled my guts. I let it all out. She was a great listener. She didn't just pat me on the back and say, 'Everything's fine.' She reflected things back, including the things she thought needed correction. The next day I got an invitation from her, so I agreed to stay with the community for a week. During that time, every one reached out to me. I was messy. I was crying a lot. Jack, one of the pastors, agreed to mentor me. It was a very slow and painful process, but the community nursed me through. I stayed on, but for me it wasn't love at first sight. It was a very bumpy road. I thought, 'What am I doing here?' But in time, the church was able to minister to my need, and I received that."

One of the most difficult challenges for some people in communities like this is strangely enough . . . dinner.

It was certainly a struggle for Zoe, who was assigned a dinner group when she first arrived. "Everybody ate together regularly with their own small group of five people. I'd say, 'What if I want to have dinner with someone else tonight? What if I just don't feel like it? What if I want to eat at eight instead of at six?' It felt very constraining and sort-of arbitrary and small. It felt unfree in the way that I was used to feeling free. It took me a long time to recognize how small commitments like dinner, over time, allow you to bond with people."

"Eating meals together is kind-of a foundation of Christian life together," Zoe explains. "Breaking bread together is very significant. It's part of family life. You just need it. It builds up that ineffable thing that a family is."

This simple and surprising truth is even supported by modern science. Research shows that children who eat together regularly with their families are healthier, less likely to be obese, at lower risk of abusing alcohol and drugs, and perform better at school than kids from families who don't eat together.[7]

I observed this health-building practice in action at Church of the Sojourners, where households regularly pray, talk, laugh, and eat around their tables. Joan and I certainly enjoyed sharing these sacred moments with our hosts. My understanding further deepened as Zoe started talking etymology, a topic I rarely discuss in mixed company. (*Just kidding!*)

"The word *companion* has at its root the word 'bread,' or *pan*," explained Zoe. "So a companion is someone with whom we share bread. We share a similar journey and destination with our companion. That's a very different story than a lone traveler with an individual destination."

As she explained this concept of sharing bread, the story of Christians in the early church took on new meaning for me.

> And they, continuing daily with one accord in the temple, and breaking bread from house to house, did eat their meat with gladness and singleness of heart . . .
>
> —Acts 2:46 (KJV)

Similarly, I was reminded of the many examples of companionship that Jesus gave us.

> While they were eating, Jesus took a loaf of bread and blessed it. Then he broke it in pieces and handed it to the disciples, saying, "Take this and eat it. This is my body."
>
> —Matthew 26:26

As these revelations took root in my heart, I knew that I had discovered the very core and center of Church of the Sojourners.

Where is that center?

At the dinner table.

---

7. Timi Gustafson, "Eating Together as a Family Has Multiple Benefits," *The Huffington Post*, September 20, 2012, accessed June 2017, www.huffingtonpost.com/timi-gustafson/family-dinner_b_1898387.html.

Church of the Sojourners has about twenty-five members and four houses in the Mission District of San Francisco. This area gets its name from the nearby Mission Dolores, built by Spaniards in the seventeen hundreds. Sojourner's families and singles have private rooms with shared kitchens and common rooms. The core, covenanted members pool their finances together, as did the early church in Acts 2:45 and 4:32. Members get a small allowance for personal needs, and they share resources like cars and appliances.

"The number one resource we share together is time," says member Lee Kuiper. "We like doing a lot of things together. This might seem kind of odd in a place like San Francisco where everyone is pursuing their own path to truth, where they're on their own individual journeys. So commitment in Church of the Sojourners means investing and building a relationship with the person down the hall. We commit to come to dinner with our households. We commit to prayers and Bible study. Our commitment has a lot of lived-out realities, and if you want to be a participator in this community, when the rubber meets the road, you are showing up. You are physically, emotionally, and spiritually present."

Households eat meals together on Monday, Tuesday, and Thursday nights. The whole community has a meal together on Friday night, which includes a Bible study. Their Sunday evening church service also includes a meal. Households have prayer and meditation in the morning before going to work or school. Community meetings are scheduled for Tuesday nights, and Wednesday nights are used as a date night or free night.

The community practices a quiet and contemplative time of Sabbath Sunday mornings. Everyone is encouraged to have a quiet time to connect with God in whatever way they think is best. Sunday afternoon worship begins at 4:30, and includes communion and a shared meal. They don't have a church building, but they sit in a circle in one of the homes.

"We have a time for affirmation at these services," says Zoe. "It's a time of speaking appreciation and encouragement to the people around us. It's acknowledging God's active presence in each other's lives. It can be quite remarkable. It's a very encouraging time."

For the record, the Church of the Sojourners is, in fact, a bona fide *church*, in the legal, non-profit, 501(c)3 sense of the word. The rationale behind this, according to Zoe, "is the idea that a church is people who are deeply invested in each other's lives. Our church is not just Sunday worship. It's being deeply committed, deeply *there* for each other in extraordinary ways. So the whole vision and theology around this community is that church can be more than how traditional American Christianity imagines it to be. Our community grew out of the deeper, bigger vision of what church should be."

Church of the Sojourners takes its stand against Western culture's hyper-individualism by covenanting with one another to be present and committed to each other with a strong sense of permanence. They are committed to stability. They have seen how American transience is destabilizing to families and churches.

"I love our covenant," says Zoe. "I think it's really beautiful. It talks about abandoning ourselves to God in service to one another. It's that kind of self-sacrificing love that we're trying to live out with particular people in a particular place. This is not a big theoretical concept. This is very practical, and that's why I love it."

A common joy mentioned by members of Church of the Sojourners is the practical love and support that ebbs and flows throughout the community. Parents appreciate the many blessings that surrogate aunts and uncles bestow upon their children. Singles like having families to plug into and children to play with. The young appreciate the experience of the elderly, and the elderly receive valuable support from the young.

"The sense of extended family is very important to me," one member said. "I don't feel isolated. I can't imagine not having these people around."

Lee spoke about one memorable birthday celebration.

"Rebecca, my housemate, was turning ten years old," he said, "and she was big into Greek and Roman gods and goddesses. So we planned a city-wide scavenger hunt, where we'd have people from the community stationed throughout the city playing different gods and goddesses. I was supposed to be Poseidon, and I was out at the Pacific Ocean. Before Rebecca and the others arrived, I received a text message of what I was to read as Poseidon. So the kids showed up and I walked out into the waves, which were really big and choppy that day. I was really acting the part. I was shouting, 'Come into the ocean and play. Have fun!' The waves were crashing and the kids were all excited. Then just as I raised my phone to read my part, Rebecca threw her arm up and it hit my hand, and my phone went flying up into the air, and it was gone. Immediately gone. I lunged and grabbed in the water, but it wasn't there. The waves had just sucked it away. Obviously, I abandoned the Poseidon script, but we still had a lot of fun that day."

Just for the record, that's why Lee's phone service went so quickly from five bars to sand bars.

Lee has more to say about both the ups and the downs of living in community: "It seems to me that the longer I stay a part of this community, the wider and deeper range of emotions I experience. I've had moments when I expect people to be there for me, and then they don't show up. It can be hard, because community has the expectation that these people that surround you are going to be God's palpable, practical hands and feet, to be there for you, to serve you, to love you. But yet there's something that's lost in translation at times when people's sin and people's brokenness get in the way. That helps keep me grounded in my personal relationship with Jesus Christ, because the community is not my savior. Jesus Christ is my Savior."

Stability is an important value to Sojourners members, who have covenanted to be together for as long as God allows. They understand that God's richest blessings for community don't happen overnight.

"I really enjoy watching the kids grow up," says Zoe. "I also love watching the spiritual growth, how people grow and change over time. I like seeing trajectories. I like seeing long stories, and this is a good place to see long stories. I love being a part of that. I love having people to worship and pray with, day after day, in both mundane and spiritual ways. That's very satisfying to me. It feels like a rich life. Rich is the word that always comes to mind. It feels *rich*. When you have rich food, it has a lot of flavor. There's a lot of stuff going on. It has a lot of content, a lot of meatiness, a lot of complexity. Even when life here is hard, it's not boring and it's not meaningless. I feel like our life here is chock-full of meaningfulness. Even when things are at their hardest, I never feel like it's without purpose. I never say, 'Why are we doing this? Why are we beating ourselves up?' It always feels like we're trying to do something that matters. We may be struggling or failing at that, but we're trying to live lives that are giving to God in the best way that we can imagine. We're *trying* to do that. We may not be very good at it. We may even be terrible at it. But our intentions are to do something that matters. That just really makes life *rich* to me. It's meaningful. Yeah. It's *rich*."

Jesus said, "The thief's purpose is to steal and kill and destroy. My purpose is to give them a rich and satisfying life." (John 10:10, NLT)

That's exactly how I felt that night while singing Christmas carols to grinning folks out on the streets. I don't remember seeing any silver or gold out there, but I do know that it sure felt rich.

DATHOUSE

Address	516 Lincoln St., Indianapolis, Indiana 46203
Phone	317-737-1537
Email	brandon@dathouse.org
Website(s)	https://dathouse.wordpress.com/
Type of Housing	Private homes
Urban/Rural/Suburban	Urban
Founded	2007
# of Core Members	Four to six
# of Residents	Six to eight
Property and Financials	Private financials and property
Community Businesses	Lincoln Lane Coffee Company
Common Meals	Biweekly neighborhood meals
Other Shared Activities	Spontaneous events and meetings
Leadership and Decision-making	Modified consensus
Outreach Ministries	Lincoln Center activities for kids; neighborhood projects; low income housing
Christian Affiliation	Non-denominational
ICC Association Membership	None
Non-Profit Org.	Yes
Key Values	Be a good neighbor; invest in young people; encourage Christian community development

A guy named Bob walks into the Lincoln Lane Coffee Company and orders a cup of coffee. He makes small talk with Sue, the barista, as she pours him a mug. Bob hands her a dollar and takes a seat at the bar.[8]

A handful of people are chatting at nearby tables. The coffee shop is stylish and a bit trendy, with just the right amount of charm to attract the

---

8. This fictional account is based on a typical scenario at Dathouse's coffee shop. The names have been changed.

young professionals who have recently been moving into the neighborhood. Two moms watch their children play in an open space for kids. A backdrop of tasteful music and the rich aroma of organic, farmer-direct coffee add a peaceful comfort to the setting.

Bob chuckles. He remembers when the atmosphere in this building was so crazy that it wrecked the lives of countless men and women. Back then it was a strip joint. In fact, the bar he sits at today served the poison that caused so much trouble for too many people he knew back then.

Things are a lot better now, he says to himself. He takes a sip of coffee and leans back against the bar.

"Hey Sue," he calls out. "How's business? Are we gonna be able to keep the lights on?"

Sue laughs. "Business is good, Bob. Actually, it's been pretty busy for the last few days now, and I'm looking forward to taking some time off. You got any plans for the weekend?"

"I'm hoping to work tonight," he says. "They been cutting back on my hours. As long as I can pay the rent, that's all I care. By the way, guess who I saw at Speedway last night?"

As Bob continues talking, a young couple walks in. They are smartly dressed, as if on their way to big corporate jobs in downtown Indianapolis.

"I'll have a caramel chai latte," says she.

"I'll have a triple-shot cappuccino," says he.

They pay and step to the side to await their order. They look blankly out the window at the flow of traffic on Lincoln Street.

"Are you new in the neighborhood?" asks Bob.

The woman and man become animated, as if recognizing human life in a place where they had not expected to find it.

"Yes," says she.

"Not really," says he at the same moment.

Laughter.

"Yes and no," says Bob. "Now, that's as clear as mud."

"Well, we bought this home over a year ago," says she, "and it took us forever to get all the permits and stuff."

"About half the work is done now," says he, "and we moved in a few weeks ago."

They continue chatting as their drinks arrive. Bob asks what street they live on, and they tell him. Then Bob gives them a little history lesson about the neighborhood. Before they know it, ten minutes have passed.

"Don't want to be late for work," the man says as he reaches for the door. "It was nice talking."

"Yeah," says Bob. "See you later."

"See you."

The couple steps outside.

"That was a nice guy," she says to her partner as they get into the car.

"Yeah," he says. "He could probably talk your ear off, but he seems like a great guy."

"I love seeing that kind of interaction," says Brandon Mott, one of the Dathouse founders. "It might not happen without the coffee shop being here."

When Dathouse started in 2007, there were crumbling houses on nearly every block of the Bates-Hendricks Neighborhood. A lot has changed since then, and today you'll find home restoration projects everywhere. Gentrification brings people together who are on very different courses in life, and Dathouse's Lincoln Lane Coffee Company is the intersection where many of these folks meet.

Brandon explains, "Some people who have lived their whole lives in this neighborhood come in for a dollar cup of coffee, because you can't even get a cup that cheap at the Speedway gas station. Then someone else is coming in for a nice, six dollar, soy chai latte, but these people are in the same space and they see each other. That's when these cross-cultural interactions occur, and I love it. I love it! It's the reason we're here. Our mission is written on these cards that we hand out to new customers, and it says, 'At Lincoln Lane, we want to create space for all of our neighbors—regardless of socioeconomic status—to gather and conspire together on how to improve the community, all while enjoying an amazing cup of coffee.' That's why we exist, and I love seeing that happen."

Bear with me while this narrative takes a little diversion, but here's a new spin on an old theme.

Jesus walks into a coffee shop. *WWJD (What would Jesus drink?)*

Would Jesus order a One Buck Brew or a more expensive Dirty Chai? (*That's an actual drink at Lincoln Lane.*) Or would he take a cup of water and turn it into wine?

Here's my take on that question: Maybe the drink in his hand wouldn't matter so much as the fact that he would be connecting with every kind of person, breaking all socio-economic taboos. It doesn't matter what he's drinking. What matters is the love and respect that he gives to everyone.

And that's the mission of Lincoln Lane Coffee.

This coffee shop is part of the larger Lincoln Center, established with the help of Dathouse's many friends and neighbors. The effort was started by other people in the neighborhood who had been working to get the strip club shut down. A church that had been thinking of planting a new Christian fellowship in the neighborhood liked Dathouse's Lincoln Center concept so much that they provided funding to acquire the property. Many other aspects of the work were freely donated. The exhausting renovations took two and a half years, and the Lincoln Center finally opened in the fall of 2014. That's when Dathouse hired Brandon Mott as Director of the Lincoln Center. He was their first employee, and other part time staff followed. Most of what they do, however, is fueled by a strong volunteer base.

The Lincoln Center provides after-school programs primarily for kids from James A. Garfield School, which is only a block away, although children from any school are welcome. Most of these kids are unattended after school, and they like coming to the Lincoln Center for games and crafts. Some of the greatest benefits are realized as loving staff and volunteers help them to work through conflict with their peers.

Dathouse has always hosted meals for parents and children in the neighborhood, and today these happen about twice a month at the Lincoln Center. They used to provide the entire meal, but eventually they changed it to a potluck, which they call "pitch-in" style meals.

Pitch-in is an important concept for everything that Dathouse does. They strongly believe that everyone has something important to give, no matter how small the contribution might appear to be. They live by this quote, which has been made popular by Christian civil rights activist Dr. John Perkins:

> Go to the people. Live with them. Learn from them. Love them. Start with what they know. Build with what they have. But with the best leaders, when the work is done, the task accomplished, the people will say "We have done this ourselves."
>
> —Lao Tzu[9]

---

9. Lao Tzu was an ancient Chinese philosopher. Goodreads, "Lao Tzu quotes," accessed June 2017, www.goodreads.com/quotes/215411-go-to-the-people-live-with-them-learn-from-them .

Finding Intentional Community

The name Dathouse was created by one of the founders, Derek Abner, who prefaced the word "house" with "dat," an acronym created from the

Featured Communities: Dathouse

first letters of the Greek words *doulos* (servant), *agape* (love), and *tapeinoo* (humility). Dathouse hopes that their every thought, word, and deed will spring from a place of servanthood, love, and humility.

In 2007, two couples and two singles all moved into a house together in the lower-income Bates-Hendricks Neighborhood. It's not the most pleasant-smelling neighborhood, being downwind from one of the largest pharmaceutical factories in the country. Plenty of people thought they were nuts for moving here.

"They said we were moving into a dangerous neighborhood," says Brandon. "They thought we were crazy for living communally. They said we weren't working toward the usual stuff. They didn't think it was appropriate to live in community when we were married. The whole idea of valuing relationships more than work and money was foreign to most of them."

Within a few years, four babies were birthed into the community, and two foster kids were adopted from the neighborhood. To keep the walls from bursting out, some of the members bought houses nearby and moved out. They still did most of their ministry in their homes, hosting a weekly dinner and activity night for kids. They hung out with their neighbors. They helped fix up people's homes. They had a weekly meal just for Dathouse members and their children.

The base for their ministry to kids and families changed in 2014, when the Lincoln Center and coffee shop were opened. Dathouse appeared to be reaching its stride, when they entered a very difficult time. That happened when Derek and Laura left in 2016, with the blessing of the others. The community intellectually encouraged this couple to follow God's leading, but they were emotionally broken. The bonds forged in nine years of community life together cannot easily be severed.

"This last year has been a challenging one for us," wrote Brandon in the Dathouse blog. "Throughout this journey, one of the things I am most thankful for has always been and continues to be community. Losing Derek and Laura as a part of our daily team was a big hit. Their love for people and their commitment to community are unparalleled among anyone I have ever known. However, in their absence, God has slowly but surely been placing new people in our lives to dream with, work for, and love our community here in Bates-Hendricks. With this new life, I am reminded this morning that community is never the goal. There is no place that you can arrive at and say, 'We have accomplished community.' Instead, community is something we are constantly becoming. It is not static, but it moves and changes and adapts. In the recent months . . . we have had an incredible amount of people join our team and have expanded our ability to be good neighbors, invest in young people, and foster Christian community development. Thank you! We know God is faithful, and is continuing to do a good work here in Indy!"

This was a very difficult season for Dathouse, and yet God in his wisdom and mercy ordained that in the natural order of things, springtime follows winter.

As I discussed this with Brandon, he shared this gem of wisdom: "I think a lot of people have this goal of feeling like you arrive at a certain destination, but really the journey is the destination. We are constantly becoming something. The journey is constantly changing. Beauty is found in the temporal, in the fleeting, in the good, and even in the bad. That is community, the ever-changing, always learning movement of life."

Dathouse's threefold purpose is to be good neighbors, invest in young people, and foster Christian community development. The most public and visible expressions of this happen through their interactions with people of all ages at the Lincoln Center. Less visible expressions include picking up trash in the alleyways, driving neighbors to appointments, or fixing leaky roofs or plumbing. In the beginning, most of the Dathouse members worked in construction so they easily slipped into the handyman role.

However, being a good neighbor requires wearing more than a hardhat. You might, in fact, need a pair of nurse's scrubs.

"My neighbor was having a rough week," Brandon said. "His dog passed away, which was really hard on him. Then he came knocking on our door one night with a gash by his eye. He had hit a doorway and it was cut really bad. I helped him clean it up and he wondered if he should go to the hospital. I said, 'If you go in they might give you a stitch or two, but it will probably heal up on its own.' He liked that idea, so we put a couple butterfly bandages on it and taped it up real good. It ended up healing just fine."

Dathouse members view all their work as a group effort in partnership with neighbors and volunteers. They are active in the Bates-Hendricks Neighborhood Association, which is a huge advocate for this area of Indianapolis. An army of volunteers comes out several times a year for a citywide event called the Great Indy Cleanup, filling big rollaway dumpsters with trash, discarded mattresses, and broken furniture that they gather from streets, vacant lots, and alleyways.

A few years ago, the neighborhood converted an abandoned lot into a park, in partnership with a group called Keep Indianapolis Beautiful. Overnight, a tangle of weed trees and rubbish turned into a grassy field with walkways and attractive native plantings. A mulched area harbors a modest playground that Dathouse got for free off Craigslist, but Brandon is working to find a grant to replace it with a more swanky playground. That big workday included hot dogs and cold drinks. The highpoint of the day was a rousing speech by the mayor of Indianapolis.

Gentrification poses a unique challenge for people who have lived the longest in the Bates-Hendricks Neighborhood. When Dathouse moved here in 2007, as many as two hundred homes were abandoned in less than one square mile. As derelict houses were bulldozed or renovated, the area began to look more attractive to professionals, who especially liked the neighborhood's affordability and accessibility. Improvements caused property values to rise, along with rents and mortgages. Those whose roots were deepest here quickly had to decide whether they could even afford to stay. To move often meant downgrading substantially into substandard living conditions.

Dathouse's mission to be a good neighbor instinctively motivated them to reach out to these disadvantaged neighbors in various ways. One successful plan has been to buy abandoned homes for as little as four thousand dollars, with the help of investors or grants, fix them up, and sell them to those who could otherwise not afford to stay. They have acquired three such homes in the last seven years.

"One woman who bought a house from us a couple years ago had some health problems and had to go on disability," Brandon said. "That led to her losing her job, and then she was struggling to make mortgage payments to us. It was especially hard because she's very conscientious and always on time with her payment. She comes to all of our community meals and always asks what she can bring. She gives a lot of support to the community. We know a lot of people like her who will not accept a handout. She has self-respect and wants to work for what she gets. When all that happened, we tried to work with her. We let her skip payments on the house for a few months, and she was so grateful. She kept saying, 'As soon as I'm done with these hospital bills, we'll get right back on track.' We worked with her and helped her through that difficult period."

I can't imagine where this woman might be today were it not for the Dathouse team. I was surprised to learn that Dathouse had given this woman a five-year mortgage.

"Five years?" I said. "That's a sweet deal."

"Yeah," Brandon replied. "I wish I could get a deal like that."

But he stressed the fact that Dathouse does not use a dysfunctional, top-down model of "charity."

"This is definitely good for both of us," he said. "Sure, it might not be that beneficial *financially* for us, but more importantly, we have invested in a stable community person who is now able to give back to the community. People like this have things to contribute that the community needs, and they are more than willing to give. So the benefits go well beyond the finances. They show up at community events. They help children at the community center. They volunteer at the coffee shop. They have a willingness to support one another. This is almost like a pay-it-forward kind of thing. They know that they've been helped, and now they're looking for opportunities to help others."

In God's economy, there are no "needy people." Everyone has something to give. Everyone is respected. Everyone has dignity. Everyone has something to pitch in.

Dathouse believes that love for one's neighbor does not stop at the edge of the neighborhood, but sometimes it reaches into city hall or the state capital building. They have defended legislation that would keep property taxes low for longtime residents in areas of gentrification. They brainstormed with the mayor and food advocates about ways to address food insecurities in the poorer areas of town. Their concern for neighborhood health is also one of the reasons why they partnered with neighbors who are raising chickens and creating urban farms.

The Bates-Hendricks Neighborhood is one of America's food deserts. According to the United States Department of Agriculture, food deserts are urban areas where at least five hundred people or more than 33 percent of the population live over a mile from a supermarket. A mile might not seem like much, but it's a huge distance for families with kids who don't have cars. The government is especially concerned about childhood obesity in food deserts. People in Bates-Hendricks have access to plenty of quickie marts that sell cheap, processed foods, but fresh fruits, vegetables, and healthy whole foods are not so easy to find.[10]

"I'm working with investors," says Brandon, "talking with them about investing in real estate *not* for profit maximization, but to create unity and to make this a better neighborhood. Yes, they will still get a return on their investment, but the investment in the community is worth so much more than the numbers on their quarterly statement. We have lost some neighbors because of the wrong kinds of investments. A significant number of them haven't been able to afford places to live in our neighborhood. That's been a difficult reality. Now we want to leverage property development to benefit our neighbors across the board, not just for the more affluent ones."

Dathouse is seeking to help people not only buy residential property, but commercial property as well. They have a vision for helping local entrepreneurs.

"We would love to find people within the community who have the skills to start and run their own businesses," says Brandon. "A lot of the buildings in our area are commercial-residential mixed use, so it would be really neat for someone to buy the building and live upstairs and run the business downstairs, like people used to do. We want to find investors who can help them do that. And our coffee shop is setting the precedent of hiring people from this community. We hope to instill that value in other businesses that come into the neighborhood. It would be great if someone wanted to run a local ice cream shop in one of these commercial buildings, or a thrift store, or a small, healthy restaurant. There's a lot of opportunity like that here."

The more I spoke with Brandon, the more I sensed that Dathouse was playing by completely different rules than those set by the dominant spirit of the age. The world teaches us to judge people's worth based on their looks, their wealth, their productivity, and their accomplishments. The Bates-Hendricks Neighborhood has a safe place where both latte sippers and buck brew drinkers can stand on equal ground. Dathouse members do not believe in "have-nots." Everybody here is a "have."

---

10. American Nutrition Association, "USDA Defines Food Deserts," accessed June 2017, http://americannutritionassociation.org/newsletter/usda-defines-food-deserts.

People may occasionally do bad things, but according to Brandon: "We don't believe there are bad people. I say this all the time. Some people ask, 'Isn't your neighborhood scary?' I say, 'No. These are just people, like anywhere else. Some of them are struggling, just like the next guy. Some of their problems might be a little more visible than your problems, but that doesn't mean they have more problems than you.' I hear those kinds of questions a lot. Some people have their own preconceived notions or biases or stereotypes, but those begin to completely change when they come face to face with people from the other side, when they get to see people as people. That happens all the time in our coffee shop. I see that daily."

Brandon has some helpful thoughts for people like me who don't generally worry about paying the rent or having enough food on the table.

"Just having money or not having money isn't really a blessing," he said. "The most valuable economy we can experience is to find God's provision wherever it may be, whether in relationships or social connections or possibly through material things. Experiencing love and giving love in return is the greatest blessing. We don't put a high value on production and the work that we do here. We don't live to work. We work to live. It's like when Jesus said that the Sabbath is made for man, not man for Sabbath. We believe the same is true about work and money. They are our slaves, not our masters. They are gifts to use appropriately and that's kind of our worldview. Love is the main thing."

That a solid worldview! It's the kind of worldview that Jesus modeled, and it has the power to cultivate community among people from radically different backgrounds.

I asked Brandon for his opinion about tithing, and how Christians like me might be comfortable setting a target 10 percent figure for helping people in need.

"Jesus did not ask us to give 10 percent," said Brandon. "He asked us to give it all. Ten percent giving is not a New Testament principle. Jesus asked us to give everything. Romans 12:1 says, 'offer your bodies as a living sacrifice, holy and pleasing to God—this is your true and proper worship.' So we offer up our whole lives. When there's a need in our community, we give whatever it takes. We work alongside them. This is so much more personal than writing a check for 10 percent. You can't love your neighbor very well if you don't know your neighbor. You can't share very well if you're not in a relationship them. That kind of giving you are referring to is part of a very individualistic kind of Christianity which I really don't know how to address anymore."

As we were concluding our conversation, I brought this sentence to Brandon's attention that I had found on the Dathouse website:

We firmly believe in sacrificial love and the reality of RESURRECTION!!!

"Why did you write the word resurrection like that, in such big letters?" I asked.

"Because we believe in practicing resurrection.[11] That's what happened with the strip club. It was a place that brought death, and now it brings life. That's the whole cycle of life. Struggle leads to new life. Hardship leads to something new. Death leads to resurrection. That's what we are all about, trying to bring newness to something that is old or neglected."

If you're ever looking for evidence of Jesus Christ's resurrection, try taking a road trip to Indy. You just might be able to watch resurrection happening in real time on the streets of the Bates-Hendricks Neighborhood... whether you are sipping an organic, farmer-direct One Buck Brew... *or a six dollar Dirty Chai.*

---

11. Brandon credits Wendell Berry with the concept of "practicing resurrection." See: "Manifesto: The Mad Farmer Liberation Front," a section of the book: Wendell Berry, *The Mad Farmer Poems* (Berkeley: Counterpoint Press, 2014).

GOOD WORKS, INC.

Address	P.O. Box 4, Athens, Ohio 45701
Phone	740-594-3339
Email	goodworks@good-works.net
Website(s)	http://good-works.net/
Type of Housing	Private homes and apartments; community rooms for interns
Urban/Rural/Suburban	One urban ministry home and thirty-five rural acres
Founded	1981
# of Core Members	About twenty-five
# of Residents	Includes people in transition who stay in the Timothy House
Property and Financials	Private property and financials; paid staff
Community Businesses	Bed and breakfast; Good Gifts retail business
Common Meals	Sunday and Friday evenings; households eat together more frequently
Other Shared Activities	Friday Night Life; Sunday evening worship and meal; Friday meeting
Leadership and Decision-making	Board of Directors; director; delegated leadership teams
Outreach Ministries	About twenty outreaches to Athens County
Christian Affiliation	Nondenominational
ICC Association Membership	None
Non-Profit Org.	Yes
Key Values	Hospitality; justice; empowering people in need; compassion; friendship

It's Friday afternoon, and you're traveling. You are a long ways from home, but you're thinking how nice it would be to do something social this evening . . . something that feels like being with friends and family. You happen to be in Athens, Ohio, a quaint, little college town in the Appalachian foothills. So you set a course for downtown, touching down in an

Featured Communities: Good Works, Inc.

out-of-the-way coffee shop tucked in among pubs and restaurants, along brick-paved streets.

As you embrace a warm cup, you can't help but overhear a conversation at the table next to you about a dinner tonight.

"And it's absolutely free, no strings attached," the young lady says. "Everyone is invited. No invitation required. Just show up, and trust me, you will have a *great* time. During the warmer months they gather outdoors, but this time of year it's at a local church."

"Wait a minute," the guy says. "It's at a church. That means you have to get all dressed up and sit through a long, boring service, just to earn a cheesy little box lunch."

"No! People don't get dressed up, and you don't have to sit through anything! Just come and enjoy the great food. The people are really nice . . . "

As they continue chatting, you surreptitiously jot down the time and place.

At 4:30 that afternoon, you somewhat nervously park your car and slip into the church's fellowship hall. It is filled with the animated conversation of about 150 people. The aroma of delicious herbs and spices makes your mouth water. A guy with a Kermit the Frog puppet is making the rounds. As he passes you, he sprinkles you with some invisible "mingle dust," explaining that it will instantly help you meet new friends.

That's goofy, you think.

"What the heck is *mingle dust*?" a guy next to you asks.

"I hope it's vegan," says a woman.

"You can get anything on the Internet these days," you add.

The chatting continues. The mingle dust must be effective, because twenty minutes later you feel as if you have a lot in common with these new friends of yours. You sit down together at a table. Everyone sings *Happy Birthday* to a six-year-old and an eighty-four-year-old, then someone asks folks what they are thankful for today.

A host of hands shoot up into the air.

"I'm thankful for my mother."

"I'm thankful that I was able to pay the rent this month."

"I'm thankful for ketchup!"

"I'm thankful for these friends of mine, because if it wasn't for them, I don't know how I would've made it through . . . "

The speaker's voice begins to break.

" . . . the most difficult time in my life."

The tears start to flow. Friends get up and the speaker is buried in a huddle of hugs.

Everyone pauses to thank God for the food. You enjoy the blessings of roasted vegetables, chili, black beans, fruit salad, and friendly banter. After dinner, there are a number of different options including a poetry reading, a prayer group, games, music, and more. You stay at your table and enjoy an informal conversation.

Someone is playing light, acoustic music in the background, and you hear the clinking of plates, pots, and pans in the kitchen. You learn that volunteers have donated and prepared the dinner, and they send extra meals home with many of the families.

You glance at the time, and you can't believe it's 7:30 already. You leave with some new names in your contact list, and several invitations for things to do in the coming week.

So this is Friday Night Life at the Good Works community, you say to yourself as you slip back into your car. *Hopefully, I'll be back in Athens next Friday.*

Good Works was launched in 1981 when Keith Wasserman began sheltering people who were experiencing homelessness in his basement. The ministry draws purpose from Job 29:11–16, which outlines God's special compassion for widows, fatherless, and strangers. Good Works does not *fix, enlighten, sustain*, or even *give stuff to people*. Rather, they *partner with* people who have in many ways been marginalized by society.

Friendships and *partnering* are at the core of both their ministry and their community.

"About twenty years ago," says Keith, "we came to the awareness that we needed to move away from ministry *to* the poor, toward a ministry *with* the poor. That was a significant paradigm shift. I'm not a big fan of the phrase 'the poor' anymore. I don't like to use it, particularly if my friends who are poor are in the room. It makes me feel really uncomfortable."

Language is very important to the members of Good Works. They recognize that labels like "the poor" and "the homeless" (as opposed to regular "people") devalue self-worth and tarnish the true identity of God's image-bearers. These and other labels put them in a different class than "normal" people, robbing them of dignity. Members reject society's measures of self-worth that are based on a person's accomplishments, possessions, and social status.

Featured Communities: Good Works, Inc.

A man named Kevin who was staying at Good Works once told Keith, "I'm homeless."

"You are not homeless," said Keith.

"Well, I'm living in your shelter," Kevin said.

Keith looked him in the eye and said, "You are not homeless, Kevin. You are a *man* who does not have a home right now."

"I do not like to say that people are homeless," says Keith. "They are people without homes. We must separate what is happening to people from their identity."

This move away from ministry *to the poor and homeless* means demolishing dysfunctional patterns that reinforce dependency. Keith calls it "Stuff-Mart," where you expect people to show up at a certain place and time so the righteous and blessed people can give them stuff. This system breeds codependency, disrespect, and helplessness.

Instead, Good Works has learned to use the "language of mutuality and reciprocity." Mutuality puts everyone on the same playing field. Reciprocity blurs the lines between "givers" and "receivers." People gain dignity *not* by receiving free stuff and being told to come back when they need more, but by being given an opportunity to give something of value to the community and receive something in return. Meanwhile, those who are more abundant in resources learn to receive gifts from their brothers and sisters who are rich in other areas. Mutuality and reciprocity make everyone more prosperous in the end.

"Reciprocity and mutuality are these diamonds in the rough," says Keith. "As you uncover and discover these things in each other, and as you affirm them, something changes in your relationship. It's no longer a one-way street of dependence, but there's mutuality. There is reciprocity. In my view, this opens new avenues of conversations about who Jesus is and the power of the gospel to change our lives."

Newcomers to Good Works might not hear words like *mutuality* and *reciprocity*, but they *feel* their effects in the way they are welcomed and valued, no matter how "poor and helpless" they are in the world's eyes. Good Works strives to make everybody feel as if they are standing on equal ground. Their goal is to create an environment where people feel safe, where they receive appropriate touch with permission (which could be a handshake or a hug), where people feel listened to, and where they feel respected.

Keith Wasserman has learned a thing or two about marginalized people because he has experienced homelessness about a dozen times in as many cities, voluntarily living on the streets and in shelters. This is not something that people do for fun. In fact, Keith admits that these experiences have made him feel uncomfortable, exhausted, afraid, humiliated, discredited, and dishonored.

Why did he do it?

"I go to live on the streets to expand my perspective and understanding of the situation people without homes are in," says Keith. "I believe that since Christ incarnated himself into our world in order to be a bridge for men and women to have a relationship with their Maker, we too then, must incarnate ourselves into the world of those whom we care about in order

Featured Communities: Good Works, Inc.

to understand how they think and how they feel, in order to really love and help them."[12]

So far, I haven't said much about the Good Works *intentional community*. Why? Because you need to step back and observe their *works*—and come close enough to see their *heart*—before you can fully understand *who they are*.

This intentional community is, primarily, made up of about twenty core members, but it also includes many dedicated volunteers, friends, and interns. At its center is the Good Works, Inc. non-profit organization, which is governed by a board of directors. Keith Wasserman is the Founder and Executive Director. (*BTW, he hates that title. How about a "Name the Director" contest?*)

The Good Works organization owns the Timothy House in Athens for sheltering people who experience homelessness. It also owns thirty-five rural acres just outside of town. On this property are:

- The Good Works administration building
- The Transformation Station facility, for helping people give, receive, and earn much-needed resources
- The Hannah House, a residence for interns, and single men and women who are working toward independent living
- The Hope Center, a large gathering space for the many groups that volunteer for Good Works
- The Carter Cabin, a small, personal retreat space
- A picnic shelter, amphitheater, basketball court, volleyball court, and playground

Core members of the Good Works community are paid staff, and nearly all of them live in private homes in and around Athens. The ministry has a huge support base: about eleven thousand volunteers serve with them each year, and a dedicated core of about a hundred volunteers serve at least monthly.

---

12. Good Works, Inc., "Homeless by Choice?" by Keith Wasserman, accessed June 2017, http://good-works.net/keiths-homeless-stories/.

Finding Intentional Community

If you are looking for a precise line between *bona fide* intentional community members and "outsiders," you won't find it. In the spirit of mutuality, Good Works has worked hard to erase distinctions between servants and those being served. Still, as you might expect, most of the guiding and planning is done by core/staff members, who meet regularly to eat, pray, teach, learn, encourage one another, and have fun together.

Good Works receives donations that allow them to serve twenty-one thousand individual meals and give shelter to around 150 people each year. They receive income from two small businesses: a bed and breakfast on their rural property, and the Good Gifts business for selling locally-produced Appalachian goods.[13]

Good Works is a busy place, and these are the main ministries that it oversees:

- The Timothy House, which provides food and shelter for one to two hundred people each year
- Friday Night Life dinners, which provides activities and sit-down, nutritional meals for about 130 people
- Friday Night Kid's Club for children
- Neighbors Helping Neighbors, which helps fix and maintain homes and property primarily for widows
- Good Works Gardens, planted at the homes of fifteen to twenty widows or people with disabilities
- Two Good Works community gardens, for supplementing the ministry's groceries (They also raise chickens for eggs and meat.)
- Transformation Station, which enables people to earn and acquire vehicles, bicycles, appliances, and more (over 150 cars have been provided to date)
- Senior Friends, which facilitates friendships between volunteers and older adults[14]
- Summer Kids' Discovery Club, providing activities and lunch for children during the summer months
- Praxis, an opportunity for Ohio University students and faculty to receive educational experiences related to homelessness and poverty

---

13. This business has been affiliated with Ten Thousand Village outlets in the past.
14. This ministry is seasonal, depending on the availability of staff and interns.

Featured Communities: Good Works, Inc.

- Hannah House Life in Transition, providing a stable environment for people in transition out of homelessness
- Good Works Walk, a regular fundraising event in support of the Timothy House

Transformation Station is a good example of how the Good Works community practices mutuality and reciprocity. Each year, Good Works accepts applications for fifty to sixty people with needs. Meanwhile, they accept donations of items including cars, washers, dryers, refrigerators, stoves, bicycles, air conditioners, furniture, and crates of food. People earn these items by helping Good Works and others in Athens County.

Receivers feel a strong measure of self-respect, knowing that they have *earned* these much-needed items. Their family members can take pride in the hard work they invested to bring these items home. One woman who received a car said Good Works "helped me get independent, and I want to give back to them and other people if I can. I intend to come back once a month."

Meanwhile, donors are encouraged to help re-home their donations, building relationships in the process. A woman who donated a car explained, "One of the major challenges [here in Athens County] is keeping transportation, and it is expensive. This is a way for us to offer an asset to the community through a group that we trust, to find a person who can use that asset, and in the process the person who gets that asset is helping the community because they do community service to earn it, so it's just good all around."

Members of the intentional community see each other regularly as they work together in ministry. They go to movies and artistic events together. They have a "business" meeting each Friday afternoon. They meet Sunday evening for worship and a meal called Life Together. They meet Tuesday mornings for worship and prayer.

Oddly enough, while most Americans strive for greater efficiency and productivity, Good Works is cultivating an entirely different ethic.

"We have this ethic of inefficiency," says Keith. "It's kind of a challenge to the concept of efficiency, because if you're not careful, any one of us can fall into the idea that the primary governing principle of everything is efficiency. Well, I don't think so. I think that the primary governing principle should be relationships with each other and with God. That's an important piece of our Christian community."

A scriptural foundation for this ethic of inefficiency is found in the story of the woman who "wasted" perfume on Jesus feet.

> Then Mary took about a pint of pure nard, an expensive perfume; she poured it on Jesus' feet and wiped his feet with her hair. And the house was filled with the fragrance of the perfume. But one of his disciples, Judas Iscariot, who was later to betray him, objected, "Why wasn't this perfume sold and the money given to the poor? It was worth a year's wages." . . . "Leave her alone," Jesus replied. "It was intended that she should save this perfume for the day of my burial. You will always have the poor among you, but you will not always have me."
>
> —John 12:3–8

Keith explains, "A lot of our time is kind of wasted on Jesus, like when we're just listening to people. Sometimes the conversation goes on and on and on, because some people want to talk and talk and talk. At a time like that, I'm often thinking, 'How can I get out of this?' Then I hear the Lord saying, 'You need to listen as an act of worship. This is not for you. You need to have a higher level of reasoning or commitment, because this is for me.' So the higher value is worship. And the same is true whether you're cleaning a bed, driving someone home, or weeding a garden. It often seems to me like worship got kidnapped and held hostage in church buildings, ten to twelve o'clock on Sunday mornings. I don't want to discredit worshipping God with singing, and we like to do that here, but we've expanded this vision of worship to be much larger than that. Who said worship should be limited to pianos and guitars? Why can't the instruments of true worship be rakes or lawnmowers or chainsaws or shovels? Why can't a hammer be an offering of praise? How do you teach a seventh grader to worship God? I say, give him a lawnmower and tell him to play it in Thelma's front yard. Go out there and worship God with a heart of service. In fact, this is the number one thing that sustains me, because I grow weary in doing good. We seek to see everything we do as worship. It's so broad. From our first waking moment to the last breath we take each day, we give thanks to the Lord. We say, 'I love you, God.' This is our heart of worship, but again, it's not always *efficient* in the world's eyes."

Featured Communities: Good Works, Inc.

To prevent Good Works members from working *too* hard, they have systems for protecting time off and personal space. They have a secluded retreat house for private getaways.

Keith has a friend named Ken who spent nine months in the Timothy House when he was in transition. After he left the Timothy House, Good Works invited Ken to come back and help make spaghetti for Friday Night Life.

Ken didn't see this as a request to do a dirty job that nobody else wanted to do. He saw it as an invitation to worship.

"I made spaghetti for two years straight," says Ken.

And he loved doing it.

What was Ken's job description?

He served spaghetti on the worship team at Good Works, Inc.

Oh, yeah, and he's pretty good at playing tongs.

HILLSIDE FELLOWSHIP

Address	2322 Hobson Rd., Fort Wayne, Indiana 46805
Phone	—
Email	info@hillsidefw.com; info@thefirehouseprojects.com
Website(s)	www.hillsidefw.com/; www.thefirehouseprojects.com/
Type of Housing	Private homes; a monastic home; property in Nicaragua
Urban/Rural/Suburban	Urban (and one rural acre in Nicaragua)
Founded	2005
# of Core Members	Thirty-five
# of Residents	About sixty regular participants
Property and Financials	Private property and financials
Community Businesses	Community event space; had a coffee shop and might again
Common Meals	Spontaneous
Other Shared Activities	Weekly gathering; regular spontaneous shared events
Leadership and Decision-making	Consensus
Outreach Ministries	Urban ministry; property and ministry in Nicaragua
Christian Affiliation	Non-denominational
ICC Association Membership	None
Non-Profit Org.	No (although the Firehouse Projects is non-profit)
Key Values	Living in grace; Acts 2:42–47; Spirit-filled life; gospel to the nations

Urbaite, Nicaragua

March 12, 2017

"La niña está muerta."

Featured Communities: Hillside Fellowship

A group of villagers were speaking in hushed tones outside the house. Some of them had been inside to see Gesalene, who was eighteen months old. The fever had gotten out of control. She had turned blue. She had stopped breathing. They were all in agreement now.

"The girl is dead."

Perhaps some were already thinking of the funeral. Perhaps they were planning what gift of food they could bring to the grieving family. But apparently the child's mother had not given up hope. She was a believer, having sung in the church choir just that morning.

Someone suggested that they take the child to the hospital.

Who takes a dead person to the hospital?

For whatever reason, the woman and her husband walked out to the main highway, carrying the child. It was Sunday, when all of Nicaragua shuts down for the day. Even ambulances don't run on Sunday.

Josh Wildstar and Matt Spinks happened to be driving through the village of Urbaite when some people flagged them down. An interpreter helped them understand that someone wanted to get to the hospital in Moyogalpa, twelve miles away.

"Sure," they said. "Get in. It's not a problem."

The mother and father climbed into the backseat of the car, along with a man who spoke broken English. Their faces were distraught. Josh and Matt saw that the mother was holding a small child wrapped up in a blanket.

So they drove past coffee plantations, green pastures with livestock, fields of plantains and bananas, and stands of forests with monkeys and parrots hiding in the shadows. They were driving halfway around the island of Ometepe in Lake Nicaragua. There are no shortcuts across the middle of the island, because such a road would go right through the middle of an active volcano. Josh and Matt could see the Concepción Volcano rising to over five thousand feet as they drove around its circumference.

The back seat of the car was quiet and somber. Worship music was playing in the front. What were Josh and Matt thinking?

"We're not fluent in Spanish," said Matt, "so we thought the girl was sick. We were just worshipping God and praying in tongues under our breath. Then, about halfway through the ride, Josh, who knows more Spanish than me, says, 'Hey Matt, I think they said she's dead.' I say something like, 'Oh my gosh,' but then immediately I have this really strong conviction in my heart. 'I don't feel like she's dead,' I say. And Josh says, 'I don't think she's dead either.' At that moment, we felt like the Holy Spirit was doing something powerful, so from then on, we both agreed that this girl was gonna live."

Josh and Matt kept praying as they had before. At one point, Josh, who was driving, reached one hand back and placed it on the bundled child.

"Life," he prayed. "In Jesus name, we release life."

It was a simple prayer . . . little more than a breath.

As Josh brought his hand back to the steering wheel, they heard a small cough and then some crying. The mother pulled back the blanket to look inside, and the parent's conversation became more animated.

"At that moment," says Matt, "we felt like something amazing had just happened in the car. I was like, 'She might have just gotten raised from the dead.' And Josh said, 'Yeah. I know.' Then we just kept praying until we got to the hospital."

The girl's parents took her inside, but only for a few minutes. The doctor sent them home, saying, "I don't know why you brought her here. This girl is fine."

"Was she dead?" Matt asked the interpreter.

"Yes," he said. "She was dead. All those people at her house knew she was dead."

But now, as they could plainly see, the girl was very much alive, alert, and active in her mother's arms.

You can watch this girl squirming in and out of her mother's lap in a video captured later, with all the spark and charm of a healthy toddler. You can see friends and family gathered around her as the mother recounts this miraculous event.[15]

The village was so excited to learn that Gesalene was alive, especially since so many of them had witnessed her death. The word spread rapidly, as they told everyone they knew about this miracle.

"People from all over Nicaragua have heard about Gesalene's healing," said her mother, who gives all glory to God for her daughter's life. "The one who was driving put his hand on the girl and prayed for her. At that moment, the girl was healed, just as he was praying to God."

The child's grandmother added, "He was sent by God to save the child."

15. The Fire House Chronicles, "Raised from the Dead!" accessed June 2017, www.thefirehouseprojects.com/raised-from-the-dead-the-fire-house-chronicles/.

Featured Communities: Hillside Fellowship

Wow.

That story describes just one part of one day in the life of Hillside Fellowship . . . and we haven't even gotten to Fort Wayne, Indiana, yet.

How does one small community get from the mundane streets and everydayness of life in an unexceptional American town to the miraculous works of God at the foot of a volcano in the middle of Lake Nicaragua?

To answer that question, let's go back to the starting line.

Matt Spinks's spiritual journey began in a mainline church, receiving a huge spark after his first mission trip as a teen. After high school, he joined Youth with a Mission and lived in India for four years, soaking in all the radical teachings and experiences that communal life in missions could give him. But after a while, something didn't feel quite right to him.

"I loved the amazing culture of those mission bases," says Matt. "We had this excitement and enthusiasm for God and evangelism and worship that I never experienced in my church back in Fort Wayne. I really loved the YWAM culture. We were living in community, but the turnover rate was so high. We'd form these close friendships and have an amazing community for a few months, and then half of the mission base would leave and go back home. Then you had to start over, because the project was always more important than the relationships that we were building. It's funny because the YWAM base would have so much more movement of the Spirit than the local church, but the average church would have so much more long-term relationships than the YWAM base. I wanted to see both of those combined."

In 2004, Matt sent an email to about fifty friends who he thought might be interested in forming an intentional Christian community. About ten people accepted the invitation to pioneer the Hillside Fellowship in Fort Wayne, moving into a north side neighborhood in 2005. They met daily for prayer, worship, and meals. Their teachings relied heavily on YWAM, the International House of Prayer in Kansas City, and the Boiler Room and 24–7 Prayer movement. This is when Matt met his wife Katie, who was also attracted to community.

In time, Hillside developed a covenant that still binds them together to this day. They agree:

- To be true to Christ
- To be kind to others
- To take the Gospel to the nations

- To do these things together in the spirit of Acts 2:42–47

The book of Acts is much more than a historical reading for Hillside. In the early days, they studied it from start to finish, seeking ways to walk out this reality in today's world. One day, they sensed a divine calling from this particular passage:

> But you will receive power when the Holy Spirit comes on you; and you will be my witnesses in Jerusalem, and in all Judea and Samaria, and to the ends of the earth.
>
> —ACTS 1:8

They felt like God was saying, "Fort Wayne is your personal Jerusalem. It's your hometown. If you are faithful here in your backyard, then I will release you to Judea and Samaria, which is the United States. Then I will send you to the ends of the earth."

"Exactly ten years to the day after we started our community," says Matt, "we met Josh and Judy Wildstar, who shared our passion of taking this Gospel and the presence of God in community across the country and to the ends of the earth. We travelled with them for a couple years in the U.S., just talking to everyone we could about Jesus. We saw God healing people and setting people free in amazing ways. Then we said, 'Why not Nicaragua?' Julie had been there before, and we always had this idea of doing a bus tour. Everyone loves the idea community on wheels, right?"

I'd like to jump into the middle of Matt's story to say that their organizational style is sometimes wacky and spontaneous, but (hopefully) always Spirit-driven. For example, their online promotion of this 2016 trip to Central America was an open invitation that simply said, "No-time-to-explain-just-hop-on-the-bus."

Matt continues: "So we formed a caravan and drove all the way to Nicaragua. It was an amazing, super fun, community experience, just reaching out to people on the streets wherever we went. At the end of the trip, we drove back home, while Josh and Julie stayed and looked for land. They even gave birth to their first daughter in Costa Rica. Then they found about an acre of land on the island of Ometepe, which we all ended up buying for one thousand dollars. Our heart was to build a permaculture farm there and reach out to the local people, following that Acts 1:8 vision. So we built a three-story worship room and sleeping quarters. We have an outdoor kitchen. The volcanic soil is extremely rich. It's one of the easiest places on the planet to grow things. We already have plantains, bananas, avocados, an amazing mango tree, several coconut trees, sugar cane, kale, lettuce, spinach, an old tamarind tree, hot peppers, and a lot more. It's kind of a Garden of Eden, the perfect place for a permaculture farm."

If you're like me, you're wondering how smart it is to pitch your tent on the side of an active volcano. If it's any consolation, archeologists say that the island has been inhabited for thousands of years. Small eruptions and earthquakes occur every few years, but the last significant eruption was about one hundred years ago, affecting only a small part of the island.

Gesalene's story didn't end on March 12th, 2017. About a week after she was raised from the dead, the Hillside team organized a feast and invited the village to her parent's house. About fifty neighbors and fifteen Hillsiders showed up for fish, rice, beans, juice, and testimony. Neighbors were excited, telling what part they had played in the miraculous event. The father shared a few words. The mother recounted on video what had occurred. Everybody heard how Jesus is alive and still working miracles, how God is active and present today. Little Gesalene was the star of the show, bubbling with childish antics and effervescent life.

Josh and Matt extended an open invitation for people to visit their community anytime for prayer or encouragement from the Lord. They closed their talk by inviting people to step forward for prayer.

"Literally, the second we said that," says Matt, "a big line of people formed for prayer. That was what we did the rest of the night. There were about six little prayer sessions going on at the same time. It was pretty awesome."

One woman was experiencing significant pain and bleeding from a menstrual problem. As the team prayed for her, she felt the pain subside. They saw this woman a few days later and she said that she had been completely healed.

A man from the neighborhood said he had struggled as an alcoholic for many years. After prayer, he said he felt like he was set free and that alcohol would not affect him anymore. The team has not seen him since, but they are encouraged by his profession of faith. Statistically, about 40 percent of men on the island are alcoholics.

FINDING INTENTIONAL COMMUNITY

Today, Hillside Fellowship in Fort Wayne, Indiana, numbers thirty-five to forty core members including children. About twenty-five additional friends visit on a regular basis. Hillside has an annual ceremony renewing their covenant with each other, while at the same time bringing new members into the community.

For several years, Hillside ran a coffee shop for ministry, income, and music events, although that has now closed. Today they host a facility called the Glory Hub for Christian concerts and events. Members are free to come to this rental space for a quiet place to read, pray, meet, or just relax. There are no community businesses, and members work in various professions. Matt and Katie run Firehouse Projects as a loosely-related non-profit ministry.

Members consider Hillside to be their primary church home, although some also attend other churches. They meet Tuesday nights for dinner, fellowship, and an occasional worship service. They share deep friendships and enjoy getting together for fun and social events. Most of the members still live in the same neighborhood.

For about five years, Hillside ran a community house called the Monastery. Members and guests paid rent to live in the Monastery, or they could work in the coffee shop in exchange for rent. Hillside ended up closing that first Monastery, but they are taking a second run at it in 2017.

"We learned a lot that first time," says Matt, "and we're doing things a little different now. Back then, when people wanted to move into community, we saw two scenarios. If they were stable and doing well financially, they'd usually get their own house or apartment nearby. If they weren't, they'd move into the Monastery. With that model, we kept taking in so many needy people that the Monastery ended up being a really needy place, while the people who pioneered the vision mostly moved out. We ended up just living from crisis to crisis. That was definitely a challenge, so we stopped doing it for a while and took some time to reevaluate. Our hearts were in the right place and it was a very welcoming place, but we decided we aren't a rehab facility or a homeless shelter. We can't always be in crisis management. Sustainability is the key, which means we don't accept just anybody in this new Monastery. We have an application process to see if it will be a good fit for everybody. We have discipleship classes and different tracks of prayer and teaching and involvement. It is definitely more intentional and more monastic. It's more intense spiritually. It's a community hub, a part of the Hillside community. The Monastery is a sacred space for deeper spiritual pursuit, where we just bask in the Father's presence. It's actually more like the old school monastery, with rhythms of prayer and study, where we do outreach together, make meals together, and create a place of sanctuary that the rest of the community can enjoy. We want to develop these more intense expressions of community. We want to make it accessible to families and individuals of every walk of life, not just singles. Not everyone in the Hillside community will live in the Monastery, but everyone is welcome to come and receive from it."

A handful of Hillside members live in Nicaragua all the time, and others like Matt, Katie, and their two kids plan to spend time there each year. They invite others to join them to rest, garden, build, and fulfill Jesus's command "to be my witnesses . . . to the ends of the earth."

Nicaraguan culture is much more social than the United States. People there spend a lot of time together in homes, shops, and on the streets. Locals are constantly walking by the Hillside property, starting conversations, sharing fruit or plantains, and checking up on Hillside's projects. In a way, the opportunities for building relationships with neighbors are as rich as the volcanic soil.

Through a number of divine appointments, Josh and Matt were introduced to a missionary couple from California who had been living in Nicaragua for thirteen years. This couple helped the newbies assimilate into local culture, and they shared resources with them, including the use of a school building along a main highway.

On their 2017 trip, the Hillside team held several spontaneous worship nights in this school building, which was little more than a concrete shell. They would bring a guitar, djembe, and a dozen or more sets of vocal chords, and sing praise music or make up songs on the spot. People walking by would frequently come in to see what was going on, since they could easily hear the music from the road. Many would accept the team's offer of prayer, and they'd often communicate by way of a translator.

One evening, an eighteen-year-old girl came in with several of her friends. She had dark hair and was neatly dressed, but she was obviously struggling to walk. She wore orthopedic shoes, and her face couldn't hide the fact that she was in a lot of pain.

Jackie and Stephanie went to greet the girls. They asked, "Is there anything you'd like to pray for?"

The young woman hesitated, as if not knowing how to respond. It's not every day that a stranger will ask you that kind of question.

Then she found the courage to say, "You could pray for my feet. I've had this problem all my life."

Jackie and Stephanie nodded. The girl removed her shoes and sat down in a chair. It was plain to see that her feet were deformed.

Several people surrounded her and began to pray, asking God to heal her feet. Everybody was in agreement, and their prayers rose like incense to the God who loved and cared and was watching so intently over them.

"Are you experiencing anything?" someone asked.

"Yes," the girl said. "It's warm. I feel a lot of heat."

Several people were watching as the girl's feet began to change. The unnatural curvature straightened, and a natural arch returned to her feet.

The girl's face was changing too, filling with awe and wonder.

"The pain is gone," she said in amazement. "It's gone."

As she stared at her feet, her eyes grew as wide as the sky. It happened so quickly. She didn't know what to say.

"Maybe you should try walking around," someone suggested.

"This is amazing," she said as she walked around the room without a limp. "I can hardly believe it!"

Every eye was on the girl now, and many eyes were filled with tears.

"This is the first time I've ever been able to walk like this!"

Her sense of shock had now turned to excitement. Someone gave her a pair of running shoes. She put them on and began running without any pain whatsoever, smiling from ear to ear. The other girls who came in with her were as thrilled as she was. They were chattering in Spanish now, and many people started laughing and praising God. They were overjoyed, unable to contain themselves. People shouted out words of thanks and praise to God, worshipping him for his goodness.

The girls stayed for quite a while that evening, talking and singing. They were so joyful, in huge contrast to how they had come in. Someone even took the girl's hand and danced with her, in expression of joy and thanksgiving to God.

The team has stayed in touch with this girl, and learned she went to visit her doctor the very next day.

"Your feet are completely fine," the doctor said. "But you better get some new orthopedic shoes . . . just in case."

"No thanks," she said.

I asked Matt if those kinds of stories also happen in mundane places like Fort Wayne, Indiana.

"Absolutely. We've seen a number of people healed in Fort Wayne. We have so many stories of the miraculous things that God is doing here."

"Why do healings and miracles like this occur?" I asked Matt.

"Because God loves us," says Matt." Sickness and disease were never a part of God's original design. Jesus came to restore and redeem us back to the original design, not just spiritually, but in all ways. He simply loves us and wants our lives to be filled with joy, and to know that he wants to have

FINDING INTENTIONAL COMMUNITY

a relationship with us. Miracles bless our lives and open us up to see the goodness of God and to live in his power. Healings reveal who God is and what he can do. People are drawn to God because of that. Anytime there's a miracle, it affects the person involved, but it also attracts other people. It intrigues them, and that can lead them into a relationship with him, although some people need to hear about a hundred miracles before they are ready to open up to that."

I thought of Hillside's mission to take the Good News to the world, which reminded me of a verse from the Old Testament:

> How beautiful on the mountains are the feet of those who bring good news, who proclaim peace, who bring good tidings, who proclaim salvation, who say to Zion, "Your God reigns!"
>
> —ISAIAH 52:7

If there was a *Hillside Fellowship Translation* of that verse, it would read: "How beautiful on the volcanic slopes are the feet of those who bring Good News."

And speaking of beautiful feet, I doubt if there was one person who saw that Nicaraguan girl that night . . . who wasn't simply *adoring* her feet.

Praise God for beautiful feet, and for Hillside Fellowship, who is bringing theirs to the slopes of Concepción Volcano.

THE JULIAN PROJECT

Address	P.O. Box 1744, Julian, California 92036
Phone	760-519-1149
Email	wolfboyparker@gmail.com
Website(s)	www.facebook.com/julianproject/
Type of Housing	Privately-owned community house; smaller rental house on nine acres
Urban/Rural/Suburban	Small-town suburban
Founded	1998
# of Core Members	About six
# of Residents	About ten
Property and Financials	Private property and financials, members help with expenses
Community Businesses	No community business
Common Meals	Spontaneous meals together, occasional planned meals and celebrations
Other Shared Activities	Movie nights, outdoor activities, chores, help with retreats, house concerts
Leadership and Decision-making	Modified consensus
Outreach Ministries	Hospitality; music and social events; personal choice of involvement in social and environmental issues, local school outreach
Christian Affiliation	Non-denominational
ICC Association Membership	None
Non-Profit Org.	No
Key Values	Hospitality; creative arts; environmental issues; social justice

A few years ago, a Christian couple named Mark and Donna spent the morning driving the streets of Julian, California. They were full-time artists seeking like-minded companions and a retreat-like home base for a possible relocation.

By mid-day, their tangled path through rambling neighborhoods had not produced any good possibilities. So they paused for prayer.

Then Mark had an idea. "Let's just walk down the main street in town," he said.

Donna agreed, so they explored the town center by foot, but that search was also in vain.

Finally, Donna asked, "Are you ready to go, Mark? I think we've exhausted our possibilities."

"Not quite yet," said Mark. "I feel like God wants us to go stand by that pole over there."

As strange as it might sound, they stood at the lamppost outside the Cider Mill to see what might happen.

Minutes passed. Mark looked around at all the pedestrian traffic. He watched the cars go by.

Suddenly, something in front of the Cider Mill caught his attention. There, with her back to them, was a young woman with familiar long, straight, blond hair.

It could only be Debby, an old friend whom they hadn't seen or spoken with in many years.

Donna saw her too. "Debby!" she called out.

Debby turned and dropped her jaw.

"Donna?!" she exclaimed.

Her husband Mike, who had just stepped out of the store, looked at Mark and Donna with amazement in his eyes. The two couples greeted each other with warm embraces.

"Of all the places to meet!" exclaimed Donna.

"We live up here now," said Debby, "What are you doing here?"

Then a knowing expression crossed Debby's face. "Are you looking for a place to live?" she asked.

Donna and Mark nodded. Within minutes, Debby and Mike had organized a personal van tour of the area. The grand highlight was a drive by the beautiful Julian Project home.

"You really need to connect with these people," Debby said. "They do similar work as you. They also have apartments to rent in the smaller house on the property."

Not long after, Mark and Donna connected with the Julian Project and met them in person. They ended up living with the Julian Project for over two years, fitting right into the community. They even hosted epic reader's theaters in the Julian Project's living room. In so many ways, it turned out to be the perfect season for Mark and Donna and the Julian Project. Eventually, they purchased their own home in the area while continuing their close relationship with the community.

And all of that wouldn't have happened without the lamppost incident.

The Julian Project has a peculiar gift for attracting the right kind of people who approach their orbit. Mark and Donna aren't the only ones who arrived by way of an unusual "lamppost" type of experience.

As for Joan and me, it's worth noting that it took some divine intervention to get us to visit. This is my true confession: When we were out on the road visiting communities, I decided to skip the Julian Project.

Why?

Well, I'm embarrassed to say, but my wee, little brain equated the word "Project" in their name with *doing, achieving, promoting,* and *proselytizing*. I imagined all the dreary things that Cold War socialists do in the basement of a gray, 1960s-era office building.

I'm not kidding. I am biased against the word *project*.

Having visited the Julian Project at the robust recommendations of our friends at Riverbend Commons in Corona, California, I now understand how my narrow-minded conclusions couldn't have been farther from the truth. Our delightful visit inspired my imagination to rise from the cool and damp basement and shoot into the skies, like festive fireworks. I see the Julian Project as a kaleidoscopic burst of sound and light. It is a colorful collage of art, music, and hospitality. It is a perfect patchwork of nature, health, and civic engagement.

What do I mean by civic engagement?

That's a fancy way of saying that these folks are really good at connecting with their neighbors and their town. For example, Tricia Elisara (who has kids in the local public school system) helped to reform the formerly anemic cafeteria menu. She works part-time as an "in-school garden educator," teaching dirt-related topics like gardening, ecology, nutrition, and healthy cooking. Her kidsingardens.com blog is a winner with many parents and kids in Julian and beyond.

Tricia's husband, Chris Elisara, is an educator and spokesperson for Bible-based creation care and new urbanism.

Gregg Parker teaches outdoor education at nearby Cuyamaca Rancho State Park. He is involved with the Julian Mountain Lion Project, the national Mountain Lion Foundation, and the Julian Dark Sky Network. His passion for environmentalism and outdoor education has opened the door for him to write a weekly column in the local newspaper.

Maril Parker assists in organizing annual local events, including the Julian Family Fiddle Camp and the Julian Fiddle and Picking Contest. She's a gifted networker, and she has a lot of fun playing fiddle in a local band.

The entire community pulls together when it comes to hosting house concerts, outdoor music events, retreats, and bed and breakfast guests at their lovely home.

Perhaps the Julian Project's most important means of civic engagement is that they simply know the art of friend making. Sure, it's a small town, but when we went out to dinner with Gregg and Maril, everybody seemed to know and love them.

You will get a kick out of the remarkable story of Julian Project's inception.

First, you should know that they have a big, gorgeous home in a picture-perfect setting. My wife Joan and I drove to Julian, California, on a late December day, wearing short sleeves and sandals. We had just come from the beach. As we climbed to four thousand feet in elevation, we were surprised to find a couple inches of snow on the ground. This added a sprinkle of Christmas allure to our visit, even under a golden sun and sparkling blue skies.

The home with its sumptuous great room, large deck, and wood-burning stove, instantly has the feel of a mountain lodge. The open kitchen could accommodate a small village, and the bedrooms are absolutely lovely. The house sits on nine acres of land with the perfect accent of flowers, shrubs, apple and pear orchards, red-skinned manzanita bushes, and breathtaking mountain vistas.

Maril's introduction to the house came around 1990 when she attended a house church meeting in what is now called the music room.

I'll never live in a house like this, she thought while adoring the architecture. *I would love to live in a house like this! But I'll never live in a house like this.*

Then in 1997, the recently-married Parkers and their good friends the Elisaras were dreaming about doing something that seemed innovative and adventurous: moving into a house together and living in Christian community. Not long after, Gregg and Maril were driving by the house where Maril had attended church when they noticed it was for sale. Nobody was home, so they spoke with the neighbors.

"The owners are out," the neighbor explained, "but you can leave them a note on the door."

So they left a note on the door. About a week later, Gregg and Maril were seated at the kitchen table with the owners.

"So what are your hopes and plans for the property?" the owners wondered.

"We have this crazy idea," Maril explained, "where we do hospitality and host people for different kinds of events. You see, we're Christian, and we want to do this community thing, and . . ."

That's when the woman's eyes started getting wet. As Maril continued, tears began streaming down her face.

Then the woman simply said, "I've been praying for you for two years."

"What do you mean?" Maril asked. What she was really thinking is, *What!? No way!*

"For two years, we've been praying that God would bring someone like you to this house," the woman explained.

Not only that, but Gregg and Maril later learned that the first owners who sold the house to this couple had been praying from the very beginning that the house would be dedicated to God's service. They were the people who had built the house, and the same ones who hosted the house church that Maril had attended.

The short version of this long story is that eventually, God—in his extravagant mercy—made it possible for the Parkers and Elisaras to receive an extravagant home that they couldn't afford at a ridiculously affordable price.

"We could see God's fingerprints all over the whole process," says Maril.

To sweeten the deal, the owners threw in all kinds of free kitchenware, appliances, furnishings, and extras.

"It got to the point where the miraculous seemed common," Maril recalls. "We just prayed and waited to see what God was going to do next."

Says Gregg, "It was a very clear, real-life example of how God can do more than you can ask or imagine."

The Julian Project continues to run the place as if it is God's home, not their own.

"It's way too big for us alone," says Maril. "There is no way we would live in such a big house unless it's for ministry."

They share the house with a handful of others who are committed to the Julian Project mission. Several years into the project, the Elisara family moved into a nearby home that could accommodate their expanding family.

Featured Communities: The Julian Project

Not long after that, the community began renting rooms to vacation-seekers on Airbnb.com. It's a win-win situation, a friend-making opportunity that also helps pay the mortgage. Julian, California, is a desirable tourist destination, so it's easy to fill their rooms when they aren't occupied by other friends and pilgrims. The home has also become a regular retreat center, especially for groups from nearby San Diego. As mentioned earlier, in addition to the big house, the community also owns a smaller rental home on the property.

The entire community gathers regularly for Monday morning devotions, prayer, and coffee. They also meet for meals once or twice a month, for fun and recreational activities, and to host larger gatherings. Community chores and maintenance are shared by the Julian Project team.

Our visit to Julian Project was somewhat spontaneous with very little forethought or preparation. Perhaps we didn't time our arrival well, because when we arrived, Maril (who is the Princess of Gracious Hospitality) said, "I only have a few minutes because I'm off to band practice tonight."

"Cool," I said. "Can we come?"

It sounded like a fun adventure, so Gregg drove all of us to a little hippy shack in the woods. As we warmed up to a wood stove and hot tea, the lilting harmonies and subtle rhythms quickly swept me away to some gypsy camp along a darkly flowing river in a mysterious land far, far away.

The musicians call themselves the Haywire Band from Julian, and they describe themselves as eclectic and folksy with classic rock influences.[16] Their original and old timey tunes are performed with guitar, fiddle (played by Maril), accordion, drums, and vocals. Together with friends like the Julian Project, the band hosts two popular music events each year: the Spring Thing, and the Applepalooza festival, which is held at the Julian Project house in the fall.

About 150 people come each autumn to Applepalooza, as the last of the apples are being harvested. People bake pies, press cider, cultivate friendships, and enjoy great music.

The Julian Project is a greenhouse for the arts. They display their friend's original artwork in the great room and offer it for sale to guests.

---

16. Haywire Band from Julian, "Haywire: The Band," accessed June 2017, www.haywire.band/.

"We like to support artists with works in progress," says Gregg. "We've had several people come and work on books here, or write the next couple of songs for an album, just seeking a change of scenery and atmosphere that encourages creativity. I remember one musician working on a song late into the night. She was trying not to play too loud on her guitar, but of course it wasn't bothering us at all. In the morning, she said, 'I was able to write a complete song last night.' We love to hear those kinds of stories."

Joan and I hadn't taken two steps inside the house before experiencing a peace that transcends human understanding. Apparently, we aren't the only ones who notice it, because reviews from guests who have booked stays at the Julian Project through Airbnb.com include phrases like "warm and inviting," "a relaxed, laid-back atmosphere," "absolutely wonderful," "comfortable and warm," and "you won't believe how beautiful the house is unless you see it." Guests love the delicious coffee, homemade muffins, pastries, fresh daffodils, cozy wood-burning stove, large wooded lot, and expansive mountain views.

"We had a gal come to stay with us from the city," says Gregg. "She had been dealing with a lot of stress. She stayed two days, and most of the time she just sat on the porch wrapped up in a comforter, looking out at the view. Her review said, 'This was just what the doctor ordered. I didn't want to leave, and you won't either.'"

The Julian Project team is quick to give God all glory for anything good that happens here. "God has been stewing something long before we arrived," Gregg explains, "and I hope it continues long after we are gone. It's been a great season, going on twenty years now."

Says Maril, "It's huge to know that just because we provided a place, people have felt loved or rested or happy or peaced-out by God's Spirit. Just because we provide the place. That comes back to us as a big, fat blessing, just to be able to participate in that."

Julian Project is doing a great job of bringing life, light, and love to their broader Julian community. Their involvement is as natural and organic as it gets, overflowing from their God-given gifts, passions, and friendships.

Featured Communities: The Julian Project

Here you will find a holistic integration of arts, ecology, hospitality, healthy living, and spirituality.

The Julian Project team successfully promoted a bond measure to establish a badly-needed municipal park, in partnership with other like-minded friends. They hosted a meeting of influential environmentalists who were working to protect and preserve Vulcan Mountain, which can be seen from the Julian Project house. When that group stepped onto the deck for a break, two bald eagles soared into view—a sight never seen before, according to Gregg. The birds of prey outlined a few lazy circles before flying away toward Vulcan Mountain.

The Julian Project history is filled with so many stories of inspiration, beauty, restoration, and creativity.

What hopes and dreams do they have for the future?

"We would love to see new blood buy into the intentional community lifestyle and further expand it, maybe even redefine it," says Gregg. "We'd like to see the gardening and orchard potential grow. We could see producing more vegetables and eggs, maybe even for the local farmer's markets. I'd like to see a greater diversity of people using the property. We just hope that if we decrease in our role, the people who take on a more leading role would represent the Kingdom of God in a way that we have been representing it, with a soft edge on theology, with the welcome mat out for everyone."

Historically, Julian, California, boomed as a gold-mining town in the late eighteen hundreds. Today, I sensed we had hit another mother lode when Maril shared this quote by Kenneth Caraway with us:

> There is no box made by God nor us but that the sides can be flattened out and the top blown off to make a dance floor on which to celebrate life.[17]

"I feel like this home has been a place where we have been invited to dance on God's dance floor and celebrate life," says Maril. "This has been a great party! It sure has been hard at times, but we're loving it. And when it's time for God to shut the doors, okay. But until then, what an amazing ride! We're so fortunate to participate in this."

---

17. Kenneth Caraway, as quoted by Tim Hansel, *You Gotta Keep Dancin'* (Colorado Springs: David C. Cook, 1998), 143.

"It *has* been a great ride," adds Gregg. "It's something that we can't take a lot of credit for. Sure, we had to say, 'Yes,' but God is doing his work in his crazy and mysterious way. We only had to open the door, or just provide a couch for someone to sit on it. That was it. That's all it takes."

"The Holy Spirit does it all," says Maril. "We just get to watch. The only reason it's us versus someone down the street is because we said, 'Yes.' We just opened the door. Anybody can say 'Yes,' but not everybody does. You have to join the party for the fun to begin."

So in the final analysis, the Julian Project *is* a project. This project is exploding boxes and—like Jesus—freeing people from bondage.

Leave your chains at the door if you come to the Julian Project. It's a terrific place to get on the dance floor and celebrate life. In all honesty, you can expect to see difficult days here, just like you'll find anywhere on this side of heaven. But overall it's a great party. You'll find joy and beauty. You'll meet some of the best dance partners that you can imagine.

Best of all, just wait until you see who's calling the dance!

KOINONIA FARM

Address	1324 GA Highway 49 South, Americus, Georgia 31719
Phone	877-738-1741
Email	info@koinonia.org
Website(s)	www.koinoniafarm.org/
Type of Housing	Twelve community-owned homes and apartments on 573 acres
Urban/Rural/Suburban	Rural
Founded	1942
# of Core Members	Eight
# of Residents	About fifteen
Property and Financials	Shared property and financials; living allowance
Community Businesses	Agriculture; bakery; camps
Common Meals	Shared lunch Monday through Saturday; Sunday potluck
Other Shared Activities	Morning devotions; pause for prayer 3x daily; Sunday worship and potluck
Leadership and Decision-making	Consensus and prayer
Outreach Ministries	Prison ministry; food pantry; affordable housing; community service; camps
Christian Affiliation	Non-denominational
ICC Association Membership	None
Non-Profit Org.	Yes
Key Values	Justice, peace, reconciliation, hospitality, sustainable farming, service to others

The late afternoon sun burns hot over Koinonia Farm. Mercifully, a thick canopy of pecan trees provides the shade you seek. You're still sweaty from picking blueberries—you wanted to experience the life of a farmer while visiting Koinonia, so you volunteered in the fields for the afternoon. Now, you enjoy a stroll past pens of chickens, turkeys, and pigs before returning to your apartment for a shower.

After grabbing a bite to eat, you head toward the dining hall where you've been invited to play games. Instead of going inside, you take a seat at a picnic table beside the playground where kids are laughing and playing. Beyond the playground, an expansive lawn is rimmed with several homes, apartments, pecan groves, and the pecan processing plant.

A retired couple joins you at your picnic table. You've seen their RV parked in the neatly mowed camping area behind the pecan operations, on the edge of a broad cattle pasture. The woman has come to teach classes at a camp for middle school students. The man has been volunteering in the commercial bakery, making granola. Earlier, you saw the Koinonia granolas, nuts, chocolates, preserves, and frozen meats in the gift shop and welcome center.

You watch someone drive a tractor toward the storage barn, followed by a riding lawn mower. The summer sun is still fairly high, but work seems to be winding down for the day.

One of Koinonia's core members takes a seat beside you.

"I wanted to thank you for your hospitality," you say. "I really feel like I'm part of the family here."

"We love having guests," the Koinonia member says. "We always have. Our basic theology is to treat everyone as if they are Jesus."

You chat about your stay and the questions that you've had while here. "I was wondering," you ask, "do you ever feel like you're cut off from the real world out here on a five hundred acre farm?"

"Not at all," she says. "Our lives continually overlap with the world outside of Koinonia. We have ongoing prison and food pantry ministries, and we've always been very involved with people who are poor. There's hardly a day when we're not hosting visitors and camp attendees. Guests come and go all the time. We are definitely well-connected with the world."

The evening cicadas begin to sing their chant. They don't disrupt your conversation, but the gnats do.

The Koinonia member takes notice of your swatting. "We live below the gnat line," she says.

"What's the gnat line?" you ask.

"It's a lateral line all across Georgia, just south of Atlanta, above which gnats are not a problem."

"Below, which, we are now sitting," you observe, waving the little devils away from your eyes.

Sounds of laughter come from the kids on the playground. Beyond them, middle schoolers are playing soccer on the large green lawn.

"Some of the girls playing soccer are wearing Muslim head scarves," you observe.

"That's right," she says. "Although we come from a Christian perspective, our Peacebuilder camp attracts kids from all different religious traditions. People respect our deep roots in the civil rights movement, and they appreciate our perspective on injustice, oppression, and racial reconciliation. We consider this to be an important part of our mission."

By now, more than a dozen adults are seated at the picnic tables. You see other clusters of people gathered around the campus and in the dining hall.

"How many Koinonia members live here?" you ask.

"There are only eight core members," she explains. "We are the ones who make the key decisions and share in the common treasury."

"And yet I've seen well over fifty or sixty people here today," you remark.

"Not everyone who works here is a member," she says. "During the summer we have maybe thirty people living and working here, although the number is a lot less in the wintertime. We also have about twenty kids and leaders at our Peacebuilder camp right now, in addition to a half dozen visitors. You'll also usually find a handful of former members and close friends who stop by to help out or just to keep in touch."

"So Koinonia as like an attractive little planet that sucks people into its orbit," you suggest.

"I guess you could say that," she says, smiling.

A young man walks across the playground with a concerned look on his face. "Has anyone seen Judah?" he asks.

Nobody has, but those who know him promise to watch out for the boy. There's not much trouble to get into around here, apart from stepping in chicken poop or getting zapped by an electric fence. There is an occasional snake, however . . . and the highway. The father takes off in the direction of the main road.

Finding Intentional Community

Two minutes later, a woman walks up with little Judah in tow. Someone quickly sends the woman and child in pursuit of Daddy.

The Koinonia Farm member bids you farewell and steps into the dining hall. Soon, an older man approaches your table.

"My name is Nash," he says, stretching out his hand to you.

Something about his stubble beard and rough style makes you wonder if he just got off the chain gang, although his clear eyes and casual smile put you somewhat at ease.

"Looks like you're visiting," he remarks. "What have you seen so far?"

You give him a summary of your visit.

"Have you been up to Picnic Hill yet?" Nash asks.

"No," you say.

When he offers to take you, you hesitate a moment. But only for a second.

"Sure," you say. The emails you've been meaning to write can wait until later.

Nash leads you to a dirty van. "It's not mine," he explains. "Belongs to Koinonia. I'm one of their unofficial tour guides." You refuse to let his gangster chuckle disturb you.

As he steers the van down a clay track between pecan groves and open pasture, Nash tells you stories about his checkered past. Somehow you're not surprised when he says he killed a man when he was nineteen. Thankfully, God's amazing grace set him on a better course in life. He was released from prison in the 1990s, and that's when Koinonia received him with open arms.

"They were the family I needed," Nash says. "This is a place where you can really start to grow. It's where you can unload all the stuff that society piles on top of you—the things that hold you back and bring you down—where you can push all that junk aside and just live life how it should be lived. Yes, you can really grow here."

As he speaks, you sense that the Georgia clay under—and on the sides of—this van is indeed sacred ground.

When the rutted road gets too step, you dismount to climb Picnic Hill by foot. Here you discover a beautiful little overlook with a swinging bench and a screened-in gazebo. From there, Nash walks you through a pecan grove with its cathedral-like ceiling. You ask about the tombstones peeking from the edge of the woods, and Nash tells you the story of each one.

Then he leads you to a mound littered with rocks, sticks, and leaves.

"This is Millard Fuller's grave," he says with reverence. "My friend and I were drowning in sweat by time we'd finished digging it. I told his wife Linda I'd make the coffin as well, but she had already bought one."

Nash tells you that Millard Fuller was a member of Koinonia and the co-founder, with his wife Linda, of Habitat for Humanity. He describes the simple burial ceremony in the woods, and how Koinonia's founder Clarence Jordan, Millard Fuller, and both their wives had asked to be buried in unmarked graves here on Picnic Hill. You see how swiftly the forest has crowded in around them.

Nash picks up a rusty hammer and taps several times on a tree beside the grave. "We do this to let them know we're here, that we still honor them. I don't know if they hear it. I'd like to think they do."

The sun is just tipping over the horizon, and the cicadas have reached their climax. Beyond an electric fence, a herd of cows beds down for the night under the pecan trees. You walk back to the van, and Nash drops you off at your apartment.

The next morning, you attend devotions in the chapel across the highway. After a quiet time for prayer and meditation, Koinonia member Bren Dubay shares a few words.

"One of our co-founders, Clarence Jordan, said, 'You have to *be* something before you can *do* something.' We have a busy day ahead of us, but we take this quiet time—as well as the three times we pause in prayer each day—to remember who we are. We are the body of Christ. Our mission is to live, pray, study, and serve together. We are family. Our outward work is not who we are, but rather our work flows from our inward life, from the heart of our identity in Jesus. This work is temporary, but our relationship in Christ will last forever. So we take this time to center ourselves and remember who we are."

After prayer, you take a self-guided tour of the small museum in the back room of the chapel. The photos you see bring the stories you've heard to life. A short video of Koinonia's history amplifies your respect for God's work on this ground that is truly hallowed.

FINDING INTENTIONAL COMMUNITY

Pastors Clarence Jordan and Martin England, with their families, founded Koinonia Farm in 1942. Many years before most Americans could even define "civil rights," these white men and their wives were answering God's call for racial reconciliation in the Deep South. In the museum, you see black and white images of black and white people working, playing, and schooling together. You see hooded men burning crosses, black men being

Featured Communities: Koinonia Farm

beaten in the streets, a long line of ominous cars on the highway leading to Koinonia, stern men with legal papers in hand pressuring Clarence Jordan to exclude the black man, to sell his land, to move away. You learn how local churches refused fellowship to Koinonia members; how shotgun blasts tore through their homes; how men, women, and children dove to the floor; how farm stands were dynamited; and how a Ku Klux Klan boycott nearly ended Koinonia. You learn how workers smuggled fertilizer into the farm at the risk of their lives.

The thing that kept Koinonia's finances afloat was a shift to pecan production and a mail order business to the northern states. "Ship the nuts out of Georgia," was Clarence Jordan's clever marketing slogan. His positive attitude and sense of humor helped Koinonia survive those turbulent years before the federal government became willing and able to enforce civil rights throughout the South.

In that museum, you learn more about Koinonia's partnership housing ministry for people in need. This ministry spawned Habitat for Humanity, which has since built homes for seven million people worldwide. In the 1980s, Habitat attracted the attention of former President Jimmy Carter, who still lives nine miles away in the small town of Plains. Today, Habitat's International office is in Americas, Georgia, just down the road from Koinonia.

You take a walk outside the chapel, past pecan trees and blueberries fields. Down the road, you wander through a tidy neighborhood of small homes that were built in partnership with Koinonia. You greet several people who you've seen working at Koinonia or attending community meals.

Returning to the Koinonia campus, you get a sense that life here is never without purpose. It's a big place with a big mission and a long list of daily chores. You see work put in its place, as relationships are cherished, faith is nurtured, and Sabbath rest is protected. Work stops five times a day when the bell is rung for prayer and meals.

You sense that life at Koinonia is both full and fulfilling. The eternal fruit of Koinonia's work is tangible and satisfying. The sense of family is strong. Racial reconciliation and justice are not trivial pursuits; rather, they are the core and essence of Koinonia. The rural setting is peaceful and protected, but at the same time not isolated from the culture. Opportunities for

Finding Intentional Community

ministry are abundant. Life here is a big step toward the church you've read about in the book of Acts.

Is Koinonia for me? You wonder.

It's not an easy question to answer, so you head over to the gift shop to stock up on chocolate pecan bark, stuffed dates, blueberry granola, and pecan brittle. You see some of your new friends kicking a ball around on the lawn.

"Hey," you call. "Anyone want to hike up to Picnic Hill with me?"

A couple of them accept your invitation. So you walk together, enjoying the conversation and laughter.

You and your friends stop for snacks at the gazebo on Picnic Hill.

I could get used to this lifestyle, you think. *If Clarence Jordan and his friends didn't let a few pesky gnats get in the way of their abundant life, then I won't either.*

LIFE MISSION FELLOWSHIP

Address	111 8th St., Hammonton, New Jersey 08037
Phone	609-561-8105
Email	admin@life-mission.org
Website(s)	www.life-mission.org/
Type of Housing	Seven apartments on ten acres
Urban/Rural/Suburban	Suburban
Founded	1989
# of Core Members	Twenty-two
# of Residents	About thirty-two
Property and Financials	Shared property and finances; monthly allotment (allowance)
Community Businesses	Window cleaning and power washing business
Common Meals	Several lunches and dinners
Other Shared Activities	Weekly church service; celebration nights; small groups; community school
Leadership and Decision-making	Consensus, with elders and deacons
Outreach Ministries	Partner with various local and international outreach ministries
Christian Affiliation	Non-denominational
ICC Association Membership	None
Non-Profit Org.	Yes
Key Values	Nurturing community; witnessing; helping people in need

Let's pretend we don't know anything at all about Life Mission Fellowship.

Okay. I hear you saying, "But I don't *know anything!"*

Well, just pretend, okay?

Imagine we don't know anything, but our curiosity is piqued by the name: *Life Mission Fellowship.*

Finding Intentional Community

"What's in a name?" Shakespeare wanted to know. And so do we, because (*I forgot to tell you*) I am Sherlock Holmes and you are Watson.

We're just pretending, remember?

"My good Watson," I say. "What is the significance of that name, Life Mission Fellowship?"

"The significance?" you say thoughtfully. "This sounds like a mystery that would baffle Scotland Yard."

"Which is precisely why we are on the case," I say. "Now let us look at the clues and analyze the evidence."

After a moment's silence, you tap your brainy cranium and say, "I believe that *life* . . . " (You pause significantly.) " . . . is important to these people, because it is the first word in their moniker."

"Superb, Watson," I say. "A stroke of genius. And building upon this growing body of knowledge, I might be so bold as to conclude that life, for these people, is a mission, or conversely, that the mission . . . is life."

"Why was this not taught at university," you say with unbridled exhilaration. "Therefore, it stands to reason that this life mission for these people is meant to be undertaken in *fellowship* . . . " (You pause significantly.) " . . . with other people."

"I shield my eyes from the brilliance of your logic," I say, "and I can see no other reasonable explanation than the one which you have so eloquently presented."

At this juncture, you recommend picking up the telephone and ringing Life Mission to cross examine them on the finer points. But since no corded phones with rotary dials can be found (*a must for this to be a proper investigation*), we decide to check them out on the Internet.

I type *life dash mission dot org* into the machine.

Like a London taxi in the fog, the website slowly comes into view.

"Look here," you say. "It's a baby announcement. Thomas John is born to Sam and Kelcy, seven pounds fourteen ounces. If that's not evidence of life in community, I don't know what is."

"Quite right, Watson. I wholeheartedly agree. Now, here's a similar announcement. Luke Anthony, six pounds nine ounces. And here's Aimee. And Hannah. Here's a set of twins. My goodness, Watson. Could Life Mission possibly be a maternity ward?"

"I think not," you say, "but let us continue our examination."

We find evidence of music concerts, skits, barbeques, pool parties, people working, people playing, people eating, and people praying. We see photos of apartments where families and singles are living as neighbors.

"It's a foregone conclusion," I assert, "that this is a community of people . . . a fellowship which, indeed, is on a life mission. I'd say, my good Watson, that this case is solved."

"But wait," you say, as you slowly raise your hand. An ashen look has paled your face. "Read this."

I look over your shoulder, and read the post aloud.

"Remembering Karen . . . as the wonderful wife, mother, daughter, sister, and friend she was."

"Well, I say now, Watson. It's not all about life, after all. This evidence fairly jams a monkey wrench into our machinery. It looks as if we might be beat."

"No, no," you say. "Keep reading."

"We look forward to the day we are reunited with her in the New Creation," I read.

"By, Jove," you say. "They must be referring to the resurrection of the dead. How could we have been so blind?"

"That's right, Watson," I say. "Now keep reading."

"In this memorial blog we remember and celebrate . . . " (You pause significantly.) ' . . . her life."

We stare at each other, dumbfounded.

"Her life," I repeat, astounded at the significance of these words. "So Karen lives on."

"She lives on," you say, "and so does her fellowship of friends in this mission of life."

With apologies to the good people of Life Mission for that playful introduction, I have to say that in a small part, they are to blame for this vignette. They are a bunch of people who love to laugh. The scrapbook page on their website, for example, is a colorful montage of photos, artwork, outreach events, skits, competitions, tasty treats, concerts, and much more. These folks even have their own YouTube Channel.[18] Holmes and Watson were right: The place is bursting with signs of abundant life.

I confess that while I was looking at videos, I skipped over the more serious sermons and music concerts, and instead went straight to the goofy

---

18. YouTube, "Life Mission Fellowship," accessed June 2017, www.youtube.com/user/LifeMissionMedia.

skits. I found some comic material there. So yeah, these folks sent my mind slouching off into that Holmes-Watson scenario.

But hey, if laughter is a significant part of Life Mission Fellowships, it can't be half bad. Right? God himself is the author of life and laughter. The thief comes to kill, steal, and destroy (John 10:10).

Which brings us back to Karen. I still get sad remembering Adam Krell's halting voice as he told me about Karen's passing. Adam is Pastor and Director of Life Mission.

"It was a difficult season," Adam said. "She died of leukemia, and it was pretty tough. She was a founding member, and one of my best friends. You never expected that to happen. It caught you by surprise. And yet, it was a lovely environment for everyone to say goodbye to her. The community was a wonderful support for her husband and kids, who are still here today."

As mentioned in Karen's memorial blog, there will be a happy reunion someday. But while we stand on this side of the curtain, life also includes death, and it would be a half-truth to say that every day at Life Mission is a smiley day.

Still, they do seem to have a lot of fun together.

Adam Krell's pathway into community began with a radical conversion to Christianity as a teenager in the 1970s. He became a very religious young man, a scholar of sorts, with an impressive library of books on theology. He made what he considered to be some significant sacrifices to become a missionary in Atlantic City, New Jersey.

Adam was giving a fundraising presentation for potential donors one day, trying to impress them with his religious knowledge, when he returned home to read a passage about Simon the sorcerer that changed the course of his life. In this story, Simon was trying to buy the power of the Holy Spirit to impress people and improve his reputation. That's when Peter confronted Simon and said, "Repent of this wickedness and pray to the Lord in the hope that he may forgive you for having such a thought in your heart" (Acts 8:22).

Featured Communities: Life Mission Fellowship

"Those words were for me," says Adam. "Then in the Gospel, I read Christ's diatribe against the Pharisees and hypocrites for their religious pride, and each one of those verses hit me square center. I had no defense. I was so convicted. It was like in the words of that old hymn, 'My hope is built on nothing less, than Jesus blood and righteousness. On Christ, the solid Rock, I stand, all other ground is sinking sand."[19] I suddenly saw how everything I had been doing was sinking sand. I saw how the books in my library were like bricks in my salvation wall. They were false proof of my security, and suddenly God was just ripping that away. I saw for the first time that I had to throw myself on Christ if I wanted to be saved. The change in my heart was so radical, it was as if I'd been living by candlelight and suddenly the stadium lights went on."

Adam talked with his missionary friends about this revelation, and they too saw things that needed to change in their lives. Their interactions with another Christian community challenged them spiritually in a good way, sparking renewal and revival.

"We knew about total commitment to Christ," says Adam. "We had that clear. We taught about that. We knew about commitment to Christ's work. We were big on that. But what we didn't know about was commitment to Christ's people, the ecclesiological part of it. Immediately, my attitude toward my brothers and sisters changed. I remember thinking, 'I have to take liability for them. I cannot let them become impoverished. I have to be committed to them.' That was the beginning of community for us. When you give your life to Christ, it's three-dimensional. It's a total commitment not just to Christ and his work, but also to his people. That's what too many Christians leave out. That's the ecclesiological dimension."

A core group from this missionary team reorganized themselves as a church and committed to live in community together. They pooled their resources together into a common purse, a practice that continues to this day. In 1989, they established Life Mission Fellowship. They received mentoring from the son-in-law of Ted Hegre, who is one of the founders of Bethany Fellowship in Minnesota.

Today, Life Mission describes their community as a Protestant monastic order. Their church liturgy is Anglican and they are members of the National Association of Evangelicals, although they have also been influenced by Catholic and Orthodox teachings. Members come from many different backgrounds, and all members attend their community church. They build bridges with other people of faith in South Jersey through their involvement in the local ministerium.

---

19. Edward Mote, "My Hope is Built on Nothing Less," 1834, public domain.

Community life for the thirty-some members of Life Mission revolves around a neat complex of three buildings with apartments, offices, a common dining and meeting room, kitchen, and school. Their community sits on ten wooded acres in Hammonton, New Jersey, a small town midway between Philadelphia and Atlantic City. A couple older cabins on the property are used for hospitality and laundry services, and the woods create a terrific space for kids to play and build forts.

Life Mission has a solid niche in the local job market with their professional window cleaning and pressure washing business. This business employs about twenty staff, most of whom are community members. Members are free to work elsewhere if they like, and some teach in the academy.

Life Mission Academy belongs to the Garden State Association of Christian schools. Grade levels go from kindergarten to thirteen, and students in the final year can attend classes at a community college or receive vocational certification in their areas of giftings. The curriculum is heavy on arts, culture, and classical education. All kids learn to play a string or orchestral instrument.

"We are big on classical learning," says Adam. "It's an intense learning environment here. We're monastic in the sense of how culture has often been preserved or treasured in monasteries. We like to learn. That's the culture here. We value traditional learning with a strong emphasis on the arts. We also have a P.E. program, and we occasionally compete with other schools in academics or sports. The students are encouraged to create and experience beauty. We have a dedicated gallery where they can display their artwork."

The academy is a small school with about ten students, taught by parents. "It's like a one-room school house," says Adam, "except we have more than one room."

Children are not officially community members, having no direct relationship with the community. Business regarding children is mediated through parents.

"We believe in the subsidiary principle," says Adam, "which means that those closest to the responsibility have the greatest authority. So parents, not the community, are responsible and have authority over the children. The community would never override parental authority."

Children are seldom involved in off-campus groups or clubs, but they like to go on field trips. In terms of social engagement, children are very much integrated into community life.

"Their opinions matter," says Adam. "We don't segregate them by age groups. We don't talk baby talk to them. We treat them respectfully, as we expect them to be respectful in return. And they are. They are very well behaved. I'm not saying they're perfect, and we don't expect them to be. They are certainly an important part of our community."

Let's talk membership. Life Mission's perspective on new members has matured through the years. Some decades ago, they hosted display tables at national Christian gatherings, handing out tracts and information to prospective members.

"That was a bad idea," says Adam Krell. "People would come to our table and say, 'So what have you got for me?' Then it dawned on us that this wasn't the right way to do it. That's not how God's Kingdom grows. We're not trying to make sales. We stopped doing that. We don't recruit. We're not even trying to grow. That's not our mission. That doesn't mean we are inhospitable. We host and welcome many guests, and if someone feels called here, we make them feel at home. But if they don't have that calling, we're not going to change to make our community more attractive."

At any point in time, about a half dozen people are somewhere along the five-year path toward community membership. Folks who are interested in joining the community, including children who are coming of age, begin by attending the year-long Christian Foundations Training. This is a no-commitment training year which covers many of the basic tenants of the Christian faith.

After that first year, those who choose to continue move into a one-year Pre-Candidacy program. This is a good experiment in learning what it's like to live in a monastic order or intentional community. These people move into community housing, if they are not already there.

A three-year Candidacy program follows that Pre-Candidacy year. At this time, candidates start participating fully in the common purse, and their capital assets (cars and house, for example) are held in escrow. They have an option to back out at any time and retain control of their assets.

At the end of five years, the candidate is expected to sign the covenant and contribute their capital assets to the community. At this point, an individual retirement account is opened up for the new member. In the future, the community continues contributing to that IRA, which will belong to the member should they ever decide to leave the community.

Any employment income is deposited directly into the joint community account, and members are given a monthly stipend to cover clothing and personal items. All members are provided with health insurance.

Life Mission has community-owned vehicles. Usage and mileage are tracked on an online calendar, and personal mileage is deducted from each member's monthly allotment. Accountability structures are in place to fairly allocate expenses, although nobody is looking over people's shoulders. Personal accountability is built on trust and self-management.

Guests are welcome at Celebration Nights, and members often invite non-community friends into their apartments for meals. Many members choose to participate in local ministries that help people who are poor or elderly. They have formed long-term relationships with local people in need.

A normal day in community might begin with a private breakfast within each family group. Then it's off to work or school. Those who are on campus often eat lunch together, and everyone eats most dinners together in the common area. Sunday church service and lunch are also joint community events. Members attend a weekly business meeting. Friday evening is Celebration Night, which could include sock hockey, crafts, games, movies, pumpkin carving, skits, or concerts. Celebration Nights in the summer are typically held on the deck around the swimming pool, accompanied by barbeque and pool games like Marco Polo.

Saturday is a great day for cleaning and maintenance. Everyone has a stewardship, which basically means a chore. Stewardships include washing cars, maintaining equipment, cleaning bathrooms, spackling walls, and touching-up paint. Facilities are kept in tiptop condition.

Personally, I was intrigued by the characteristically un-American, un-capitalistic view of work that is held by Life Mission Fellowship. Service is not something that is pulled out of people, or coerced. It is not a duty or obligation. Rather it is offered freely, like lettuce in the garden or peaches on the tree.

Adam explained, "We don't have rights and duties with each other. We don't measure things legally or forensically. Our relationship is mutual fellowship. It's more of a communion. This is family and friendship, not a social contract. Everything I do should be from love for God and others. Sure, it's my responsibility or role, but I don't consider it my job. Everything is ministry. It's a stewardship. It's a service of love for one another."

Finding Intentional Community

I thought about how some members might sweat all day long at work in a hot city somewhere, knowing their paycheck is fattening the community bank account, while others might teach kindergarten classes in the air-conditioned school, bringing in no pay at all.

"Did that kind of scenario ever created problems for community members?" I asked.

"It did in the early days," says Adam. "Someone who had an outside job would come home and feel they should have more privileges than someone who was teaching here, and they might take more liberties with resources. It's like the stereotypical husband who worked hard all day at his job, not caring that his wife was also working hard all day at home. Then he comes home and says, 'I should get more because I paid for all this.' That was something we had to talk about. It became one of our covenant points and we have a much better attitude today. We recognize that everyone does their best, as if they are working unto God. If it earns money, that's secondary. Jesus said the widow who gave the mite was greater than the large donors, because she gave her all, and that's our standard.[20] That's how you measure if you are successful, if you are being a good steward and serving man the same as if you are serving God. Some people's responsibilities make money, and some don't. They are both good at what they do. That's the principle of stewardship."

I was impressed by Life Mission's language and attitudes about community life. For example, Adam says, "You can't commit to the community. You can only commit to individuals. Take away this abstract concept of community, and only Gretchen exists. Only Lisa exists. Only Butch exists. Only Brett exists. We do not commit to community. We commit to these particular people. That's the question for people who might want to join the community: 'Do you want to be with these people?' They should know that they are joining a network of relationships, not some amorphous organization."

Adam spoke to me about Jesus's Sermon on the Mount as if it was the best Ted Talk ever (times thousands). This sermon contains Jesus's classic teachings about loving enemies, not worrying, storing up treasures in heaven, caring for people in need, and much more. When Jesus said, "Blessed are the poor in spirit, for theirs is the kingdom of heaven" (Matthew 5:3), he was being countercultural.

---

20. Mark 12:41–44

"He was showing us how to order our lives," says Adam, "not with those who are upwardly mobile, but with the downcast in society. Jesus was saying, 'This is what humility looks like in my Kingdom. This is cruciform love. This is sacrificial, self-giving love.' If there's a choreography of cruciform love, it's called the Sermon on the Mount. Jesus was teaching us the Kingdom vision. He was showing us how to look like the Trinity, the Community of the Trinity, and what that looks like in human relationships. The problem is, we try to find significance in what we do or what we own. If we have a nice car, we think that makes us special. People compete to get the most friends on Facebook. They try to find identity in all kinds of places. Instead, we present our life to each other as a stewardship. It's a gift from God for us to offer back to him by serving others. So everything we do is for the Master. It doesn't matter if I'm at the top or the bottom of the ladder. I'm not gaining my identity from my position or how much weight I pull, by what I know or how many books are in my library. That's the insight I got from Simon the sorcerer. I wanted the gift of God so that I could make a name for myself. Scripture made it clear that that's detestable. Instead, we are walking together on a discipleship path, using life's experiences to become more like Jesus and to grow in love. The object is to become like Christ."

Adam pointed me to Philippians chapter 2:

> In your relationships with one another, have the same mindset as Christ Jesus, who, being in very nature God, did not consider equality with God something to be used to his own advantage; rather, he made himself nothing by taking the very nature of a servant, being made in human likeness. And being found in appearance as a man, he humbled himself by becoming obedient to death, even death on a cross!
>
> —PHILIPPIANS 2:5–8

"This is what it means to be cruciform people," says Adam, "to practice self-giving, self-sacrificing, status-renouncing love. Jesus humbled himself, and humility is the main feature of this life, to humble ourselves like children, to give up our reputation and be willing to lay down our lives for each other. When Jesus washed the disciple's feet, he wasn't doing anything different than God has done from eternity past. In fact, his servant posture is one of the evidences that Jesus is God. He put God the Father on demonstration, saying, 'If you've seen me, you've seen the Father.' Jesus is our ultimate example of how to be restored and made whole, and it happens in community with God and others."

Wow! My wee little brain is still spinning, processing those priceless gems of wisdom. How do you summarize that?

Hey, I know!

Let's return to that goofy little scenario about Sherlock Holmes and Watson.

Let's pretend we don't know anything about cruciformity or ecclesiology or stewardships. In fact, let's pretend we're turning the volume all the way down, and we can't hear anything at all.

Let's just look at the pictures!

Let's pretend that all we know about Life Mission is what we *see*.

So what do we see?

We see children laughing, learning, playing music, and mingling with people of all ages.

We see adults working shoulder to shoulder, not working against each other, but bearing one another's burdens.

We see classes, services, community meals, barbeques, chores, pool games, and skits.

We see people shedding tears at a graveside.

We see real people who are working through disagreements, tensions, and disappointments.

We see worshippers pressing together into the heart of God.

"My dear Watson," I say, "What does it all mean?"

"The evidence is incontrovertible," you say. "These people do indeed care for each other."

"Quite right," I agree. "What we plainly see is a transcendent and divine trait that cannot be quantified in our laboratory, but which can readily be observed, felt, and simply labeled as . . . love."

And that's how Sherlock Holmes and Watson solved the mysterious case of Life Mission Fellowship.

LOTUS HOUSE

Address	St. Louis, Missouri
Phone	314-977-2856
Email	—
Website(s)	https://lotushouse.wordpress.com /
Type of Housing	Two privately owned houses
Urban/Rural/Suburban	Urban
Founded	2008
# of Core Members	Ten
# of Residents	Ten
Property and Financials	Private property and finances; 25 percent of income dues
Community Businesses	None
Common Meals	About five meals shared together weekly
Other Shared Activities	Morning prayer; fun activities; celebrations
Leadership and Decision-making	Consensus
Outreach Ministries	Volunteer at a local school; racial reconciliation; urban ministry
Christian Affiliation	Non-denominational
ICC Association Membership	Shalom Mission Communities
Non-Profit Org.	No
Key Values	Faithfulness, simplicity, service together, sharing, justice, New Monastic

The Lotus House members were not born on the wrong side of the tracks, but they got there as fast as they could.

Some college students in St. Louis were becoming interested in New Monasticism in 2008 when they decided to establish an intentional community in a poorer neighborhood of the city.

"A very nice realtor agreed to show us some houses," Alden Bass recalls. "We were clear in saying we wanted a large house on the north side.

Instead of going north, she showed us several fine houses on the south side. When we protested that we *really* wanted to look in north city, she shook her head and assured us that a nice couple like us would be more comfortable on the south side. What she really meant was 'a nice *white* couple.'"

The students found a new realtor who led them to a big old house that suited them just fine on the north side. This is where the Lotus House community now resides. In many people's eyes, they live on the "wrong side" of the Delmar Divide, which is an invisible socio-economic barrier that has stood longer than the Berlin Wall. Cross Delmar Boulevard and you can't help but notice how skin tones grow paler while resources grow richer. On the south side of the divide, you'll see preppy people patronizing fancy restaurants, chic boutiques, and outdoor cafes. On the north side of the divide, you'll find vacant lots, abandoned businesses, and bombed out houses. Literally, it looks like bombs fell on them, with whole sides of the houses slumped down to the ground, the floors exposed like doll houses. This happens because of neglect and abandonment.

Living here, you can't help but get hit in the face with the realities of racism, poverty, unemployment, and extreme segregation. It makes you wonder:

Why has Lotus House allowed these awkward realities to take a center stage in their family story?

Doesn't their privileged birthright give them license to (in good conscience) find themselves a nice home and church in the suburbs where they can insulate themselves from the injustices of life in modern-day America?

Like other intentional Christian communities, they specifically mention the words of Apostle Paul from Philippians 2 as inspiration for their actions:

> Have the same attitude that Christ Jesus had. Although he was in the form of God and equal with God, he did not take advantage of this equality.
>
> —Philippians 2:4–5
> (God's Word translation)

Featured Communities: Lotus House

The Lotus House community stresses that even though they live on the depressed side of the Delmar Divide, it's still a safe place to live and raise their kids. They've developed deep friendships with many of their neighbors. In the summer, the street is covered with a beautiful canopy of towering sweet gum and maple trees. The lawns are done up with flowers. The houses on their street are mostly occupied, which is unusual for this part of town. They're on a cul-de-sac of larger, three-story houses built in the early 1900s and occupied by prosperous black professionals.

Most days when the weather is nice, you can see kids playing ball and riding bikes in the street. Some of the Lotus House members ride their bicycles to work. Unlike folks in the sprawling suburbs, they have the privilege of actually coming face to face with their neighbors on a regular basis.

They like to sit out on the porch and read or talk to people going by. They spend a lot of time out there, especially during the hotter months of the year.

Lotus House had a quarter-acre garden that never really thrived, although they want to grow more of their own food in the future. They currently have a small but prosperous vegetable and berry garden in the backyard of one of their homes. Their weekly community meals are open to neighbors and friends who in the summer months gather around the picnic table.

The Lotus House community has loved this neighborhood ever since the first day they saw the "For Sale" sign in the front yard, back in 2008.

Says Alden, "We were welcomed by the neighbors who showed us the house themselves and talked to us for a while. It's a very stable street. Some of the neighbors have lived here for fifty to sixty years. They were excited that young people were moving in to take care of the house and help the street be stable. Stability is so important, and you can't always have that in rental property where transient folks are cycling in and out."

Still, the frank reality is that tough streets are just a few blocks away, and personal possessions can sometimes be quickly converted to cash at one of the local pawn shops.

"Sure, we've had some lawn mowers stolen," said a community member, "but we don't feel personally at risk. This feels like home for us and the kids."

In 2014, America's attention was drawn to Michael Brown's shooting by a Ferguson, Missouri, policeman. While most Americans were watching the story unfold on their television screens, the Lotus House community was viewing it from the streets of their neighborhood which is 99 percent African American. The killing happened less than ten miles away from their front porch.

After Ferguson, there were opportunities not only to talk with neighbors, but to become more directly involved in the larger civic conversation. You'll often find the Lotus House community attending civil rights marches, immigration reform rallies, and events promoting social and racial justice. A cursory glance at Lotus House's portfolio of community involvement might lead you to believe that they are political activists. They have participated in marches, but they do not consider themselves to be an activist community.

If political activism is not their main purpose, then what is?

Featured Communities: Lotus House

In a word...

...love.

Their decision to slip beneath the superficialities of class norms and leave their birthrights in the suburbs made them witness to some messy problems that others would rather forget. It put them in the uncomfortable position of truly learning what Jesus was thinking about when he asked his followers to love their neighbors. They quickly learned that love was more than sending your neighbor a quarterly shipment of food, clothes, and rent subsidies. They learned that love meant standing in your neighbor's shoes.

Love, therefore, is the simple rationale behind everything at Lotus House. The well-crafted Lotus House Covenant puts a high premium on doing things for others, and doing things *together* . . . things like morning and evening prayers, volunteer work, meals, sharing 25 percent of their income with the community, and just having fun together.

The Lotus House community covenants to serve together. That happens most regularly at a nearby inner-city church, through an after-school tutoring and mentoring program. They've made long-term relationships with some of the kids there, including one boy who ended up living in foster care at the Lotus House for close to a year. He left, but then returned several times. He's in his twenties now, doing a lot of time on the streets, but Lotus House has always been a haven for him. The community members stress that this is not a matter of give and give, but give and take, since they always receive blessings in return.

These days, Lotus House's first ministry is to their own families. New children in the community have occupied what were previously spare bedrooms.

I asked Alden for a cherished memory of living in community.

"One day stands out," he said, "although there are a lot of little moments like this one. We got a big snow storm here in January and everything closed down, so nobody could go to work. Our whole community ended up spending the day together, playing cards, hanging out, and eating together. It was one of those magical, unplanned days that only happens every once in a while. It was just good to be together. We all remember that day fondly. There was nothing we were supposed to *do*. We just got to *be*. It was very special."

Lotus House members continue to carve out time for a retreat or two each year. That's a time when they come together, usually out in the country, and spend time together. They reflect on the year behind and the year ahead, and they just have a lot of fun together.

The community shares kitchen duty for their twice-weekly community meals. Friday evenings, they enjoy open dinners where up to twenty guests may show up. They enjoy sharing game nights and birthday celebrations together with the community.

Some of their best times together happen in the evening after prayer, which lasts about twenty minutes. They sit around and chat. Sometimes someone will get the idea to do something like a handstand competition or a silly game. As with any healthy family, they simply enjoy being together.

The Lotus House Covenant is indeed suggestive of a marriage or family covenant. These folks have pledged to stick together through thick and thin, in good times and bad. They helped a member who was having some significant health challenges, taking her to appointments and supporting her in all the ways that a loving family can do.

"The greatest benefit," according to Alden, "is that we're not just a community of friends with common interests, but we're called together as disciples. We're not together just because we like each other, but because of our commitment and our calling in Jesus. We're still getting to know each other, even though some of us have been together for eight years or more. So it's a deeper kind of relationship. It's more profound than simply choosing to be friends."

The Lotus House stands together as a community because they have covenanted together. Even on those rare days when people start to get on each other's nerves, you won't see members jumping ship. They have pledged to work things out, because this commitment is based on the whole person, not on common interests like hobbies or athletics.

Lotus House has been blessed not to have any major, community-wrenching conflicts. Most disagreements are not over big, ideological stuff, but petty things like who finished the last box of cereal. It's all ordinary stuff, and it all has to be worked out. Living in community, it's not possible to avoid things or bury these small conflicts. You can't get away from people for long. Everyone knows there's a problem if you stop showing up for prayers. Everything at Lotus House is structured in such a way that it's better to deal with things than to avoid them.

The community was childless until a few years ago when Alden and Candace adopted three siblings.

Featured Communities: Lotus House

"We have really been blessed in how our community has served as an extended family to our children," said Alden, "especially since our biological extended families live far away. The community has helped care for them and just been family to them. It's been a huge blessing for us and the kids. For a long time, one of the members gave us a standing date night, allowing us to go out for the evening. He would have dinner with the kids and take care of them. It's also good for single folks who might be used to living alone to have this feeling of family."

The Lotus House community has a bit of an academic feel to it, which does nothing to overshadow their foundational heart of love. At any given time in their history, there have been two or three members who are associated with St. Louis University. It is common to hear discussions of new and old monasticism here, with quotes from people like Dietrich Bonhoeffer, John Chrysostom of Antioch, or the Benedictine saints. It's not all theoretical stuff, though. The practical applications of monasticism among the urban poor today are all around them, as they seek to walk in the footsteps of Jesus in north St. Louis. The Rule of the Lotus House offers a short primer on these New Monastic ideals, and how the Lotus House is "living together in an area abandoned by the Empire as a community of disciples committed to sharing our property, our gifts, and our lives."[21]

Lotus House members have created a very practical structure for their common life, which enables them to effectively love and care for each other and their neighbors on a daily basis. This is monasticism at its best, whether it's old or new. One thing is certain, though: the fact that this monastic expression is flourishing north of the Delmar Divide is definitely something very new, indeed.

So what is the bottom line of the Lotus House?

I've already stated it. In a word, it is . . .

Love.

Love for their neighbor is never something this community talks about without grounding their words in action. Love here is tangible. It is instinctual. When they see a need or an injustice, they do something about it.

You would do the same thing if you lived north of the Delmar Divide.

---

21. Lotus House, "The Rule of the Lotus House," accessed June 2017, https://lotushouse.wordpress.com/rule/.

Love for neighbors within the house is just as tangible as love for those on the streets. The Lotus House is a safe and healthy environment for reconditioning the typical America knee-jerk reaction to feed one's own desires first and watch out for Number One. It's an incubator for growing God's greatest fruits of the Spirit, while keeping both feet in the real world.

You can't give to others what you haven't received yourself, and this is especially true with the love of God. The starting point for Lotus House, therefore, is resting secure in the knowledge of God's boundless love for each individual. As beloved children who are always accepted and always forgiven, they embrace the freedom to love others in the same way they have been loved by God.

So in a sense, the road to Lotus House begins by journeying toward the Father. Receive his love first, then ask what he wants you to do with it.

While you're in the presence of the Father, why not ask him what he thinks about these crazy Lotus House folks in north St. Louis?

If you do, I suspect you'll see a huge smile cross his face.

REBA PLACE FELLOWSHIP

Address	737 B Reba Place, Evanston, Illinois 60202
Phone	847-328-6066
Email	RebaFellowship@gmail.com
Website(s)	www.rebaplacefellowship.org/
Type of Housing	Twenty-four community-owned properties in two locations; one rural home
Urban/Rural/Suburban	Urban, in two Chicago suburbs
Founded	1957
# of Core Members	About forty-five
# of Residents	About sixty
Property and Financials	Shared property and financials; living allowance
Community Businesses	Property management; furniture store; office jobs
Common Meals	Most meals are eaten with household members
Other Shared Activities	Weekly church service at community churches; occasional potlucks, discussion groups, work days, fun outings
Leadership and Decision-making	Consensus and committees
Outreach Ministries	Urban ministry; food, clothes, and support for poor and immigrants; individual local and international outreach
Christian Affiliation	Mennonite
ICC Association Membership	Shalom Mission Communities
Non-Profit Org.	Yes
Key Values	Hospitality, discipleship, spiritual growth, urban outreach

When I close my eyes and think of Reba Place Fellowship, I see a mighty oak tree in the middle of the sprawling Chicago suburbs. At its base I see squirrels and birds, green lawns, and healing streams of water.

I am reminded of the prophet Isaiah's description of God's faithful people:

> They will be called Oaks of Righteousness, the Plantings of the Lord, so that he might display his glory.
>
> —Isaiah 61:3

Reba Place Fellowship is that oak with mighty roots and branches.

Its broad branches are multi-cultural and intergenerational, offering material, spiritual, relational, occupational, and educational blessings. Its fruit is as full and diverse as Chicago itself. Its sturdy roots and trunk anchor the uncertain future in the fertile past, drawing wisdom from those who have walked in community for many years.

Reba offers a rich and diverse variety of ways to be involved in community. On any given day, community members might:

- Share breakfast and devotions with housemates and friends
- Work with Reba's properties or for their Plain and Simple furniture store
- Volunteer at a nearby school or childcare facility
- Help distribute food, clothes, and furniture to people in need from Reba's food pantry and thrift store
- Help immigrants become better grounded in the Chicago suburbs and American culture
- Assist the older Reba members with adult care
- Enjoy an evening potluck at one of the Reba houses
- Clean up, cook a meal, or shop for one of the households
- Play games together or attend a discussion group
- Go for a hike or attend a music or art event in the metro area with Reba friends

Reba Place Fellowship owns about twenty-five homes and apartments in two different suburbs of Chicago: the Rogers Park neighborhood is older and more diverse, and the Evanston community is a little more upscale. Each of the two locations has its own community-run Mennonite church, attended by community members and non-members alike. The two Reba

Featured Communities: Reba Place Fellowship

churches were established so that friends who did not want to become full members could still participate in the spiritual life of the community.

The Living Water Community Church in the Rogers Park neighborhood has been blessed to become the church home to a flourishing immigrant community. Here you can expect to be greeted in eight different languages: English, Spanish, French, Kirundi, Swahili, Khmer, Nepali, and Hindi. An animated Swahili Unity Choir regularly contributes to the worship experience, and hymns are sometimes sung in other languages. Splinter groups gather after services to study the sermon text in Khmer and Swahili. These related activities are encouraged by Reba members, who do much more than talk about racial and intergenerational diversity. They take God's Word very seriously when it says that God is a defender of the weak, poor, widowed, fatherless, foreigners, and oppressed.

Reba Place Fellowship is, indeed, a mighty Oak of Righteousness, where all of God's creatures—no matter how strong or weak—can find a home.

My wife and I arrived at Reba's Clearing household one morning at seven a.m. for breakfast and prayer. The three-story home was built in an era when extravagant craftsmanship was the standard, with tall ceilings, exquisite woodworking, large front porch, and an impressive entryway. The wood-banistered, open stairway has been retrofitted with an elevator for disabled members.

Over hot oatmeal, soft-boiled eggs, coffee, and fruit, we read together the words of Eberhard Arnold, a founder of the original Bruderhof ("house of brothers") community in Nazi Germany:

> Life in community is no less than a necessity for us—it is an inescapable 'must' that determines everything we do and think. Yet it is not our good intentions or efforts that have been decisive in our choosing this way of life. Rather, we have been overwhelmed by a certainty—a certainty that has its origin and power in the Source of everything that exists. We acknowledge God as this Source. We must live in community because all life created by God exists in a communal order and works toward community.[22]

---

22. Shane Claiborne et al., *Common Prayer*.

Reba receives wisdom from Christians like these who have lived in community much longer than they have. Their maturity has been seasoned through years of their own successes and failures, across a quilted landscape of victories and struggles.

Since 1957, they have been giving shape and form to a picture of Jesus's people living in community in an urban setting. Today there is a great sense of Reba being a calm place in the storm, but it hasn't always been that way.

Long-time Reba members confess that in the 1970s—when the adolescent community was growing exponentially while struggling to find its identity—they experienced awkward struggles with over-commitment, overbearing male authority, and self-righteous attitudes. That's when they joined the Mennonite Church, building upon the experience of those who have lived in community for centuries, finding stability in Anabaptist roots. Rejecting prideful individualism, they joined with other intentional communities to form the Shalom Mission Communities, an umbrella organization that anchors them in accountability with others.

In more recent years, Reba discovered ways to become more relevant to younger generations, which was especially important as their median age ticked higher. Today, young people are attracted to many aspects of Reba, including its practical application of the biblical concept of younger apprentices being discipled by older mentors.

There are always new issues to address in the context of communal living. One common challenge is when members' opinions differ about finances and decision-making. This is something that less-connected Christians who aren't involved in each other's finances and decision-making processes rarely if ever struggle with. But when communities share a common purse, opinions can clash. Reba's modus operandi is to encourage members to elevate other's needs and desires above self, and to learn to listen effectively to God and to others.

People who live in community are challenged to resolve conflict, release hurt, and give and receive forgiveness. Good communication is essential for healthy community life. Members also learn to define personal boundaries and know when to say no.

Featured Communities: Reba Place Fellowship

Reba members agree that the strengths and blessings of living in community far outweigh the challenges. These are some of the things they like best:

1. Members experience the joy of being committed to radical discipleship and authentic, heart-felt worship
2. They find fulfillment in engaging with the urban context in a loving and relevant manner
3. They experience the rich fruit of engaging in long-term relationships with other brothers and sisters in Christ, navigating conflict and learning from mistakes; these spiritual fruits are not possible in the context of more shallow relationships
4. Shared economics allows members to accomplish much more than they could on their own

Finding Intentional Community

5. Younger members build upon the maturity and experience of all those who have walked this community road before them

Add to this the fact that Reba members simply enjoy each other's company, and you arrive at a pretty good way of life.

"A lot of people come from wounded backgrounds," says Reba member Sally Schreiner Youngquist. "They didn't have what they needed growing up, and they want to do things differently now. This is a healing environment, and people feel like that's so much more important than earning lots of money and having lots of stuff. There is a relational richness in being a vehicle for God's love, in experiencing God in the midst of community. That's especially true in the context of this lonely nation with so much alienation, addiction, and mental illness. I'm happy that many young people are discovering this, and that old people feel vitally connected. The intergenerational connections here are strong. All different kinds of people are committed to one another. So many people here say that the things they treasure most are the loving relationships and the mutual support."

"We have a man with muscular dystrophy," says Sally. "We have people in their nineties. These people are well-cared for, better than the care they would expect to receive at most retirement centers. It's amazing what is possible when you have a commitment to care for one another."

Reba's experience caring for their own elderly has enabled them to start a professional in-home healthcare business. Another community-run business is their Plain and Simple furniture store, which imports Amish products from Indiana. Reba owns apartment buildings that they offer as affordable housing to Evanston seniors and low-income renters. These apartments provide a setting for community jobs in property management and maintenance. Members who do not work for one of the community-owned businesses find jobs in Chicago and its outlying areas.

Reba's core members pool their income and assets into a common fund from which all community needs are met. They receive a nominal allowance for their personal expenses. At the core of the community is a stalwart determination to love and support each other through thick and thin, being the church as Jesus intended for it to be. "There were no needy persons among them," says Acts 4:34, and that's the mission of Reba Place Fellowship, as members care for one another.

FEATURED COMMUNITIES: REBA PLACE FELLOWSHIP

Reba Place Fellowship has about forty-five covenant members today. Like planets in orbit around the sun, Reba is in relationship with people of varying commitment to their core values and practices. Neighbors and friends are always welcome at open potlucks and discussion groups, and some of them have been coming for many years. Reba offers internships for people wanting to test the waters of intentional community by living onsite and immersing themselves in community life. Members and interns alike enjoy working in the urban garden, which produces a bounty of tomatoes, lettuce, and greens in the warmer summer months.

"Some of the people going to our churches have bought houses nearby," says Sally. "They want to live close together and walk to church. That's a distinct feature of community, rather than being in commuter churches where people have to hop in the car and drive across town to see their Christian friends. Intentional proximity makes your life less bifurcated. You're close to your brothers and sisters. You share prayer concerns. You can share cars. You interact freely with one another. This is very important."

One can scarcely live in Christian community in the city while ignoring the needs of poor people. In addition to offering affordable housing to neighbors, Reba picks up leftover food from local grocery stores and gives it away twice a week to people in need from their Manna Garage. They also have a free thrift store called The Pick in the basement of one of their apartment buildings.

Their outreach actually extends far beyond Evanston and Rogers Park. They have partnered with the village of Valle Nuevo in El Salvador, helping them buy land for homes and agriculture. Additionally, they are active in the Black Lives Matter movement in the greater Chicago area.

David Janzen, author of *The Intentional Christian Community Handbook*, is a member of Reba Place Fellowship. He's also one of the foremost champions of intentional Christian community.

"A lot of people imagine that the Great Commission is about evangelizing," says David, "but Jesus is more specific than that. He asked his followers to make *disciples* of all nations. Making disciples is different than evangelizing. If you're just trying to save souls, the common life is not that important. But making disciples is much different than saving souls. Making disciples is done within the context of a common life. The things that Jesus teaches about loving one another, caring for one another, serving one another, sharing resources with one another, bearing one another burdens—these things are very much accomplished as a way of life together. In Jesus's society, many people were already doing those things, because there was a lot of sharing of resources, sharing of needs, taking care of people, and common work. This all happened within the social structure of the extended family. That is not the structure of our lives anymore, because we are economically, personally, spiritually, and relationally independent of one another."

"What is the goal of the Great Commission?" David asks. "If the goal is to get people to be disciples, intentional community is very essential. It is a recommended way to get serious about knowing and following Jesus. You can see how well it works in the New Testament. When people come alive in the Gospel, they are led into intentional community. The sharing of gifts, experiences, and resources is the way of the Kingdom of God. Intentional community is where the ego is de-throned. It is where the kind of discipleship that Jesus had in mind begins to take place."

Discipleship is the spiritual target that Reba Place Fellowship is moving toward. Discipleship is at the heart of all they do.

The unfortunate truth is that many people who faithfully occupy a space on a pew each Sunday morning have never been discipled. Many Christians are still infants in their faith (1 Corinthians 3:1). Pastors of all denominations yearn for more than one passive hour of church attendance per week from members, so that true discipleship can occur.

The men and women of Reba Place Fellowship take discipleship very seriously, and they have a lot of fun doing it. This mighty oak is bearing much fruit, and there's always room in its branches for one more nut.

There might even be room for you!

RIVERBEND COMMONS

Address	Corona, California
Phone	—
Email	drew@riverbendcommons.org
Website(s)	http://riverbendcommons.org/
Type of Housing	One privately-owned home
Urban/Rural/Suburban	Suburban
Founded	2000
# of Core Members	Five
# of Residents	About ten
Property and Financials	Private property and financials; shared food; monthly rent
Community Businesses	None
Common Meals	About four times weekly
Other Shared Activities	Weekday morning devotions; weekly prayer night; monthly meeting; celebrations, retreats, and fun outings
Leadership and Decision-making	Modified consensus
Outreach Ministries	Individual outreach to poor, Muslims; arts group; neighborhood outreach
Christian Affiliation	Non-denominational
ICC Association Membership	None
Non-Profit Org.	No
Key Values	Hospitality; sustainability; creativity; simplicity; suburban outreach

One of the women at Riverbend Commons was getting married, so Riverbend offered accommodations to the wedding party at their large home in Corona, California. Apparently, nobody explained to a groomsman from out of town that he would be staying at an intentional community. So when he arrived, he soon decided that the bride's housemates were actually the parents of the bride, since they lived with her. Still, he thought it extremely strange that the "mother of the bride" was so relaxed as to be sitting in casual clothes on the couch working Sudoku puzzles on the day of her daughter's wedding.

When the groomsman met Drew Ward of Riverbend Commons, he assumed Drew was just visiting the house, since he was another adult male who obviously wouldn't be living with the "parents of the bride."

Moreover, the groomsman assumed that Drew was giving him a key to another house when Drew said, "This key will get you into our house tonight. Just lock up after yourself." Then when the groomsman's ride dropped him off at the Riverbend home late that night, he asked, "Are you sure this is the right place?"

His ride assured him that it was, but he approached the front door with some misgivings. Having no other options, he tried the key in the door . . . and it worked.

Strange.

The next time he saw Drew, he approached him with a questioning look on his face.

"So . . . whose house is this?" he asked.

"We like to think that nobody owns it," said Drew. "It's really God's house, and we're stewards of it."

Right, thought the groomsman, not much closer to enlightenment than before.

Drew would have explained more, but he still didn't know that this guy didn't have a clue what was going on. And the guy didn't ask.

His confusion only mounted as he watched seemingly unrelated people walk upstairs and into rooms and through doors that were obviously private. It all seemed so random to him. Finally, he could stand it no more.

Drew and his friends were talking in the family room when the groomsman came in with exasperation written all over his face.

"I just need to understand something," he said. "I just need to know who *owns* this place . . . "

The Riverbend folks were a little caught off guard.

" . . . because . . . I need to know who to ask to get some milk out of the fridge."

There it was. The young man's confusion was out in the open.

"You don't have to ask," Drew said. "The fridge is open to you. So is the pantry. Just take what you need."

Featured Communities: Riverbend Commons

They spent the next fifteen minutes unpacking his misunderstandings and describing the basics of living in community with other Christians.

Then the groomsman said something very profound: "The only thing I could figure out is that nobody seems to own anything, but everybody seems to care for everything."

"That's it," says Drew, recalling that moment. "That's what we've been after all along. That's the deal."

The Riverbend Commons folks love it when people come to that conclusion without any prompting, because it really is *the deal*.

Intentional Christian community is a peculiar concept, especially in a prosperous suburban setting where materialism and privacy are gods. The entire culture is aligned toward private ownership and rights. No wonder this young man's biggest challenge was to establish ownership so that he could abide by the cultural taboos without incurring the wrath of the principal stakeholder.

Nowhere is the division between what is *mine* and *yours* more unassailable than in the suburbs. Rewards, achievements, failures, gains, and losses are all measured in material units that are bought, sold, bartered, and hoarded.

In 2000, Drew and Nancy Ward and their friends decided to start an intentional community in the suburbs of Southern California. They shared their ideas with a friend who was living in community in the heart of San Diego.

"We found a nice place in the suburbs for our community," Drew said. "A suburban tract home."

"That is revolutionary," their friend said. "That's radical. What we're doing in the city is a piece of cake compared to what you're up against."

At that time, the fledgling Riverbend Commons community didn't fully appreciate the depth of their friend's words. They didn't understand how their values would fly in the face of materialism, consumerism, private property, private theologies, and private don't-cross-my-borders-and-keep-to-yourself philosophies. It was truly a counter-cultural move.

"We didn't bump up against the radical nature of it for several years," says Drew. "We did struggle in making connection with our neighbors. We'd watch them drive their cars into their garages, the door would come down, and we'd never see them again. People in our neighborhood rarely make meaningful contact with each other."

It is literally possible to live a lifetime in the suburbs without ever seeing your neighbor face to face in the flesh, with no protective wall of glass between the two of you. The sad fact is that many of these people have a significantly higher risk of physical and mental illness, based on research that links loneliness to shorter lifespans.[23]

According to Drew, "The suburbs are a well-manicured prison colony where we are the unwitting keepers of our own captivity—separated from each other by all sorts of fiercely defended invisible walls."[24]

Connecting with neighbors has indeed been a challenge for Riverbend Commons. In the early days, when young families were snatching up the newly-built houses, children were the emissaries between homes. But as kids grew up and moved on, houses drifted apart. Riverbend Commons made several creative but mostly unsuccessful attempts to connect with neighbors, like hosting open mike nights in the backyard and inviting neighbors over for dinner.

A huge breakthrough came as a result of an extended drought which caused civic officials to encourage homeowners to tear out the irrigated grassy strip between the sidewalk and the street, replacing it with more drought-tolerant landscaping. The Riverbend folks put their heads together.

"Why not create a neighborhood garden along the sidewalk?" they asked. "We can invite neighbors to grow things, harvest things, and make things with what they grow."

This three-foot wide strip of hard dirt might seem like an insignificant scratch on terra firma, but in fact, it became a bridge between isolated neighbors.

First, the neighborhood silently watched as Riverbend planted drought-tolerant herbs like rosemary, oregano, thyme, and mint. Then when the dump truck load of topsoil showed up, so did a neighbor . . . with a shovel to help.

---

23. Katie Hafner, "Researchers Confront an Epidemic of Loneliness," *The New York Times*, September 5, 2016, accessed June 2017, www.nytimes.com/2016/09/06/health/lonliness-aging-health-effects.html?_r=0.

24. Drew Ward, "A Sliver of Shalom in the Suburbs," *Christianity Today*, December 17, 2012, accessed June 2017, www.christianitytoday.com/thisisourcity/7thcity/sliver-of-shalom-in-suburbs.html.

Featured Communities: Riverbend Commons

The Riverbend folks were ecstatic. The first human connection had been made, and more were to follow.

They planted fourteen feet of vegetables in front of their house and put up a sign which read, "Neighborhood Garden." The results were enormous by suburban standards. One family came to help plant seeds. Others came to weed, water, and stake plants.

"It created a lot of great conversations out there in front of the house," says Drew. "Parents would love to stop and show the plants off to the kids, take a tomato or strawberry, and eat them right off the vine. We had more conversations out there than we ever had before."

Finding Intentional Community

Riverbend Commons created additional landscaping marvels in their compact front, side, and back yards. Their property was even officially certified as a wildlife habitat by the National Wildlife Federation.[25] They did it all themselves, from the jungled waterfall monolith in front (*made from up-ended sidewalk!*) to the terraced gardens with fruit trees and vines in back (*the lovely terraces are made from broken concrete!*), and the raised beds and arbor on the side of the house. The covered patio in back has been the perfect setting for house concerts and parties.

Riverbend values creativity and simplicity. They created most of the superb artwork that adorns the house. They bought and upcycled much of the furnishings from thrift stores. On the surface, Riverbend Commons fits right into this neatly manicured neighborhood. But on deeper reflection, it appears that *something is very different here*.

I confess that I'm personally prejudiced against suburbia. Why? Because my wife and I began raising our family in a prosperous, Southern California suburb just thirty minutes from Riverbend Commons, and for us, it was a very cold and lonely experience.

Something is different here, I thought as we settled into conversation and community with the half-dozen people who share the house. The wildlife habitat triggered my imagination.

Maybe it's not just a wildlife sanctuary, I thought. *Maybe it's a human life sanctuary.*

Nancy Ward validated this revelation.

"When you live in community," Nancy says, "people in need will find you. We've had single dads, foster kids, abused kids, and single moms whose husbands left them for other women. They've stayed both short-and long-term. One single mom ended up staying here for three years. Her husband left her and their three boys for another woman, so she was really grieving that first year. The second year she was just getting her feet back on the ground. They needed lots of time to heal. I bet some people look at Riverbend and think that they could never live like this. And yet, a lot of people come here when everything is falling apart. I think there's something about providing a

---

25. National Wildlife Federation, "Create a Sustainable Garden that Helps Wildlife," accessed June 2017, www.nwf.org/Garden-For-Wildlife.aspx.

place of hospitality and sanctuary. People know that they'll be safe here. We haven't gone looking for people like that, but they have found us."

Southern California is a popular vacation destination for many people. Riverbend Commons took a bold step by tapping into tourism when they put their spare rooms up for rent through Airbnb.com. For them, it's a fun ministry and a way to make new friends. Hospitality is something they do very well, and their five-star reviews prove it.

Riverbend's community structure is very loose. It's like family. Drew and Nancy's names are on the deed, but they work hard to *not work too hard*. That is, they consider their housemates to be equals. They receive inspiration and guidance from others. They empower others and refuse to become codependent dorm parents.

Riverbend has morning devotions Monday through Friday, and they share dinner Monday through Thursday. They take turns with household and gardening chores, growing what food they can in the garden. They have a monthly meeting and two retreats a year. Finances are not held in common, although everyone contributes toward monthly expenses. Each person is free to worship as they please. The community is very artistic, and they love to spontaneously do fun things together.

In an age when American sentiment is prejudiced against Arabs, the Riverbend kitchen table became a nurturing habitat for immigrants with a common Muslim heritage.

First, they connected with a woman who had an art-based reconciliation ministry to Palestinians. Then they befriended a man who had once done well on Arab Idol—which is just as popular as American Idol—but who after becoming a Christian committed himself to leading worship music in Southern California. One thing led to another, and this man introduced Riverbend to his girlfriend who was in difficult circumstances and needed a place to live. Her name was Sahar.

Sahar's story begins at age seventeen in Saudi Arabia. When she gave her life to Jesus, her brothers were bound by Sharia Law to kill her. Then in a harrowing series of events, her sympathetic father was able to help her find asylum in the United States. She was twenty-one when she first came to Riverbend Commons.

Sahar had lots of connections in the Arabic-speaking community. One day Nancy came home to find six women who were excited to meet her because she had taken Sahar in. These women were Syrian, Turkish, Tajikistani, Egyptian, Iranian, and Iraqi. All of them were Christians who had converted from Islam.

Overjoyed, Nancy sat down to tea with them and said, "Please, tell me your stories."

One by one they told her about how they had come to Christ. Some of their conversions had been at tremendous risk to their lives. To Nancy, it was like a spiritual break-out session from the United Nations, right in her own kitchen.

Nancy was thinking, *How in the world is this happening? Here I am sitting at a table in my suburban home with beautiful believers from all over the world!*

One Syrian woman told the story about how her prosperous family had abandoned ten homes and a business worth $3.5 million in the middle of the night, fleeing to save their lives. Her family was grateful to be alive and free, but here they lived in a small rental house that they could barely afford.

Sahar was an ambassador for more meaningful relationships with other Muslims and former-Muslims in Southern California. She stayed on for more than a year, and the community continues to minister to Muslims today.

Honestly, I wouldn't have believed it if I hadn't seen it.

Riverbend Commons is the real deal. It's authentic community in a well-to-do Southern California suburb. It's a beautiful home that by every measure compares favorably with the Joneses next door, but who is comparing?

"To many people this house may feel suburban," says Drew, "but it was created with an ethic that is radically different from the typical suburban home."

Unquestionably, they have the richest home in the neighborhood, and I'm not talking money. And how does Drew compare himself with the Joneses?

It's simple: "We're the freaks in the neighborhood."

And I might add . . . that's a good thing. They are a safe haven for both wildlife and human life.

"Life is something that we participate in," says Drew. "It takes a season in the garden to see that. We plant a seed. We water. We don't *make* a tomato. All we really do is participate. God makes the tomato grow. The best we can do is help promote the conditions in which God's work happens. We talk about creating habitats. So we create a habitat where prayer occurs. A habitat where selflessness occurs. A habitat here healing happens. One thing we've heard over and over for sixteen years is how this has been a place of real healing. So many people have been restored and found healing and peace here . . . not because of anything we have done, but because of what God is doing. There are moments when Nancy and I have come to acknowledge that whatever it is happening here, we're just able to participate in letting it happen. Sometimes there's this moment when, suddenly, whatever is going on around us is absolutely *not* under our control. It has moved well beyond anything that we've planned. It's far beyond any effort that we've placed, and this event and these people have taken on this wonderful, rich energy. Wherever we are—it might be a music night or a Christmas party with friends—Nancy and I just feel it. We know when that happens. At times like that, we just look across the room at each other and smile. We kind of close our eyes and nod, thinking, *This is it . . . This is it.*"

Finding Intentional Community

RUTBA HOUSE

Address	923 Onslow St., Durham, North Carolina 27705
Phone	919–578–3834
Email	info@schoolforconversion.org
Website(s)	www.schoolforconversion.org
Type of Housing	Two privately-owned homes
Urban/Rural/Suburban	Urban
Founded	2003
# of Core Members	Fourteen
# of Residents	Fourteen or more
Property and Financials	Shared and private property (flexible)
Community Businesses	None
Common Meals	Shared meals about four times weekly
Other Shared Activities	Daily prayer; occasional chores
Leadership and Decision-making	Consensus
Outreach Ministries	Prison ministry; urban development; School for Conversion; hospitality
Christian Affiliation	Non-denominational
ICC Association Membership	None
Non-Profit Org.	No (although the School for Conversion is a 501(c)3)
Key Values	Justice; hospitality; peacemaking; discipleship; New Monastic; community

If you get a chance to visit Rutba House, know that the strong sense of peace and justice that you experience here was borne out of violent times.

This community's story begins with war.

It's 2003, and Jonathan Wilson-Hartgrove and his wife Leah are serving on a peacekeeping delegation near Bagdad, Iraq. While traveling, their partners are injured in a car accident on a shrapnel-strewn highway. This is at a time when American planes and tanks are destroying Iraq, and no American in his right mind would expect to receive help from an Iraqi.

Featured Communities: Rutba House

Miraculously, Jonathan and Leah witness a Good Samaritan story being played out right before their eyes. The injured Americans receive care from an "enemy" doctor whose hospital has just been bombed by American planes. This happened in the Iraqi city of Rutba.

The experience was so profound that later that year, Jonathan and his friends named their new community in Durham, North Carolina, "Rutba House" in honor of this Iraqi town.

They intentionally settled in the depressed Walltown neighborhood of Durham where racism, addiction, poverty, and oppression had faces and names. The home they rented had just been vacated by drug dealers. "Safety" and "beauty" were fixer-upper qualities for Walltown, to be enjoyed sparingly in those early days of the community.

Walk into Walltown today and you'll say, "This isn't so bad of a place." You should know that a lot has changed since Rutba House put their roots down here. It's safer and nicer today. People are better connected. The neighborhood has had a makeover and is quite comfortable.

So in a way, an Iraqi doctor's compassionate touch has spanned continents and continues to inspire healing and wholeness in Walltown today, turning chaos into peaceful order.

And by the way . . . it wasn't until *after* they had established their new community that Jonathan and Leah learned that the Arabic meaning of *rutba* is "order."

According to Jonathan, "The heart of the Scriptures is fulfilled in what the New Testament calls *ecclesia*, or the gathering together of people. This is what Jesus was about in the world, building a community of people, and that community itself is an expression of the Good News."

Walking in the footsteps of Jesus, the Rutba community has never wondered where to find ministry. Ministry has always found them.

Their family had not finished unpacking boxes when Jonathan met with Rev. Sylvia Hayes, a respected leader in Walltown. Jonathan told her about what had happened to them in Rutba, Iraq, and how they wanted to start a hospitality house in the neighborhood.

"Hold on," Rev. Hayes said. "You're saying you want people who don't live with you to come live in your house?"

"Yeah. That's right," said Jonathan.

"When you gonna start this?" she wondered.

"Well, we already have the house. We just need to meet some people."

"Like *today*?" she asked.

If Jonathan was surprised at the question, he did a good job of hiding it.

"Sure," he said. "You got somebody in mind?"

"As a matter of fact, yes. A guy called just before you came in. He's right across the street from you all."

"So she walked us over and introduced us to a guy named Ronnie who had just gotten evicted," Jonathan recalls. "He moved in that evening, and that's how we got started as a hospitality house."

Rutba's integration in Walltown was made much easier with the help of people like Rev. Hayes. The neighborhood had no reason to trust the crazy new kids on the block. Rutba received favor from a number of respected leaders who not only introduced them to the neighborhood, but also patiently helped them learn to love and appreciate a worldview that is borne from generations of oppression and entrenchment, which is foreign to most white Americans.

Rutba House's threefold community mission is to practice *hospitality*, *peacemaking*, and *discipleship* in the way of Jesus.

Hospitality is primarily offered in their two houses for immigrants, former inmates, and people in transition. Rutba House's sixteen members are accustomed to sharing the dinner table with just about anybody you could imagine. Who knows? . . . maybe they have even shared meals with Jesus.

Peacemaking did not cease being a value for the Wilson-Hartgrove family when they left Iraq. This neighborhood microcosm faces the same racial and justice tensions that are festering in most American urban centers today, and Rutba House has a positive plan of action that is seeing results. Their faithful commitment to inmates is helping to break the cycle of generational crime. They defend the defenseless in the Durham City Hall and the North Carolina State Capitol building. They offer vocational training and job placement to people in the community. They build bridges over troubled interracial waters. They bring together the haves and the have-nots.

Featured Communities: Rutba House

Discipleship at Rutba House is much deeper than a "'crack religion' that sells Jesus as cheap comfort for whatever ails us."[26] Rutba's School for Conversion walks with local youth, adults, and inmates down a path of total life transformation. For years, Rutba members have fellowshipped weekly with inmates on death row. They disciple people on the margins. They welcome folks of any creed, belief, or status. They teach justice to those who are trapped in a master-servant paradigm, which is still surprisingly strong on both ends of the social spectrum.

"I was raised in the church in rural North Carolina by people who loved Jesus," says Jonathan. "But like much of American Christianity, it was

26. Wilson-Hartgrove, *Wisdom of Stability*, 63.

quite individualistic, a 'me and Jesus' understanding of the faith. I experienced community in this rural setting, where people's lives were interwoven by an agricultural economy. I thought there was great value in what the New Testament calls *ecclesia*, the gathering together of people. This is what Jesus was about in the world: building a community of people, and that expression of the Good News is what attracted me to community."

The Rutba House intentional community is Christian and ecumenical, meaning they profess to have faith in Jesus Christ, while not asking members to subscribe to any particular denominational tradition. They seek to walk in the footsteps of Jesus. As followers of Jesus, they open arms to people of all beliefs.

Rutba House members seriously value their "Rule of Life," which is based on tradition and the teachings of Jesus. If this sounds a bit monastic, well . . . it's supposed to.

In fact, Jonathan Wilson-Hartgrove has helped define a new breed of monk, having authored *New Monasticism: What It has to Say to Today's Church*.

The Rutba House members are New Monastics. But when you think *monk*, don't picture the jolly Friar Tuck who fattens up on homebrewed mead and loaves of fresh-baked bread slathered with honey and butter. Think urban, blue collar monks who have the same compassionate heart as Friar Tuck, but who pack way different gear. Rutba House's shared spiritual rhythms weave them together in a community fabric with common threads of prayer, shared meals, chores, personal study, and a deeply-rooted faith.

Back in 2003—the same year Jonathan and his wife returned from Iraq and founded Rutba House—they received a letter from a monastery in Minnesota.

The letter read, "We heard that you are young Christians living in community. We are excited that you are doing this, and we'd love to be in conversation with you. We'll share with you what we have learned, since we have been living in community for fifteen hundred years."

Fifteen hundred years!

It was an invitation that a baby community couldn't pass up. A Rutba delegation was soon on the plane to one of the foremost Benedictine centers in the world, St. John's Abbey in Collegeville, Minnesota.

Featured Communities: Rutba House

That letter has led now to more than a dozen years of fellowship and growth. St. John's Abby took Rutba under its wings and shared with them a rich and abiding tradition. They have woven Rutba into a fabric that extends all the way back to the early Desert Fathers. The seed planted into Rutba has germinated into a whole new understanding of monasticism in a historically oppressed, urban environment.

"New Monasticism is a way of describing this movement of people into intentional communities that has been part of the North American experience for the last eighty-five years," says Jonathan. "Throughout the history of the church, there have been movements toward monasticism, particularly in times of significant social change, when Christianity is trying to negotiate how to relate to the culture at large, and how to do that with new forms and practices. Monasticism has often been a testing ground for that. The first monastic movement in the Christian tradition was when the Roman Empire was beginning to embrace Christianity in an official way, when all of a sudden there was a social advantage to being a Christian—when it might help you get a job downtown, as opposed to getting you crucified or eaten by the lions. It was a great shift in the history of the church. At that point, it was important for people to leave the city, to leave the political life of Rome, and to go into the desert to root a spirituality that engaged the principalities and powers, but also to develop a new political way of life."

Jonathan explains how the same dynamics that led monks into the desert are now leading New Monastics into urban centers. "This movement," he explains, "is not identical with the traditional forms of monasticism that grew up out of other moments, but is in response to the particular challenges of the world that we live in today. It is a new expression of the very long story of monasticism."

You cannot help but believe that the humble tasks of mentoring middle-schoolers or visiting prisoners on death row are of significant historical importance at Rutba House. So are the more activist activities, like testifying at city hall, standing with Black Lives Matter, picketing for prisoner's rights, or attending a peace and justice event.

"This is the modern wilderness where I've tried to stay put and do battle with the devil," Jonathan says in his book *The Wisdom of Stability*. "North Carolina is a far cry from the ancient Egyptian desert, but the spiritual mothers and fathers of that arid land have become guides to me as I've learned to practice stability in this place." [27]

---

27. Wilson-Hartgrove, *Wisdom of Stability*, 35.

Finding Intentional Community

Whereas ghettoization was the greatest problem facing Walltown a generation ago, gentrification is perhaps the biggest challenge today. Property values are skyrocketing as upwardly-mobile workers snatch up Walltown homes. It's suddenly a desirable neighborhood, being in close proximity to Duke University and uptown Durham. And predictably, money trumps justice when it comes to community development.

Gentrification does not appear to be much of a problem when viewed from the upper rungs of the societal ladder. In fact, folks who are living comfortably would be hard-pressed to see one thing wrong with gentrification, as dumpsters haul away the old and home improvement vans bring in the new. But looking up from below, it's an entirely different story.

"For this neighborhood," Jonathan explains, "the challenge of simply surviving is by some measures even more severe now than it was in the mid-twentieth century. This is true in many urban areas in the country, because white flight in the '70s—even for neighborhoods that were not historically African American—meant that black and brown people moved into the cities where at that time rents were cheaper. Now it means that whole communities are displaced by people who are moving in to those areas because they want to be close to downtown. And when they move in with a piece of paper that says, 'This is my property; I bought this land,' they are displacing people. And when people who are displaced express any concern about this, the common response of the gentrifiers—of people who look like me—is to say, 'We feel threatened.' And so they call the police. Then when the police come and there's a confrontation between those being displaced and those of the gentrifying population, we see what's happening all over the country."

For Rutba House, "being Jesus" in the midst of these agitated dynamics means peacemaking and promoting healthy dialog between parties. It also means offering a practical plan of sustainable, affordable housing for people who are being forced out because of steeply rising rents. The community's long-range goals include establishing a non-profit trust that will buy Walltown homes and make them permanently affordable.

Rental rates in Walltown have tripled in recent years. The crass economic advice to renters who have lived here for multiple generations is, "You should have bought your home years ago." But they couldn't. For most of the twentieth century, local banks would not administer loans to African Americans. These are the same families who are now being pushed out.

Featured Communities: Rutba House

While most people would use attractive labels like "beautification," "revitalization," or "progress" to describe gentrification, Rutba House stands on a different definition.

"It's a justice issue," Jonathan says.

Justice is, after all, the bottom line for much of what happens at Rutba House, which is south of the Mason-Dixon Line. Little did slave owners know or care how their bent perspectives on justice would still be deeply entrenched in people of all colors throughout the South, hundreds of years after their profits had been earned and spent. Poorer people in Durham to this day still use "the plantation" as a useful metaphor.

For example, to say that "Billy got a job up at the plantation" means he'll be working for Duke University.

Old habits are hard to break.

Is the situation hopeless? Not according to the Rutba community. They remember the words of the Prophet Micah, who said:

> And what does the Lord require of you? To act justly and to love mercy and to walk humbly with your God.
>
> —Micah 6:8

However, don't think that Rutba's Rule of Life is all about serious, grown-up stuff. They also heed Jesus's words which say, "Let the little children come to me" (Matthew 19:14).

The Rutba kids like living in this attractive community with grassy lawns and stately trees. Backyards are wonderful gathering places for picnics, barbeques, and games. Rutba owns a vacant lot that they have turned into a beautiful pocket garden for vegetables and ornamentals. Folks gather for weekend campfires behind one of the houses.

What is Rutba's advice for people wanting to merge into their New Monastic experience?

"Move to Durham" is the short answer.

That's not to say that out-of-town visitors are not welcome. The School for Conversion website calendar (schoolforconversion.org) posts dates for open houses. You'll also find announcements there for Rutba House potlucks that are open to the public.

"These potlucks are a fellowship time," Jonathan says, "and sometimes they lead to further things. We often have some kind of intentional discussion, and sometimes there's opportunity to learn what's going on around town. That's kind of an easy onramp to what's happening here. There's also potential to volunteer with our programs, so if your gifts are with kids or folks getting home from prison, you could get involved in that way and see what it leads to."

Since they are a "community building community," know that the process will take some time. Rutba does offer year-long internships for people wanting to immerse themselves in this New Monastic lifestyle.

However, once you decide to test the waters, be prepared to jump right in. Remember Rev. Hayes's response to Jonathan's offer of hospitality? Be prepared for that kind of response if you ask Rutba about joining with them on one of their projects.

"Like *today*?" you might hear them say.

One thing is for certain: You'll never get bored or lack a sense of purpose at the Rutba House, where planes, tanks, and gentrification cannot stand in the way of God's peace, love, and justice.

THE SIMPLE WAY

Address	3234 Potter St., Philadelphia, Pennsylvania 19134
Phone	215-423-3598
Email	info@thesimpleway.org
Website(s)	www.thesimpleway.org; www.facebook.com/theSimpleWay
Type of Housing	Five community-owned homes and seven green spaces and gardens
Urban/Rural/Suburban	Urban
Founded	1997
# of Core Members	About twelve
# of Residents	About twelve
Property and Financials	Shared property; private financials
Community Businesses	Online bookstore
Common Meals	Several times a month
Other Shared Activities	Weekly prayer gatherings; monthly meal and discussion
Leadership and Decision-making	Modified consensus
Outreach Ministries	Urban outreach and beautification; peace and justice events; neighborhood celebration events
Christian Affiliation	Non-denominational
ICC Association Membership	None
Non-Profit Org.	Yes
Key Values	Justice, discipleship, racial reconciliation, urban renewal; urban farming

I wandered into a Christian bookstore recently, where I discovered a few books on *justice* shivering under a cloud of self-help and devotional resources. Justice seems to be a depreciated topic in Western Christianity, when in fact, God crammed every corner of the Bible with themes and stories of justice and oppression.

Consider this one simple verse: "For I, the Lord, love justice" (Isaiah 61:8).

This bold statement becomes even more striking when you consider that it is the keystone verse of the remarkable chapter quoted by Jesus when he began his public ministry. After proclaiming this call to end oppression, Jesus sat down and said, "Today this Scripture is fulfilled in your hearing" (Luke 4:21).

As I spoke with The Simple Way members, Isaiah 61 kept popping into my consciousness, over and over again. I saw how The Simple Way has literally brought beauty from ashes, after a devastating fire leveled a block of their neighborhood in 2007. I saw how they are tangibly bringing good news to poor people. They are outspoken advocates for prisoners, foreigners, and oppressed minorities. They are literally rebuilding ancient ruins in the Kensington neighborhood of Philadelphia. They are bringing beautiful murals and healing gardens to a ruined city. To me, these acts sound like a litany from the prophetic words of Isaiah:

> The Spirit of the Sovereign Lord is on me, because the Lord has anointed me to proclaim good news to the poor. He has sent me to bind up the brokenhearted, to proclaim freedom for the captives and release from darkness for the prisoners, to proclaim the year of the Lord's favor and the day of vengeance of our God, to comfort all who mourn, and provide for those who grieve in Zion, to bestow on them a crown of beauty instead of ashes, the oil of joy instead of mourning, and a garment of praise instead of a spirit of despair. They will be called oaks of righteousness, a planting of the Lord for the display of his splendor. They will rebuild the ancient ruins and restore the places long devastated; they will renew the ruined cities that have been devastated for generations.
>
> —Isaiah 61:1–4

The Simple Way is by no means the only group bringing good news to the poor in twenty-first century America, or in Philadelphia, for that matter. But it doesn't take long to see that justice is more than a weekend hobby for The Simple Way.

Featured Communities: The Simple Way

The Simple Way describes itself as a village within the greater Philadelphia area. About a dozen core members live in five community-owned houses. The Simple Way also manages several green spaces, playgrounds, gardens, and a small park that can be reserved for barbeques, weddings, and celebrations. They have an online bookstore. Their "modified common purse" means members contribute a portion of their personal income for community expenses. Key values include community, friendship, justice, racial reconciliation, and urban renewal. They meet weekly for prayer and community meals. Their mission is, simply stated, to love God, love people, and follow Jesus.

Since its beginning in 1997, The Simple Way has reimagined ways to breathe life into this neighborhood that was abandoned by the unemployed working class in the 1950s and 60s.

"We talk about practicing resurrection here," says member Shane Claiborne, author of *Irresistible Revolution; Living as an Ordinary Radical*. "Bringing dead things back to life. Making ugly things beautiful. Turning vacant lots into gardens."

The Simple Way delights in planting gardens and trees in every available patch of dirt. They grow organic vegetables, fruit trees, and flowers. They even have koi swimming in their hydroponics greenhouse. Compost bins and rain barrels have edged out dirty mattresses, trash bags, and discarded tires. Open walkways bring neighbors together who were formerly divided by chain link fences.

"Simple living doesn't mean ugly living," says Shane. "It can be beautiful living. There are murals everywhere. There's artwork. There's a dynamic of imagination and creativity. It's like the grass piercing through concrete. In fact, one of our neighbors said it looked like we were bringing the Garden of Eden to north Philly."

Reimagining communal life in Philadelphia means reformatting architecture. Low-income projects here were built without dining rooms, porches, and community spaces. Every new green space and home improvement project is designed with intentionality for cultivating community. The Simple Way did not come up with these ideas alone, but they delight in helping to strengthen the values held by their neighbors. The Simple Way members have learned much and had their lives greatly enriched by their friends whose roots grow deep in this rich, urban soil.

"Our neighbors value community," says Shane. "They kick in for a cousin or for someone on the streets. We have a friend who made a huge holiday meal for people next door who were working at the scrap metal yard. When people lost their homes in a big fire a few years ago, the Red Cross shelter wasn't even needed because people opened up their homes to each other."

The Simple Way is also reimagining inner-city health.

"One of the first things I noticed when I moved into the neighborhood was this epidemic of malnutrition, obesity, and diabetes," says Shane. "We have corner stores, but a lot of them are selling food that has absolutely no nutritional value. Kids are buying cupcakes and chips when what they really need is *food*!"

To that, one community member said, "It's easier to get a gun around here than to buy an organic head of lettuce."

That was a few years ago. Urban gardening is helping to change things. To The Simple Way, healthy food is just one component of justice. But it's not easy getting kids to understand how injustice can taste so sweet, while being sold in attractive plastic packaging at the corner market.

A woman in Kensington who was a caretaker for her grandkids had a small kitchen fire. After the fire, she was devastated when child protective services took her grandchildren away. She applied for a grant to help fix up the kitchen because she couldn't afford to do it herself. Then she got a letter from the government saying that her grant had been denied because they were giving priority to people who had children in the home. Her sense of despair only mounted, because she couldn't get her grandkids back without having a kitchen, and she couldn't get her kitchen without having kids.

"That's exactly what the Scriptures mean when they say that we're wrestling not against flesh and blood," says Shane, "but against powers and principalities, or against bureaucratic obstacles that are holding people hostage and pressing them down. There are a million versions of that story around here. But if we don't live near people like that, how can we help them?"

The Simple Way offers weekly food distribution, university scholarships for four students at a time, a tutoring club, school supplies distribution, a Christmas store for neighbors, and some very popular neighborhood celebrations. However, gifts do not only flow one way here. The Simple Way receives many blessings from their neighbors in return. They do not operate "programs" for the poor. They simply share life with their neighbors.

Thesimpleway.org explains, "The Simple Way is made up of *'remainers'* (long-term, indigenous residents); *'returners'* (people from the neighborhood who have come back to be a part of the restoration); and *'relocators'* (non-indigenous friends who have moved here to intentionally bring their gifts and energy)."

They stress that they are not creating a new community within the neighborhood, but rather working from within, coming alongside and strengthening the community life that is already there. In this context, the *remainers* are the real heroes, since they have a long-term investment in

Kensington. They have experienced life here at its best and its worst. They have also experienced the strongest pressure to leave.

"We have older people here who want to die with someone holding their hands," says Shane. "We have older men who are now mentoring a lot of young people who don't have a father. That's all part of living out the Gospel in the context of where we live."

Mother Teresa once said, "It is fashionable to talk about the poor, but not as fashionable to talk to the poor."[28]

Shane Claiborne agrees. "It's easier to avoid issues of justice when they don't have names and faces. The heart of the Gospel calls us to live in proximity to the pain of the world. That's the example of Jesus who was born of refugees, put in an animal's manger, and executed on a cross. He showed us the most incredible acts of divine solidarity. Immanuel is 'God is with us.' God feels our pain. He knows our loneliness. Following him means moving closer to the pain. For many of us, it's a geographical thing. We want to be closer to the streets where people get beat up and where injustice happens. It's the opposite of white flight and leaving the neighborhood. It's a call for the church to actually dive in and be a part of the solution. So that call—that invitation—is to live in proximity to people who are suffering. Proximity is critical."

Relational justice is lived out daily here in the Kensington neighborhood. As with a growing number of people today, The Simple Way is not satisfied with merely sending checks, prayers, and clothes to people in need. They want to share the same street address with them. They call them friends and family. Unfortunately, this lifestyle is foreign to many Christians in the twenty-first century.

"We don't just have a compassion problem in the church today," says Shane. "We have a relationship problem. It's not that we don't care about poor people. It's that we don't know many of them. That's also true with racial injustice. It's why a lot of white folks say, 'We don't have a policing problem.' When you ask people of color, overwhelmingly they say, 'Absolutely, we have a policing problem.' Racial violence and police misconduct are very real, because we see the world through different lenses. So that call to be in proximity to those who are suffering is absolutely critical. We need

---

28. Claiborne, *Irresistible Revolution*, 141.

to be present in the streets with neighbors, in good times and in bad. We need to be visually present at a candlelight vigil when someone gets shot."

Relational justice means sharing a meal or a bed with a neighbor who knocks on the door in crisis. It means playing with kids in the neighborhood, visiting friends on death row, and attending peace and justice marches. It means doing the laundry and weeding a garden with friends. It means picking up trash together. It means speaking with the media about racial injustice, or attending a prayer vigil at the U.S. Supreme Court.

Life is integrated here, not compartmentalized. Relational justice is a vital thread running through everything they do.

Like every other corner of this planet, life is not always easy at The Simple Way. There may be tensions to work through with your flat-mates, or the bothersome dirty dishes or messy toilet that didn't get cleaned up. Winters can feel long and dreary. Daily routines can lose their sparkle and simply become drudgery.

"There's a lot of stuff to work through," says Caz Tod-Pearson, Director of The Simple Way's operations. "Community is people just trying to live out their lives being a good neighbor and doing that alongside each other. And there's no magic bullet for that. There's no magic to working really hard and being intentional and being a good neighbor."

I asked Caz about her favorite times living in community.

"It's anytime we get to sit around the table and eat a meal together and not rush away," she explained. "It's when we linger together, when we're able to just be together with all of our differences and all of our experiences and enjoy each other, where we're not trying to fix each other. We just want to be together. We just want to belong. For me, that's happened while sitting around a meal table, or at someone's birthday party, or at Thanksgiving together. It might even be shoveling snow together after a big snowstorm. It's just having the intentionality to say, 'Hey, come over and we'll be in this space together.' Living in this diverse neighborhood means we are sharing space with people who are in very different places, so it requires something of inclusivity and non-judgment. That's what I really love. When I'm doing that, I feel like I'm doing what's really good for my heart and what's good for the heart of the person I'm with. Life is meant to be shared, and I'm only going to do well in life if that person next to me is doing well."

Finding Intentional Community

Years back, The Simple Way started a tradition that took on a life of its own. All of Kensington looks forward to an annual cycle of neighborhood celebrations, at Christmas, Easter, Mother's Day, Labor Day, and more. The back-to-school celebration attracts upwards of six hundred kids and their families for games, food, and free school supplies.

Shane Claiborne says that these seasonal events "feel like a liturgy for our community and our neighborhood. You don't find this in the Book of Common Prayer. We try to color outside the lines. Helping kids with homework might not seem like a big thing, but it's big. We are living in a time when we've lost the art of community and made idols of independence and individualism. That's why a lot of the wealthiest places in the world have such high rates of loneliness and depression, suicide and self-medication."

That's a good reminder. We easily confuse wealth and happiness. We forget that some of the happiest people live in poorer settings like inner-city Philadelphia.

"The dominant patterns like urban sprawl and American individualism have a different gravity than this call to community," says Shane. "A lot of our world is pulling us away from community, and especially away from the suffering of the world, away from neighborhoods that struggle. And yet, the gravity of the Gospel pulls us into those places."

Gravity of the Gospel.

When Shane said that phrase, it stuck like an arrow in my heart.

Gravity of the Gospel.

Gravity is something that everyone experiences equally. You can't ignore it. You can't cheat it or find any loopholes or exemptions. There's something unifying about gravity. There's something equalizing about it.

In a similar way, community unifies and equalizes, while segregation polarizes.

Shane explains, "Community isn't just for radicals. It's not just for people who feel some extraordinary call. The hunger for community is in all of us. People long to belong. They long for friendship. The church was meant to be that community, a place where we all can belong to each other, where we belong to God together. It's significant that Jesus's longest recorded prayer says, 'Let my people be one as you and I are one.' In some ways, we work so hard to pretend that we don't need other people, that we are independent. We try to swim upstream from what is good. It's actually best to be *interdependent*, to be in community with other people, to know that we need God together. Maybe that's why Jesus continually pointed towards children who are the most dependent people in the world. He said, 'If you want to enter the Kingdom, you need to enter like a child.' A child is very vulnerable—very in need—and yet that's who we're called to follow, not the princes and presidents. We're called to follow the children, and to know that we need God and other people."

Right on, Shane! I love this perspective of childlikeness and interdependence.

I think about how the dominant culture is actually swimming upstream—or fighting against gravity—trying to be independent princes and presidents. Meanwhile, the childlike Kingdom-seekers are resting, being drawn by the *gravity of the Gospel* toward community and justice and interdependence.

Pause for just a moment, and meditate on this *gravity of the Gospel* concept. Let your imagination whirl and spin out into the heavens. Imagine a dark sky and bright stars. Look to the planets. See how they are tied together in a graceful dance across the sky.

How are they tied together?

Ah, yes . . . Gravity.

Without the sun calling the dance of the planets, all would be chaos.

In a flash, we can understand the force that holds together that lovely dance in north Philly.

Of course . . . It's the Son in the center . . . and the gravity of the Gospel.

SUSANNA WESLEY HOUSE

Address	1703 Sanger Ave., Waco, Texas 76707
Phone	832–205-5074
Email	melissa.turkett@gmail.com
Website(s)	http://missionalwisdom.com/epworth/houses/susanna-wesley-house/; www.instagram.com/swesleyhouse/
Type of Housing	One house and guest cottage on one half acre
Urban/Rural/Suburban	Urban
Founded	2013
# of Core Members	Seven
# of Residents	Seven
Property and Financials	Foundation-owned home; private finances; monthly rent
Community Businesses	None
Common Meals	Monday night community meal
Other Shared Activities	Morning prayer; music nights; spontaneous gatherings
Leadership and Decision-making	Consensus, under the oversight of the Missional Wisdom Foundation
Outreach Ministries	Urban farm, house events, personal involvement in neighborhood
Christian Affiliation	United Methodist-led, but non-denominational members
ICC Association Membership	Missional Wisdom Foundation
Non-Profit Org.	Yes
Key Values	Hospitality; New Monasticism, urban farming; neighborhood involvement

It's a warm day, as usual, in Waco, Texas. You park your car at the curb of 1703 Sanger Avenue and get out.

The stately old house towers above you with its elaborate chimneys, dormer windows, and steeply peaked roof. The clapboard siding and Victorian trim is done in pastel blue and pink with burgundy accents. The only thing missing from the wraparound porch is someone with a checkered apron calling out, "Y'all want somethin' cool to drink?"

You see a man working out back, so you cross the sidewalk and climb the steps into the yard. As if welcoming you to the Susanna Wesley House, tall, purple wildflowers rise from a keyhole garden and wave at you in the breeze. You follow the tiled pathway toward the side of the house, past crepe myrtle trees and a potato tower. Raised, stone beds are bursting with tomato plants. You glance across a broad green lawn to see a young woman and child picking flowers, their picnic blanket beside them on the grass. Walking further along the pathway, you come to a wooden pergola. At your feet are Mexican tiles decorated with the brilliant, Texan sun.

The man you saw from the street is working in a bed of herbs and greens.

"Good afternoon," you say.

"Hi," says he.

You share names and shake hands.

"Do you live in the neighborhood?" he inquires.

"No. I heard about your community meal from a friend of mine who's been here before."

He knows your friend, and you chat awhile. Then he offers to take you up to the porch where dinner will be served tonight.

"Oh, don't stop what you're doing," you insist.

"Well, people will be gathering on the porch in a little while," he says. "Take a look around the place. You'll see a cottage in back that we rent out on Airbnb. Just make yourself at home in the gardens, and we'll see you on the porch in a few minutes. Okay?"

"That sounds great," you say.

You wander past dozens of raised beds containing tomatoes, cucumbers, and greens. Further back at the edge of the property, you discover a quaint, pioneer-looking cabin. A sign above the door says "Jack Bryant Cottage." You don't know who Jack is, but you wouldn't be surprised to see him sitting in a rocking chair on the little porch with a corn cob pipe in his mouth, two-day stubble on his chin.

You turn toward an old barn that looks as if it originally housed the horses and carriages. It is sagging and slanted, looking a bit tired, but still hinting of its former glory. Much of the aged barn wood has been removed from its walls.

Nearby, you look to the ground and discover a reflection of yourself framed in goldfish. It's a garden pond. You cross a little bridge and follow the trickle of water toward its source. You pause to enjoy the peaceful setting.

Walking further, you come upon the hens, their stylish house looking as if it's a miniature replica of the big house. The birds peck at a ball packed with greens from the garden. You allow the breeze to guide you through an array of lovely flowers flaunting deep purples, bright yellows, and crisp white blooms. Upon closer inspection, you see bees gathering pollen and nectar.

Suddenly, you notice that your gardener friend is gone. So are the woman and child on the lawn. You head back to the front of the house and climb the steps to the wraparound porch, where you join a handful of others.

"Would you like a glass of iced tea?" someone asks.

"I would absolutely love it!"

You take a cool sip, thinking, *The only thing missing now is the checkered apron.*

You take a seat in a wicker chair.

"We're glad you came to community night," a woman says, as she plops into a rocking chair beside you. "We'll eat out here tonight. It's not too hot, and there's such a nice breeze."

You continue chatting, and she tells you a little bit about the Susanna Wesley House.

"Who owns it?" you ask.

"It's actually owed by the Missional Wisdom Foundation. They're the umbrella organization over several community homes like this one. The Susanna Wesley House—or Swesley, as we like to call it—is actually an intentional community. We are about a half-dozen Christians who have covenanted to God and to each other. We're stewards of this house, and we really love sharing it and the gardens with friends like you. Would you like a little tour of the house?"

"Sure," you say.

You take your iced tea and follow her to the door.

"This was a Sears Kit House,[29] built in 1897," she says. "Sears sold homes like this in their catalog and delivered them by railroad to towns all across America."

---

29. Boutique version, made in New York.

Inside, the first thing that captures your attention is the ornate woodworking: the diagonal hardwood floors, the trim around the windows and doors, and the curled pine wainscoting. The ceilings are tall, and the walls are patterned with elegant wallpaper. The woman draws your attention to a "Harry Potter bathroom" tucked neatly away beneath the master stairway.

Next, she shows you the prayer and music room, with its orchestral assemblage of guitars, ukuleles, piano, harp, and banjo. The corner fireplace is overshadowed by an iconic print of the Holy Trinity, depicted as the divine guests who visited Abraham and Sarah in Genesis 18.

"This picture reminds us that we want to be people of radical hospitality," your hostess explains. "Anytime a guest walks through the door, we never know when we might be entertaining Jesus."

"No worries here," you say with a laugh. "I assure you I can't walk on water! I've tried . . . and failed miserably."

Your hostess smiles. "One can never be sure."

Next, she draws your attention to a Tibetan singing bowl, several copies of the *Common Book of Prayer*, and an ornamented Celtic scroll work piece on the wall.

"This is an illustration of our rule of life," she says. "We pray together right here every weekday morning. And on Fridays, we focus on one aspect of the rule of life."

She explains that the community is monastic, not in terms of woolen robes, shaved heads, or vows of celibacy, but in rhythms of prayer, study, meditation, hospitality, and commitment to one another.

"We're one of many New Monastic communities today," she explains.

Your hostess leads you into a room that is decorated with a wide assortment of tribal objects. Lions prowl across the wallpaper.

"This is the Africa room," she says. "You could probably guess. It's where we watch movies, play games, or just hang out together in the evening."

Your next stop is the dining room, where an enormous, chevron-patterned wooden table is overshadowed by a sparkling chandelier. You pass through a swinging door that looks as if it was heisted from a Western saloon. In the hallway beyond, a whiteboard is crammed with lists of indoor chores, outdoor chores, and shopping lists. Further along, you see scores of prayer requests posted on the wall. Your hostess approaches a magnet Jesus display, pausing to remove his white robe.

"Jesus wants to dress up for community meal tonight," she says. She replaces the white robe with a garment of many colors, then continues down the hall.

Okay, you think. *Jesus appears to have a magnetic attraction to this community . . .*

You pop briefly into the kitchen, where you are introduced to a couple who is preparing dinner. It's a spacious room with two sinks and two refrigerators. Your hostess catches you eyeing the glass-fronted fridge that is stocked with Dr. Pepper.

"You're probably wondering," she says.

"Yeah. I am."

"Since Waco is the birthplace of Dr. Pepper," she says, "we think every home in town should be well-stocked with the drink. Would you like some?"

"Thanks, no," you say, raising your glass. "I'm good."

Your hostess points to a back stairway.

"That's our shortcut to the rooms upstairs," she says. "We have a total of five adults and two children living in the house right now. So that just about wraps up this grand tour of the main floor. Any questions?"

Not having any, she leads you back out to the front porch.

"This is the perfect place to watch a thunderstorm roll by," your hostess says, "or just to chill out with friends. Sometimes the simplest things in life are the best."

The Susanna Wesley House is one of about ten Epworth Project communities located primarily in Texas. The project began in 2008, parented by the Missional Wisdom Foundation, which is itself attached to the United Methodist Church. Members commit to one-to four-years of community life, although they are often able to stay longer. Community members need not subscribe to the Methodist faith, but all agree to the Epworth Rule of Life (*see below*). The application process begins when inquirers correspond, visit, and develop relationships with members of one of the houses. It can take some time for both parties to determine if the inquirer will be a good fit for the house. This person will eventually complete an online application with the Missional Wisdom Foundation, who will consult with the house and enter into a time of prayer and consideration before making a final decision.

Featured Communities: Susanna Wesley House

Epworth Project members follow daily and weekly rhythms of prayer, hospitality, work, meals, and chores. Most of the members are church workers or religious students, although that is not a requirement. Outreach to the local community is important to the Epworth Project, and each home has its own unique focus, such as serving refugees, helping homeless people, or cultivating an urban farm. Neighbors are invited to these homes for community meals or special events. Each house is semi-autonomous, receiving council and accountability from the Missional Wisdom Foundation. Members pay rent to the Foundation, which owns each of the homes.

The five adults in the Susanna Wesley House all work outside the home. Their involvement in urban farming and healthy food production arose organically, due to one sad fact and another untapped potential. The sad fact was that the surrounding Sanger-Heights Neighborhood was a food desert. One in three Waco citizens are below the poverty line, and that rate is even higher in Sanger-Heights. The two-mile distance to the nearest grocery store made it difficult for many people to avoid buying expensive and unhealthy "food products" at the local mini-marts. Fortunately, Susanna Wesley House had a significant untapped potential, banked silently away beneath a mass of weeds in forty-three neglected, raised beds. That untapped potential . . . was dirt.

Community members spent months clearing weeds and tilling soil. They also reached out to several local ministries based right in their neighborhood, including Mission Waco, which was very supportive of their crazy idea to develop a small urban farm. In turn, the community was able to help Mission Waco open Jubilee Food Market, one of the few non-profit grocery stores in the nation. Thanks to this new oasis of healthy food, the Sanger-Heights Neighborhood is no longer a food desert. Jubilee's future plans include a hydroponics greenhouse, dependent upon funding and support from the community.

Susanna Wesley House is known in the neighborhood as a house of hospitality and beautiful gardens. Members make friends the old-fashioned way, by walking through the neighborhood and chatting with people, as well as by reaching out through social media. They invite people to garden with them, and to attend their Monday evening community meal. They met a Waco city councilman at one of the neighborhood association meetings, then connected with him again at the local farmer's market. After accepting their invitation to dinner at the Susanna Wesley House, this councilman asked how he could help their mission.

"We're hoping to start a concert series out on our lawn and pergola," a member explained. "We would love to have a different local non-profit organization sponsor each of these nights, and they could take up a donation and tell people about their organization."

"I could certainly help you promote that kind of event," the councilman said. And that was how their outdoor concert series got started.

Their Instagram account—@swesleyhouse—has helped Swesley House make a number of key connections. Among other things, it connected them with an experienced herbalist who helped launch their herb garden. None of the members consider themselves to be expert gardeners, and they appreciate all the help that they can get.

For many Americans, a perfect day would involve sunny beaches, mountain resorts, expensive spas, or shows on Broadway. For Susanna Wesley House member Melissa Turkett, the sweetest days are simpler than that. She described one of her perfect days to me.

"I came home from work late one Monday and parked behind the house," says Melissa. "As usual, my husband Patrick is in one of the garden beds, pulling weeds."

"'Hi Patrick,' I say, and we quickly catch up on our day. Then I say 'Hi' to two of the neighborhood kids who are playing with the chickens in the coop. Instead of going straight into the back door, I take the long way around and head for the front of the house. The flowers are in their prime, and the place is buzzing with bees. My housemate Emmanuel is by the porch, talking to one of our neighbors. The neighbor says, 'Hey. Is it too late for my daughter and me to come to community meal tonight?' Emmanuel is stretching his legs, getting ready to go on a run. 'Not at all,' he says. 'Just come back at six.' 'Okay. We'll see you in a little bit,' says the neighbor. Emmanuel takes off on his run and I walk up the front porch stairs. One of our neighbors is playing on the wicker couch with her baby. I smile as they laugh and babble and coo with each another. As I reach for the doorknob, I hear the deliberate plunking of piano keys. I go inside and see Claire giving music lesson to a young girl who is sister to the baby on the porch. I leave the music room and enter the kitchen, where Zach is putting the finishing touches on a delicious dinner which will be served to our family and friends tonight. I offer to help, but he's got nearly everything ready."

"That picture might seem so ordinary and mundane to some people," says Melissa, "but not for me. I see something holy there, in this peaceful space where everyone feels welcome, whether it's their home or not. To me, this is what community should look like."

Holy moments are, of course, punctuated with tedious and uncomfortable times of fixing a broken lawnmower, cleaning out the chicken coop, or even having a disagreement. Still, in a monastic setting, that is all part of the divine.

"I live in intentional Christian community because I think it gets us back to the church in the book of Acts," says Melissa. "We've made the gospel so complicated today, when it's really quite simple. We've lost the heart of it. It's really about living with people. It's loving God and loving neighbors, whether they live in your house or next door. And the more that I learn to love my neighbor well, the more I learn how to love God well.

That's why my heart beats so strong for Christian community, living with people who are on the same journey as me, who can hold me accountable. It's such a beautiful way to do Christian life."

I asked Melissa to explain, more specifically, what attracted her to New Monasticism.

"For me," she said, "there's this tension about following Jesus well and growing into his image that appeals to me about New Monasticism. It runs counter to those parts of the Western church where you don't really have to take up the cross, but only do the things that are convenient for you. New monasticism creates a tension about the inward life that is such an important part of the Christian walk and inward journey, to discover who God called and made you to be. But there's also the tension of the outward journey, to carry the Good News out into the world. For me, it's actually more than Good News. It's the best news possible, leading to the best life possible. That doesn't mean a life that is easy or without sorrow or failures, but one that leads you to say at the end of your days, 'This has absolutely been the best life that I could have lived.' That's what appeals to me about New Monasticism."

"Some people ask me how I work a full-time job and still have energy to work in the garden and do all the things that community life requires," says Melissa. "Well, I'm human, just like anyone else. I still binge out on TV shows every once in a while, but that's not the rule of my life. Christ's Kingdom is the rule, and I love it. Things usually don't happen as quick as I'd like here, but I see the beauty of allowing it to be a slow process, of coming up organically, just like plants in the garden. So much of life here happens in the small moments that we allow to influence our lives. We hope that our prayer life will help us not to miss God in those moments, to recognize, for example, that neighbors stopping by are not a nuisance. Those interruptions can be welcome breaks. So we take a moment to intentionally look back and reflect and say, 'See how the Holy Spirit was moving through each of those small moments to create a beautiful story of our community.'"

Let's assume that most of the people of Sanger-Heights are typically American in that the closest they want to come to farm life is at the drive-through window of the local hamburger stand. That being said, a good number of neighbors are still attracted to Susanna Wesley House's urban farm. They love to receive gifts of vegetables and share them with friends and family.

A small number of neighbors actually step into the garden beds and get their hands dirty, and their interactions with community members tend to be deep and fertile. This suits the community just fine, preferring quality relationships to quantity.

One day, Melissa, who works in campus ministry at Baylor University, invited her student friends to come over and help out in the garden.

"One woman was quick to accept my invitation," says Melissa. "I knew that she was having a particularly tough semester, so I was glad that we'd have an opportunity to spend some time together. And of course, we can always use help in the garden. When she came, there were a few other people working in the yard with us, while the two of us were pulling weeds and digging out a garden bed. I remember her asking questions like, 'So why do you do this?' And, 'What's the importance of gardening for you?' I felt as if one of the reasons she was asking was because she was searching for things of relevance in her own life. She was maybe looking for input on what she might do next. We were having some good conversation, while getting our hands dirty. It's hard work, and there's something of Jesus and the Kingdom of God in gardening. He certainly liked to tell parables about gardening. As we continued working and talking, some people started to file through our yard. I recognized them from Hope Fellowship, a ministry that's right next door to us. They came in and made themselves right at home, admiring the flowers and vegetables and chickens. They know they're always welcome to come in."

"What are you planting?" one of the guys asked.

"Tomatoes," said Patrick. He mentioned several varieties of heirloom tomatoes he was planting.

"I've grown that one before," said the guy. "I had so much success with it. I can't wait to come back and see how well it produces for you."

"Little things like that are so cool," says Melissa, "just the sense that he'll be back, that he knows he's always welcome to be in the yard whether we're here or not. After that, another neighbor lady walked into the yard."

"I just wanted to stop and say hey," she said. "How are you doing? I haven't gotten to see you lately."

"It's been a busy semester," said Melissa.

"Time has been flying for me as well," said the neighbor. "I just wanted to see how you all are doing."

Melissa and the woman chatted for some time. After she left, another neighbor stopped by.

"Oh my goodness," she said. "Just look at those chickens! They're nearly full grown. Last time I saw them, they were just cute little chicks. Can we go and play with them?"

"So we all went into the chicken coop and picked them up," says Melissa. "We were playing with the chickens and just hanging out and talking for a while. We fed them meal worms and some leafy treats from the garden. Again, I was just enjoying this spontaneous, organic moment. Nobody had a plan. Nobody was feeling uncomfortable. Our friend wasn't apologizing, as if she was stealing our time away from something more important. Everyone was feeling welcome. And that's how the day continued, as we went back to gardening and talking with whoever was around. Then this really significant moment came, when my college friend simply said, 'I get it.' 'What do you mean?' I asked. 'I get it,' she said. 'Now I get why you live this way.' I don't remember much of what else was said, but the words really aren't that important. The important thing is this beautiful picture that was being painted right in front of us. I could have tried to tell her and explain to her what it meant, but the most beautiful thing was for her to experience it for herself. It was another one of those holy moments, to see friends and neighbors coming by and genuinely caring for one another and being excited for the work that's being done among us."

It just goes to show you that some things never change.

You might think that the stories Jesus told of seeds and fruit and digging in the dirt are getting a little stale by now with all the inventions and improvements we've made, with everything we call "progress" in the last two thousand years.

Then suddenly, we discover that these parables are just as relevant today as they were back then.

What cheer!

Let's all grab a bottle of Dr. Pepper, dress up magnetic Jesus, and celebrate life with our Swesley friends!

The Epworth Rule of Life[30]

Our Rule of Life is based on Wesley's General Rules, the membership vows of the United Methodist Church and St. Benedict's Rule. We believe this rule opens our eyes to God's grace, balances life and enables us to pursue holiness in all aspects of daily living.

Prayers

We will pray daily

We will use a variety of forms of prayer such as the reflective reading of Scripture and other spiritual texts, confession, the prayer of examen, intercession, journaling, and contemplation

We will fast from food once a week (either a full or partial fast)

Presence

We will practice a contemplative stance in order to be present to God, the world, and ourselves

We will be hospitable to our neighbors in our families, neighborhoods and workplaces

We will be hospitable to our faith community through participation in our worship, fellowship and mission

Gifts

We will honor and care for the gift of the earth and its resources, practicing ecologically responsible living, striving for simplicity rather than excessive consumption

We will practice generosity in sharing our material resources, including money, within and beyond this community

We will use our spiritual gifts, talents and abilities to serve God within and beyond this community

---

30. Missional Wisdom Foundation, "Epworth," accessed June 2017, http://missionalwisdom.com/epworth/.

Service

> We will serve God and neighbor out of gratitude for the love of God
>
> We will practice mutual accountability with a covenant group within the community, for how we serve God and neighbor
>
> We will practice regular Sabbath as a means of renewal so that we can lovingly serve God and neighbor

Witness

> We will practice racial and gender reconciliation
>
> We will resist evil and injustice
>
> We will pursue peace with justice
>
> We will share the redeeming, healing, creative love of God in word, deed and presence as an invitation to others to experience the transforming love of God
>
> I commit to this rule of life and to the well-being of this community, out of gratitude to God who forgives, heals, and makes all things new. May my life be a blessing within and beyond God's church, for the transformation of the world.

THE WORD OF GOD

Address	3820 Packard St., Ste. 200, Ann Arbor, Michigan 48108
Phone	734-994-3243
Email	mail@thewordofgodcommunity.org
Website(s)	www.thewordofgodcommunity.org
Type of Housing	About seventy private homes throughout the county
Urban/Rural/Suburban	All
Founded	1967
# of Core Members	130
# of Residents	130
Property and Financials	Private property and financials
Community Businesses	None
Common Meals	Monthly women's breakfast
Other Shared Activities	Biweekly prayer meetings; regular small group meetings
Leadership and Decision-making	Leadership team
Outreach Ministries	Various; personal initiative
Christian Affiliation	Non-denominational
ICC Association Membership	None
Non-Profit Org.	Yes
Key Values	Ecumenical, charismatic, missionary, Christian community

Go back with me in time.

It's 1965.

A grainy black and white picture slowly comes into view, like an old tube television image. (*Tube TV? That was before solid state . . . way before digital.*)

You are looking at downtown Ann Arbor, Michigan. The streets are active and alive with art fairs, street music, student protests, anti-war demonstrations, White Panther sit-ins, and civil rights marches.

Finding Intentional Community

Back then, teachers at the University of Michigan invented all-night, anti-war "teach-ins," an idea that caught on quickly at other schools across the nation. Ann Arbor was a hip and happening showplace for avant-garde arts and music. Some of the better-known pilgrims, protesters, and performers appearing in Ann Arbor in the late '60s included Yoko Ono, John Lennon, Bob Dylan, Joan Baez, Neil Young, Joni Mitchell, the Doors, Jimi Hendrix, Janis Joplin, and Stevie Wonder.

The black and white picture slowly fades to color as flocks of hippies migrate to Ann Arbor by way of Greyhound buses, love bugs, and flowered vans. These "street people," as some folks called them, pushed the boundaries to the limits on issues of sex, drugs, and antiestablishment values. In 1968, they were even so bold as to establish a commune in two large Victorian homes near the university. Ann Arbor was so edgy that some people called it the "Midwestern Haight-Ashbury."[31]

While most Christians were keeping a respectable distance from Ann Arbor's young radicals, a few crazy believers were plunging right into the thick of things, seeking new ways to bring Jesus into the conversation.

Four young Catholic men from Notre Dame University had recently experienced the baptism of the Holy Spirit. They felt called to help bring charismatic renewal into the midst of Ann Arbor's craziness. In 1967, they made the area around the University of Michigan their home base and mission field.

Meetings in their apartment were centered on Bible study, folksy music, meals, and prayers for healings and revival. The gathering of four swiftly grew to over one hundred, necessitating a move to the Catholic student chapel. People with no religious background were attracted to these God-gatherings that introduced them to a different Spirit than the ones they met in other radical movements of the day.

The Catholic leaders called their community The Word of God. Both Catholics and Protestants were attracted to the meetings and the movement. This was at a time when significant walls separated Christian camps. One local group of Pentecostals had been praying for the Holy Spirit to move

---

31. For more information on this topic, see: Ann Arbor District Library, "The Hidden History of Ann Arbor, Michigan: A Small Town's Big Impact on the Sixties," by Alan Glenn, accessed June 2017, http://freeingjohnsinclair.aadl.org/freeingjohnsinclair/essays/hidden_history_of_ann_arbor.

in Ann Arbor long before these Catholic men arrived. When the group heard about a charismatic revival among Catholics, they were amazed and somewhat skeptical, not having any experience with Catholics who personally loved and followed Jesus. Many Protestants at this time did not even believe that Catholics were true Christians. One bold Pentecostal woman went personally to check out these charismatic Catholics. She became so convinced that this was a work of the Holy Spirit that she ended up joining the community.

The young Catholic leaders were challenged by the influx of Protestants. They, at first, assumed that everyone would be initiated into the Catholic Church. But as more Protestants arrived, they quickly felt God calling them to be ecumenical. So they instilled into the Word of God community a value of respect and honor for believers with diverse affiliations.

In those early years, many of the single members began living together in guys' or girls' communal homes and apartments. When families began to join, they often shared space in their homes with single people. In the excitement and freshness of experiencing a spiritual revival in the twentieth century, these people attempted to follow the example of the early believers by being more involved in communal life and sharing resources with those in need. The community tried pooling their finances together in a "common purse" for a few years, but stopped when they decided it wasn't practical for their purpose.

So out of Ann Arbor's hotbed of radicalism sprang this incubator of God's Kingdom where people of all backgrounds were free to bring questions, seek answers, and find friends who could walk with them through these chaotic times. It was a countercultural movement within a counterculture. These were exciting days, and the Word of God community grew in strength and influence, numbering well over a thousand members in the 1970s and '80s.

Much has changed in the last fifty years of Ann Arbor's history. The city is largely gentrified, prosperous, and stable. Its trendy pubs, restaurants, music venues, and art galleries attract a healthy flow of tourists. The university students are "better behaved" than they were in the 1960s, even if they still have an idiosyncratic bohemian bent.

As for the Word of God community, it's a tenth the size of what it was in its heyday, numbering about 130 members. Like Ann Arbor, it has lived through some wild times and is now seeking a new identity in a new age.

As I talked with Phil Tiews, who came to Word of God in 1971, I sensed a depth of maturity, wisdom, and brokenness, borne out of years of hardship and prosperity. He spoke of the challenges of attracting young people to a community that in some ways is still riding a wave that was

Featured Communities: The Word of God

birthed in the previous century. I sensed humility and introspection, and a justified reluctance to let this Word of God chapter fade away into textbooks and archival records. In this new season, these elders are becoming students of a younger generation of church leaders who are exploring new methods for a new generation.

"We're trying to learn some lessons from folks who are pursuing missional community today," says Phil. "I feel as if the values and sense of leading that moved us forty or fifty years ago has recently been finding expression in the missional community movement, with the added focus of engaging in environments where non-Christians live their ordinary lives. Our purpose during the late '60s and early '70s was not to go out and find people. Our task was mainly to have a prayer meeting and people would come to us. They would experience the renewing work of the Holy Spirit in our meetings, which is really a different environment than today, where we're trying to develop some new expressions of community life outside of ourselves."

Word of God does not have a central building or neighborhood, but is, in fact, dispersed in private homes and apartments throughout Washtenaw County. They use local churches for biweekly prayer meetings and monthly women's breakfasts. They gather for Christmas caroling and community outreach several times a year. They have occasional retreats. They rent space for their community office, which employs one and a half staff members.

Most community outreach is by personal initiative, as individuals support local formal and informal ministry opportunities. "Our community members have a finger in almost every pie in the county," says Phil.

That's understandable, given their fifty-year history. Some spin-off ministries that were originally founded by Word of God members include a Christian school, a medical clinic, a pro-life ministry, care for unwed mothers, follow-up care for infants, a prison ministry, assisted living for adults with disabilities, and aftercare for released inmates. For thirty years they ran Servant Publications, which closed its door in 2003.

Word of God has a pastoral leadership team, which cares for the common life of the community. Their leadership style nurtures fraternal relationships and mutual care. Primarily this means they are equipping members with the biblical tools they need to resolve conflict and make good decisions. Leadership is slow to step in if pastoral help is needed, and when they do, its approach is gentle.

In recent years, Word of God cleared the calendar of many community events and obligations. While this appears to be counterproductive for a community that is languishing in numbers, they made this decision at a time when community members were overly inward-focused and too busy with community events to find time to build bridges with local churches and fellowships.

"We sensed that God called us into existence as a community not just for ourselves," says Phil, "but to take the things we experienced and use them for the benefit of the whole church. So we simplified the expectations of community life, not because it isn't good for people to be meaningfully connected as a spiritual family, but because if that is all we ever do, we won't build relationships anywhere else. So we simplified what was expected or required of members so they could be engaged in churches and other areas."

It's as if a pendulum has swept from the "inward-focused" side of community toward the "outward-focused" side, although the pendulum may be poised to head back in the other direction.

"Now might be a good time to recapture a bit more intentional community life with one another," Phil says. "We have a lot of unintentional life and informal contact with one another here, especially with relationships that go back thirty or forty years. When we get together, it's easy for people to pick up the depth of their relationship and love for one another, but we don't have as much actual contact with each other as we used to have. We are looking at how to recapture that, especially so new people can have the opportunity to experience a depth of community life that is transforming."

Word of God members pay no dues and have no official shared financial responsibilities, although they are encouraged to support the community's expenses and benevolence fund with their donations. Prospective members are welcome to visit their prayer meetings and women's breakfasts.

The gifts of the Spirit have always been important to Word of God. Phil remembers meeting "a young woman who was clinically depressed. She'd have bouts where she'd wind up in the hospital. Her friends brought her to our prayer meeting where we prayed for her. She began to experience a lifting from her depression. In a fairly short period of time, she gave her life to the Lord and was completely delivered from that. She's had no reoccurrence in thirty years, and in fact, she moved into a significant position of leadership here. It was a pretty wonderful thing."

Featured Communities: The Word of God

"People experience a strong measure of the charismatic life and gifts here," says Phil. "People do a lot of prayer with folks for healing, or being set free from evil spirits. We pray for God to intervene miraculously. We don't always get the answers we want for our prayers, but we still believe he answers. We have lots of testimonies of how he's healed people and set people free."

In addition to the organized ministries that have been birthed by Word of God in the past, members continue to find creative ways of bringing the love of Jesus to their community. One community member was recently shooting the breeze with smokers who were pumping away outside his workplace.

"I used to smoke," he told them. "Did you ever think of quitting?"

"Well, yeah," one of the guys said. "I've tried a few times. Never can stick with it."

"God can help you quit," he said. "He helped me. Do you want me to pray for you?"

"Sure," the guy said.

Out of this encounter, the community member felt that God was leading him to minister to smokers by praying with them. This small, outside-the-box ministry is representative of what folks in the Word of God community are doing apart from formal outreach.

A snapshot of Word of God in the present is easier to understand after you've seen the video of their past. The vintage footage from the 1960s and '70s only tells half of the story. Keep watching into the '80s, and you'll see more growth and prosperity. You'll see Word of God leaders bringing seminars, books, and media to the nations, instructing them in charismatic renewal and community foundation. In 1982, they were instrumental in forming Sword of the Spirit, a huge international community of communities that is still active today.

However, things were getting a bit hot around Word of God's leadership team in the late 1980s. Former members accused them of being controlling, elitist, uncompassionate, and authoritarian. Some even went so far as to use the "c" word, accusing them of cultic ways and means. Inquests by the Roman Catholic Church and the Lutheran Church Missouri Synod affirmed the orthodoxy of Word of God's faith, releasing them from cultic accusations.

This crisis point caused Word of God leaders to concede that they had been overly authoritarian. They realized that they needed to make significant changes. Of that fact, there was strong agreement among leaders and members alike, but the devil was in the details. Proposed changes to community forms and structures caused dissension, leading to a split in the community. Some members stayed in Word of God while removing themselves from the covering of the Sword of the Spirit. A significant number of members left the community while remaining in Ann Arbor and staying connected to Sword of the Spirit. Those who left called themselves the Word of Life community.

Phil Tiews remembers riding that storm out in the tempestuous 1990s. "We recognized that the approach we had taken to pastoral care was more authoritarian than we thought was right for an ecumenical community that was fraternal in its nature. Some leaders were too controlling, expecting folks to discuss every significant decision going on in their lives. This was not healthy. It breeds more dependency than maturity, so one of the steps that the leadership took was to confess an excessively controlling approach to leadership and repent of it. We not only repented of the past, but we determined not to do that in future. Another thing that both leadership and community members had to repent of was a tendency toward an elitist self-image that made us think that [out of all religious movements] we had finally got it right. One practical outworking of that was to write letters to the churches that community members attended, repenting of this attitude and expressing our desire to have positive relations with them. We did, as a result of that, begin praying regularly with some pastors and developing a network of Christian leaders in the area that we have maintained to this day."

Viewing the archival videos of those stormy days, nearly a quarter century ago, provides a deeper understanding of the portrait of Word of God that we see today.

I couldn't help but wonder about Word of God's estrangement from its twin, Word of Life.

"How are you doing with Word of Life today?" I asked.

"I think we have a positive relationship," Phil explained, "just not an *extensive* relationship at this point. We've had joint prayer meetings. Both communities have people who serve together in local ministries. There's a lot of informal contact back and forth."

"Is it possible you would ever merge back together with them?" I asked.

"That's one of the options on the table, and it might be a good thing. We're open to that discussion and that possibility in the future."

I thought to myself, *That would certainly clear up the confusion I have between their names. Word of . . . whatsitcalled?!?*

Meanwhile, Word of God is mostly aging, with only a sprinkling of younger adults and children. They hope that their research into the missional community movement—in addition to an influx of new members—will shape future direction and bring new relevance to the timeless values they have carried with them from the past.

"If the Lord does indeed bring people to us," says Phil, "we expect he will use them to help shape and form the direction as we move forward. Not only will we teach them, but we need to learn from them as well."

In light of all these experiences—the good, the bad, the uplifting, and the humbling—I asked Phil to explain what the Word of God has to offer to young people today.

In a word, his answer was *mentoring*.

"We have a lot of mature Christians who have been walking Spirit-filled lives with the Lord for decades—through both good times and bad times—not only corporately, but personally. I think that the maturity and humility that has developed in people would be a great benefit to others. As I talk to younger people, I see that this is what a lot of them want. They're looking for an older brother or sister who can be a mentor. We have a vast experience of failures and successes to share in those regards. The difficulties we've experienced have helped us to be people who are strong on grace, and patient with others. God has taken time to get a lot of the arrogance out of us."

Another one of Word of God's strengths is its ecumenical focus.

"If you ask community members, 'Why are you still here?'" says Phil, "one of the first things they'll mention is the sense of ecumenical call, the opportunity to share life and have a sense of the Kingdom beyond our individual church boundaries."

The more I spoke with Phil, the more I sensed that he and his partners were on a journey that was not finished yet. They set out from the anxious 1960s and crossed tall, snowy peaks and hot, dusty deserts. They made a safe place for their tribe in the land that they discovered, and yet their village seems to be unfinished.

And I sensed that this is okay.

As if to confirm my thoughts, Phil shared this story:

"Our kids were still very young, and we were driving back from vacation in Canada. Everyone was sleeping in the car but me. As I drove, I was thinking of the Word of God community. I said, 'Lord, I don't know where we're going, but I'm very grateful that I've had the opportunity to live out this whole expression of my walk with you. I'm very grateful for the opportunity to share community life with others, and to know that this is more than just a commitment I have on Sunday morning.' Today, I still hold to the things I said that night. We experience good times and bad times. People looking from the outside might say, 'That was a period of real abundance and life, and what's happening now is more meager.' I'd say, 'No! All of it has been a gift from God. All of it is an opportunity to walk with others and try to respond with all of our heart, soul, mind, and strength.'"

So while it's fun to reminisce about the good ol' days at Word of God, perhaps the best is yet to come.

In fact . . . perhaps *these* are the good *new* days!

Chapter 6

Surprising Discoveries about Intentional Communities

Did you enjoy hearing from those seventeen communities?
    I absolutely *loved* it! I'm so grateful to the women and men who shared their joys and struggles about the mundane, thrilling, and divine aspects of living in community. Today, I have such a clearer picture of community life than I did when I set out on this journey, thanks to the friends I made along the way.
    Nearly a year has passed since I wrote the opening pages of this book. Want to know something interesting? I'm actually sitting in the same spot today as I was back then, in my familiar little coffee shop. It's a cool, spring morning now, and my bones are warmed by black coffee and golden sunshine.
    When I began this project, I actually thought I had a pretty good handle on the basics of intentional Christian community. I had done a lot of reading on the topic, and that should have made me an expert, right?
    Ha.
    That was before Joan and I completed a few road trips, visiting some of these Christian communities across the country. That was before I spent countless hours talking to these good folks on the phone.
    I learned a lot since I first set out on this journey, thinking I was so smart. Would you like to hear about the surprising discoveries I made? Some of them deeply challenged me, and I won't be startled if they challenge you as well.

HOSPITALITY

I expected communities to be hospitable, but not *that* hospitable. And yet they were, as a rule, among the best hosts we have known. They were genuine, not seeming to be put out in the least by our visits. I'm not saying that our overnight accommodations were elegant, because in fact, some rooms we slept in were very modest, although they were always clean and private. Upscale rooms and amenities are definitely not the measure of a good stay at intentional communities, although some were in fact quite nice. Still, no matter how plain or elegant the accommodations were, we always received warm hospitality.

Most communities reached out to us in advance to answer our questions and prepare us for our stay. They seemed happy to see us when we arrived. Some inquired about food allergies and prepared tasty, home-cooked meals. They gave us enough privacy when we stayed overnight, while making themselves available as needed.

As former bed and breakfast proprietors, authentic hospitality is something we recognize and value highly. It was pleasant to discover the real deal in these communities, especially since we live at a time when hospitality appears to be a dying art.

As a member of the Susanna Wesley House said, "Anytime a guest walks through the door, we never know when we might be entertaining Jesus."

Or in the words of a Koinonia member, "Our basic theology is to treat everyone as if they are Jesus."

Here's a question: How often have you invited good folks over for dinner, and they never invited you back? I would guess that in our many years of inviting people over for meals, eight out of ten people never invited us back. Our friends who have the gift of hospitality have had similar experiences.

Drew Ward from Riverbend Commons told me, "The norm is that you invite someone over for dinner, have a great time, but are never invited back. That's even typical in the church we attended for twenty years. In all those years, we can count on two hands the number of times that Nancy and I were invited to people's houses for dinner."

I may be dumb, but doesn't the Bible say that we are obligated to be hospitable? I just searched and found over twenty-five Bible verses mandating or applauding hospitality. Didn't Jesus basically say that if we are inhospitable to others, we are inhospitable to him?

Enough said.

Suffice to say, Christian communities excel at hospitality. Maybe they were simply paying attention to what they were taught in Sunday school class.

JUSTICE AND COMPASSION

I was inspired to discover such a high level of involvement by intentional Christian community members in justice and compassion issues. These folks care for and partner with people who are poor, imprisoned, fatherless, widowed, foreigners, elderly, unborn, sick, or otherwise shunned by society. This is something I expected to see in a few communities, but it really grabbed my attention as a dominant theme across the board.

It seems as if communities, in general, have taken "charity" to a new level, affirming the dignity and integrity of people in need by first of all forming friendships with them. They are learning not only what these people need most, but what gifts they have to offer. They have developed years-long relationships with people in prison, in slums, or on the streets. Some minister to their own elderly in ways that are superior to conventional nursing home care. Many offer dinner tables and beds to the types of social misfits that Jesus was criticized for hanging out with.

The Barna Group reports that Christian philanthropy is pitiful.[1] Why does it appear to be so strong in community?

First, it is my opinion that this tangible expression of justice and compassion is a sign that Christians in community are simply doing what Christ intended. Their actions might be seen as a temperature gauge, showing that the warmth of God's love is strong in community. The Bible says that iron sharpens iron (Proverbs 27:17). This principle works exceptionally well in community where believers have a high rate of interaction with one another.

Second, it might have a lot to do with location. For example, while it may be easy to ignore justice issues in a gated community or a prosperous

---

1. Barna Group, "Global Poverty is on the Decline," accessed June 2017, www.barna.com/research/global-poverty-is-on-the-decline-but-almost-no-one-believes-it/.

Finding Intentional Community

church, it's a different matter when you constantly come face-to-face with oppression right outside your door. You can easily change the channel when you see a suffering child on TV, but try turning away day after day on the city streets. In this situation, you are quickly forced to come to the place of asking, *What would Jesus do?*

Shane Claiborne of The Simple Way community says, "The communities that are thriving don't just exist for themselves. They are missional. They exist for the sake of others, for welcoming immigrants. They advocate for those who are most vulnerable. It's not just inward-focused. Yes, there are communal practices like prayer and sharing and meals and supporting one another, but there's also a strong missional element of being on the streets and helping kids with homework, of restoring houses, and planting gardens. That work is vitally important. They are in a symbiotic relationship."

I asked Brandon Mott of Dathouse Community why more church folks aren't involved in helping people who are poor or oppressed.

"Individualism is a big part of American Christianity," Brandon said. "People think they just need to worry about their own selves and their own families. Another word that popped into my head is busyness. People get busy, but busyness does not have to be problematic. It's a problem when there's a lack of focus or a lack of intentionality. I think busyness is unintentional living. It's accidental, not on purpose, just going through the motions. It's a status quo type of living. That's probably the biggest cause of people not being more involved, because they are busy, but their busyness is not focused. It's just haphazard."

Joan and I have actually been "spurred on to love and good deeds" (Hebrews 10:24) by the excellent example set by communities in caring for people in need. We had barely parked the camper van after a road trip when I asked Joan, "Do you want to teach English as a second language to immigrants in town? They're looking for volunteers."

"Let's do it," she said.

Joan tutored Ethiopian immigrants when we lived in Colorado, but it's something I've never done before. So we are absolutely thrilled to be helping immigrants come to a place where they can communicate more fluently in our culture.

Helping strangers (immigrants) is a dominant theme in the Bible.

Surprising Discoveries about Intentional Communities

> "Lord, when did we see you a stranger and invite you in?" ... The King will reply, "Truly I tell you, whatever you did for one of the least of these brothers and sisters of mine, you did for me."
>
> —Matthew 25:38,40

Naturally, nations should protect themselves from terrorists, but that's no excuse for being unkind to the people Jesus told us to love. In case you hold a view of immigrants that leads you to stand back and say, "Well, they shouldn't be here in the first place," you might ask yourself if you are treating a human being like an issue. Go back to the Riverbend Commons chapter and put yourself around the table with those women who fled from Muslim countries because they became Christians, knowing they would have been murdered if they remained. People like these may become martyrs if we send them back home. Others will die or be unable to support starving families for different political or economic reasons. Are we willing to turn our backs, shut our mouths, and be complicit in their deaths? These people might be in your neighborhood or in mine, needing our compassion.

This is how *not* to treat people in need:

> As [Jesus] went along, he saw a man blind from birth. His disciples asked him, "Rabbi, who sinned, this man or his parents, that he was born blind?"
>
> —John 9:1-2

The disciples had to establish blame, because this man might not be eligible for God's good gifts.

In today's culture, the disciples would be asking, "Is this person here legally or illegally? Whose fault is it that those people are begging on the streets? Are they worthy of compassion?"

Yikes! Are these people *human beings* or *issues*?

Even the religious leaders are opposed to helping the blind guy, condemning Jesus for healing on the Sabbath.

Thankfully, Jesus says, "While you all are arguing about this man's eligibility, I'm just going to kneel down, spit in the dirt, make a little mud, and heal this man. You can't see me, Brother, but I'm right here in front of you. Now let me touch your eyes. Here are my hands, now ... "

Jesus gives us the perfect picture of how to respond to people in need. Stop treating them like issues. Step outside of the conventional "left or right" political discussion and discover God's third way. Be willing to get down in the dirt. Talk to her. Offer him our Father's compassionate touch. Ask yourself what Jesus would do.

These thoughts were stirred up in my mind as I got to watch the hands of Jesus at work through Christians who are living in community. The people I met really do excel at making friends with, reaching out to, and rescuing those who are neglected by society.

DIGNITY AND FRIENDSHIP

I have always considered myself to be fair toward people from every race, class, gender, and orientation, especially in my writing and radio work. Then I learned a few things from people like Keith Wasserman of Good Works. Keith was so kind as to highlight some of my wording that didn't seem appropriate to him. By merely requesting some simple edits, he helped me identify subtle ways in which I was seeing "the poor" as an issue or a project, rather than as a brother and sister. (*Thanks, Keith!*) Language is one of the ways in which we can either rob or impart dignity.

As Keith said in the Good Works chapter, "I'm not a big fan of the phrase 'the poor' anymore. I don't like to use it, particularly if my friends who are poor are in the room. It makes me feel really uncomfortable."

As I read this just now, these words jumped out at me:

. . . *if my* friends *who are poor are* in the room.

This helps me to understand two very basic and biblical ways for prosperous believers like me to boost marginalized people's dignity: first, by making "friends" with them, and second, by being "in the room" and present with them.

I get it.

Keith told me about some other ways that Good Works imparts dignity: "I encourage our community to pray, 'Lord, help me to see people as you see people, made in the image of God with dignity and value and worth.' The Bible says that Jesus looked at the multitudes with compassion, like sheep without a shepherd. So I say, 'Lord, help me to see people as you see people.' Built into the DNA of a good, healthy Christian community is the ability to teach and be teachable, to help each other see things how the Lord sees them. We have to constantly help each other because we're constantly drifting. We can't buy into the national media that constantly degrade people just because they are poor or immigrants. James 1:27, says, 'Religion that God our Father accepts as pure and faultless is this: to look after orphans and widows in their distress.' That in itself is profound, but the rest of the phrase is equally significant. It says, '. . . and to keep oneself from being polluted by the world.' We need to be aware that the world pollutes and stains our view of widows and orphans. God has not given us projects who are poor. He has given us friends. The question is, 'Am I willing to develop friendships with people who are not in my social or racial class?' To me, that is one of the most significant parts of discipleship for Christian communities."

Keith is right on target. What greater dignity can you give people than to offer to be their friend?

Brandon Mott of Dathouse commented earlier about what happens when people reach out across conventional socio-economic frontiers: "Some people have their own preconceived notions or biases or stereotypes, but those begin to completely change when they come face to face with people from the other side, when they get to see people as people. That happens all the time in our coffee shop."

Brandon Mott was the guy who turned me on to this quote that was mentioned in the Dathouse chapter:

> Go to the people. Live with them. Learn from them. Love them. Start with what they know. Build with what they have. But with the best leaders, when the work is done, the task accomplished, the people will say "We have done this ourselves."
>
> —Lao Tzu[2]

That is dignity!

Bestowing dignity means building up people's sense of self-worth and making them feel like equal partners. It does not mean giving them free handouts, unless, of course, it's a matter of survival. It means being in the same room with them, and being their friend. These are some of the things I learned about bestowing dignity and making friends with people from the other side.

---

2. Goodreads, "Lao Tzu quotes," accessed June 2017, www.goodreads.com/quotes/215411-go-to-the-people-live-with-them-learn-from-them .

DIVERSE BELIEFS

I don't consider my political beliefs to be particularly narrow, but I confess that I was challenged by the wide spectrum of political views expressed by people from different communities. Politically, intentional Christian communities appear to be all over the map. But don't be too quick to write them off, as so many Christians are apt to do. Before you go ballistic, know that they are not in the enemy's camp just because their position might make you a little uncomfortable. Hear me through, now, okay?

To begin with, you and I might reevaluate some of our basic assumptions.

What assumptions? First, the assumption that *we* can be the ultimate judge of people's character based on how they stand on social and political issues.

Come on, now. Admit that it's true. I've done it. Have you?

We have blacklisted Christians who think "wrong" and vote "wrong," even though they, like us, have the same loving Father who tenderly cares for them. Or worse, I (and possibly even you) have stood in place of the Almighty God and judged their souls unworthy of salvation.

How could people who believe like that *call themselves Christians?*

Yes, I was surprised at the wide diversity of thought among the super people who live in community. Meanwhile, I observed these diverse people overflowing with compassion and unique giftings. I saw them bearing much fruit. These communities—regardless of their political beliefs—are beautifully modeling the image of God today.

Another mistaken assumption we often have is to see political and moral choices in terms of black and white or left and right. In fact, many people in community are defining an entirely new, middle way.

In the words of John Michael Talbot of the Brothers and Sisters of Charity, "We tend to hang Jesus on a particular political paradigm, be it conservative or liberal. I really think that our paradigm has to unquestionably be Jesus. When we do that, we find that our care for the poor, our care for people in need, and our care for justice issues don't fit comfortably into either the Democratic or Republican platforms. For me, it tends to spew over into both or neither. That's just the way it works."

While issues of helping needy people are typically framed in terms of funding and resources, communities in general are seeing these things

Surprising Discoveries about Intentional Communities

in terms of relationships. For example, instead of handing out food and clothes on Saturday and telling folks to come back next week for more, many people in community are sitting down for lunch with folks who are poor and developing friendships which will lead to more holistic solutions. This new path clearly breaks all political molds. Wouldn't it be convenient to pretend that our tax money and donations could solve the world's injustices? It's not that easy. At their core, these are not material problems.

Many communities are showing how the *perceived* needs of people can be vastly different from their *actual* needs. Jesus had no "programs" for people in need, but he treated each person as a unique human being, touching them, healing them, rebuking them, or feeding them. It's a very individualistic, relational approach, and it takes time and attention.

Communities are also stopping to ask themselves, "What do these needy people have that *we* need?" As one leader told me, "We didn't come into the inner-city to change the poor. We came here to be changed by the poor."[3]

All Christians who are living in community did not vote alike in the last election, nor will they in the next. Still, each believer needs the other believers, and has important things that the others need. Lord knows, we have erected enough barriers between denominational churches. God help us not to create the same divisions between intentional Christian communities. Jesus prayed, "Let them be one" (John 17:21). Thankfully, these communities are, so far, wonderful melting pots for diversity.

In the words of Keith Wasserman of Good Works, Inc., "It's beautiful when you have someone from the Catholic Church working next to someone from a Protestant church. It's beautiful to see these relationships form. On Saturday we had a young woman from a Vineyard Church volunteering next to a woman from the Church of Christ. They were of different generations, and they formed a friendship. That gives me great joy. We regularly see different churches serving dinner together at our Friday Night Life. There's such a deep respect and love, and it's been like that for many years. I call it grace from God."

DIVERSE EXPRESSIONS OF COMMUNITY

When I began this project, I imagined that most community models would either be in rural, farm-like settings with birds, meadows, and frolicking

---

3. For an excellent discussion on this topic, see Robert Lupton, *Toxic Charity*.

children, or urban communities with iron gates and graffiti. I supposed I'd see one or two suburban communities. As for monasteries, I hadn't even considered them yet (although I was soon enlightened).

Instead, I learned that intentional Christian communities—like humans—are diverse, adaptable, and can thrive just about anywhere and in many different forms. Some communities live together in homes and apartments, and others are dispersed in cities or cohousing neighborhoods. Community members have many different skills and interests. Some folks like hanging out at their homes and others at coffee shops or community centers. All use their talents and strengths to bless God and people. They express themselves in so many different ways. Some have homogenous religious beliefs and others are as diverse theologically as you can imagine.

Both urban and rural communities have terrific locational advantages. You might think that urban communities would be more effective at connecting with minorities and marginalized people, until you walk into the middle of a peace and justice camp at Koinonia Farm. There, I watched Muslim girls with head coverings kick soccer balls around with homeschooled Christians and people of who-knows-what connections and beliefs. Both rural and urban communities have thriving ministries to poor, homeless, immigrants, and single parents. They open their arms to a constant stream of guests. Even suburban communities are doing a phenomenal job of building bridges with their neighbors.

Some community expressions are free-flowing and spontaneous. Many more than I expected are highly structured monastic or New Monastic. John Michael Talbot nearly talked me into becoming a monk! Not really, but I fell in love with the Brothers and Sisters of Charity's expression of the Kingdom of God in community. What a radical new idea! (*Er . . . new? Well, not exactly.*)

Let's talk for a moment about big houses, and why Joan and I were so relieved when we finally unloaded ours a few years ago. We had experienced a sweet season with our kids and the bed and breakfast, but Joan and I became exhausted when we were pulling the weight all by ourselves. So we sold the house and farm and moved into a tidy little home.

After coming back from the West Coast, I had a surprising interaction with a friend of mine. I was telling him about the Julian Project in Julian, California, when my friend asked me, "Do you ever wish you had a big house and farm again?"

Surprising Discoveries about Intentional Communities

"Yes," I said, and my response actually caught me off guard, because we had been so glad to be free of our bed and breakfast.

I explained to my friend how the Julian house is so similar to our Fox and Fiddle experience. I said, "It's a big, beautiful home in a gorgeous mountain setting, with acreage for agriculture, a rental house, overnight guests, friends coming for music and potlucks, friends living in the spare rooms, lots of hospitality, and a great sense of community. And when I saw what they were doing at the Julian house, it suddenly hit me. We had been living in intentional community! My wife and kids and I were the core members. The friends who lived with us and worked the farm were part of the community. The only thing that was missing after our kids moved away was the inner circle of close partners. And without partners, Joan and I were overwhelmed."

That's the beauty of community. The Julian Project and others *do* have close partners who are committed to each other, and without them, community is not sustainable.

So despite my aversion to big homes, I found myself wanting a big house again . . . but only if I had some committed partners. I must confess that I could see us not only in a big house, but in many different settings. (*Nicaragua, here we come—volcano or no volcano!*) We're pretty flexible. Mostly I yearn for deeper community, wherever it can be found.

I write this in part to encourage you. As you read these pages, perhaps you, too, have had a moment of discovery. Perhaps you said, "Ah ha! We're a lot closer to intentional Christian community than we ever imagined!" Perhaps you already have a house, friends, or regular gatherings that are the seeds of rich community. If so, I encourage you to water and cultivate those seeds. Begin by taking small steps in that direction. There are so many different expressions of community. You are sure to find one that will satisfy your needs.

WRONG ATTITUDES

I learned some things about the wrong attitudes and misguided motivations for joining a community. For example, when I wrote the chapter called "Taking the Long Way Home," I hadn't visited any communities yet. In those paragraphs, you perhaps sense loneliness and alienation stemming from my past. The implicit suggestion is that once a person gets plugged into community, loneliness issues are resolved.

Not so, according to Zoe from the Church of the Sojourners in San Francisco.

"Loneliness is what drives a lot of people to community," says Zoe, "but community doesn't address loneliness in a way that people want it to be addressed. Community is not a problem-solver. It's a place of discipleship, and it's very, very effective as a place for both group and individual discipleship. It's an effective place to be a part of the Kingdom of God in a specific way. But that's not the same as what people think they're looking for when they say, 'Oh, I'm lonely. I need friends. I need community.' Some people do, in fact, find a tremendous sense of family and a decrease in loneliness in community. I'm not saying it doesn't happen, but it's not automatic when you join community. Because sometimes what happens in community is you're given a group of people to be friends with, to go deep with, but it's like family, and you don't choose your family. In a family model, you might not necessarily get along with your brother, but he's still your brother. You're still family, so you have to learn how to be a family together. I've learned to define friendship very differently in my twenty-one years here. I have deep friendships here, but they are not necessarily friendships that were born out of instant affinity. They don't come from drawing together the people I have the most obvious things in common with. It's simply a matter of seeing who's here, then saying, 'Okay, these are the people who are going to be my friends. How do we love each other? How do we go deep with each other?' It's a different model of friendship, and sometimes that's difficult for people. Sometimes we have complicated interactions with people who come here in genuine, deep need, whether mental, emotional, spiritual, or physical, and we can't always meet their needs. Community is not a problem-solver."

This is sound advice. It's a reminder for us to seek to learn and practice rootedness, commitment, conflict-resolution, good communication, forgiveness, and community in the place where we are now planted. We can't just move into community and expect everything to get fixed.

Dietrich Bonhoeffer wrote this in his book *Life Together*:

> Every human wish dream that is injected into the Christian community is a hindrance to genuine community and must be banished if genuine community is to survive. He who loves his dream of a community more than the Christian community itself becomes a destroyer of the latter, even though his personal intentions may be ever so honest and earnest and sacrificial.[4]

---

4. Dietrich Bonhoeffer, *Life Together*, 27.

This perspective definitely rubs against the grain of the popular, romantic notion of community, which places our personal wishes and dreams above everything else. I believe it reflects a mature, other-centered view of community. But don't let those words scare you away if you see them more as an ideal to aspire toward than a present reality.

Caz Tod-Pearson of The Simple Way directed me specifically to the Bonhoeffer quote just mentioned, adding, "That's definitely been my experience. When we romanticize this, then we don't live out of our true self. We don't live out of a place of authenticity, and then there's just disappointment after disappointment. For us at The Simple Way, we choose to live well where we are, just following the words of Jesus and the life of Jesus as much as we can. Sometimes that means people live together in the same house. Sometimes it means living in separate houses, maybe sharing meals together. Sometimes it means we pick up trash together. I think that looks really different based on what's going on in the neighborhood and our lives. There's no one formula for community."

This attitude definitely deflates our self-centered dreams of community and surrenders them to others. It makes *we* more important than *me*. It certainly explodes any intentions we might have of joining a community and saying, "Y'all got a good thing goin' here, but there are a few things you need to get straightened out . . . "

COMMUNITY ISN'T EASY

My general preconceptions about community life were at the start, admittedly, a bit too rosy. I met more than a few people in community who were going through tough times, who had experienced conflict with someone, or who felt lonely at times. Some communities said they had moments where they were living on the edge financially. Some of the common phrases I heard were, "It's not always easy" or "You get hurt here, just like anywhere else."

Caz of The Simple Way community said, "When people read about you, they sort of romanticize what life in community is like. Then when they come to visit, there's kind of a disappointment. We've let people down because we're not everything that they imagined we would be. We just try to be true to who we say that we are, which might be what you imagine, or it might not. I think it's really important for people to not think of intentional community as the answer to everything, lifting it up in an unrealistic way, because we're only human. It's not necessarily as romantic as everybody imagines it to be. Community is people just trying to live out their lives being a good neighbor and doing that alongside each other. And there's no magic bullet for that. There's no magic to working really hard and being intentional and being a good neighbor."

Keith Wasserman of Good Works, Inc. says, "Relationships in community experience turns for better or for worse. They take work. They take watering. They take intentionality. They take planning. There are moments of challenge as well as the good times. There are moments of struggle. It's not easy when you make close friends and they move away. Thankfully, there are people who I've known here for forty years. There is a network, and on a good day that network is strong, and on a bad day, it's like, *Does anybody care? Am I alone? Does it matter?*"

Keith dispels the myth that people who live in intentional Christian communities are perfect. "We are all fallen. We're human. What's important is not that we are perfect, but that we are growing in awareness and teachable hearts. We give each other permission to speak into each other's lives. That's what it means to be in community. We always grow and try to be teachable, helping to spur one another on to give encouragement and correction, which is rare, as we love each other and help each other have the mind of Christ. We've built reflection into so many components of our ministry, to stop and ask, 'How can we learn and do this better?' I hope people are willing to apologize and say, 'It's my fault. Please forgive me.' These are important concepts in the structure of any Christian community in which sustainability can happen."

"Being in community doesn't mean that you are exempt from the tragedies of life," says Dan Brokke of Bethany International, who lost his brother and several other community members in a horrible tornado. "It was tragic. It shook everybody, but it also brought us together."

Brandon Mott of Dathouse wrote in his Wordpress blog, "This last year has been a challenging one for us . . . two of our founding members moved far away . . . Losing them as a part of our daily team was a big hit. Their love for people and their commitment to community are unparalleled among anyone I have ever known. However, in their absence, God has slowly but surely been placing new people in our lives . . . With this new life, I am reminded this morning that community is never the goal. There is no place that you can arrive at and say, 'We have accomplished community.' Instead, community is something we are constantly becoming."

Surprising Discoveries about Intentional Communities

Do you think community members ever make crazy blunders? Well, Maril at the Julian Project remembers the busy day when she grabbed a bottle of liquid laundry detergent from the base of the surplus supplies shelf out in the garage. She poured it into the washer, but that load of laundry came out horribly blotchy, with gray and black spots all over everything.

"What's wrong?" she asked Gregg. "Did the washing machine explode or something?"

After a quick investigation, Gregg said, "Honey, you put motor oil in the washing machine."

"Motor oil?" Maril asked. "What are you talking about? It was detergent. Here's the container."

"Unfortunately," Gregg explained, "I changed the oil in the car a few days ago, and I had to put the dirty oil somewhere, so I put it in that."

Apart from the clothes being ruined, how did the story end? According to Gregg, there was some "spirited correction from Maril. I think the neighbors might have even heard that."

There are more stories where that one came from. "This would be a good reality TV show," Gregg says. "It would get good ratings."

Says Maril, "It's more of a challenge than if we were living next door to each other and collaborating with stuff. We actually live in the same house and share stuff and share the kitchen and bathroom. Most people who hear that are like, 'No way!' Sure, it comes with sacrifices. You always have to weigh the cost-benefit and make it sustainable long-term. You have to ask God what he wants, and kind of go with it."

Gregg adds, "Living with others forces a certain amount of honesty and accountability and self-checking and being real and honest about weaknesses and strengths and character. One of the best reasons to live in close proximity to people is that you want to grow and mature as a personality and as a spirit. When you do that, you learn from each other. You realize you have to face blind spots and perspectives. You get to see issues in your own life and in others where you might otherwise not know that they exist. If your goal is to become spiritually mature and grow personally and come to wholeness, then you can check yourself against these other people's journeys and perspectives. There's an opportunity for exponential growth like you won't have if you're more isolated. In a good season, the growth has been a wonderful reality. In a lessor season—or a week or month of avoiding that and just getting by—you can hold onto your mediocrity, your compromises, your immature approach to life in community. But when you purpose to go beyond that, you have built-in relationships and hearts and minds right in front of you that can help you move up to a whole new dimension."

STABLE, HEALTHY TEAM

Here's something interesting I learned along the way. It began with the questions that arose in my mind when I read these criteria for prospective monks at the Brothers and Sisters of Charity website:

> Candidates to the monastic expression must be in good health, physically, emotionally and spiritually, and be debt-free.[5]

I didn't quite know what to think when I read this, but I was a little surprised. Why? I suppose because I naively assumed that Christian communities would open their arms to anyone. I didn't want to say that these requirements were unwelcoming, because I felt there was something here that I didn't understand.

Subsequently, I heard similar remarks from other communities about their application criteria. Gradually, I began to understand that being open and hospitable to *guests* is quite a different matter from accepting any person who wants to join the core group of the community.

Then it began to make sense: in order to have a stable, healthy team, you need core members who are healthy in all dimensions and unencumbered with things that will drag the group down.

Matt Spinks of Hillside Fellowship really pegged it when he said, "Community needs to be sustainable. You need more healthy people than needy people. You need pillars of the community. There is a place in the body of Christ for taking needy people in, but you have to be very prepared for that. You can't have a small community of maybe twelve people and take in several drug addicts. You need trained staff for that. This is something we learned through the years. You need to say, 'For us to take you in here, it wouldn't help you or us, and in fact, it would just make things worse for you.' There is a lot of wisdom in knowing your boundaries and knowing your calling."

---

5. Brothers and Sisters of Charity, "Monastic," accessed June 2017, https://littleportion.org/monastic.

COMMUNITY AS A MEANS OF SANCTIFICATION

As I researched the Alleluia Community in Augusta, Georgia, one line from their covenant jumped out at me:

> We promise to love one another and to call each other to holiness. We believe that this is the way God has chosen for our sanctification.[6]

"Sanctification" is the process of becoming holy, or in other words, growing into Christian maturity.

So at first glance, it seemed presumptuous for the members of an intentional community to claim that the conditions of their covenant are "the way God has chosen for our sanctification." But as I heard similar perspectives from several community members, I began to understand.

This revelation has become much more vivid to me in the past year: Christians cannot grow to maturity apart from other believers. Sure, we can learn stories and facts about God when we are isolated from other believers, but we can only put the things we learn into practice in the context of community. The richness of the Gospel is in the "one anothering" part.

Moreover, since we have been made in the image of God, we need each other to fully visualize God's image. As Dan Brokke of Bethany International said, "The thing that is so powerful in Philippians two is that the mind of Christ can only be experienced through community. You can't experience the mind of Christ in isolation."

Christ reveals himself to us through other members of the body. And the more contact we have with the body of Christ, the better.

"Meeting together" can happen in many different ways, but believers living in close proximity interrelate more intensely. In my observation, they exhibit more tangible fruits of sanctification than those who barely know each other.

Dietrich Bonhoeffer, in his book *Life Together*, supports this position. He says:

> Christian community is like the Christian's sanctification. It is a gift of God which we cannot claim. Only God knows the real state of our fellowship, of our sanctification. What may appear weak and trifling to us may be great and glorious to God . . . The more thankfully we daily receive what is given to us, the more surely

---

6. Alleluia Community, *Our Covenant*, accessed June 2017, www.yeslord.com/about-us/our-covenant/.

and steadily will fellowship increase and grow from day to day as God pleases.[7]

I like what Adam Krell of Life Mission said earlier in this book: "We knew about total commitment to Christ," says Adam, speaking for himself and his friends who were exploring community. "We knew about commitment to Christ's work. We were big on that. But what we didn't know about was commitment to Christ's people, the ecclesiological part of it. Immediately, my attitude toward my brothers and sisters changed. I remember thinking, 'I have to take liability for them. I cannot let them become impoverished. I have to be committed to them.' That was the beginning of community for us. When you give your life to Christ, it's three-dimensional. It's a total commitment not just to Christ and his work, but also to his people. That's what too many Christians leave out. That's the ecclesiological dimension."

Therefore, community is essential for the sanctification process and Christian maturity. Community is the "real world" where we learn conflict resolution, sacrificial love, commitment, self-discipline, contentment, and other-centeredness.

MIRACULOUS SIGNS AND WONDERS

Just before Jesus returned to heaven, he said:

> And these signs will accompany those who believe: In my name they will drive out demons; they will speak in new tongues . . . they will place their hands on sick people, and they will get well.
>
> —MARK 16:17–18

I was very excited to see these signs and wonders alive in intentional communities. When God raised a Nicaraguan girl from the dead through the prayers of Hillside Fellowship members, a lot of people noticed. The word got around quickly, and many people took steps closer to see what kind of God this is who raises people from the dead. The same is true for other miracles mentioned in these pages. It is truly amazing to discover that the miraculous wonders of the book of Acts are happening in Christian community today.

---

7. Bonhoeffer, *Life Together*, 80.

Surprising Discoveries about Intentional Communities

GLIMPSES OF THE REBUILT TEMPLE

Early in this book, you heard my perspectives on the rebuilding of God's holy temple in these latter days. Now after having spoken with many believers who are living in community, I feel as if we are receiving a much clearer picture of the rebuilding of the temple.

For the record, I did not see perfect Christians. I didn't meet folks who are never hurt or offended, discouraged, or tempted. Neither are intentional Christian communities the only place where God's temple is being rebuilt today.

I did, however, receive a deeper understanding of what church is meant to be. This excites me, because quite honestly, the church soup I've sipped on for most of my life is weak and I yearn for more substance. I'm as much to blame as anyone for this shortcoming, because of my failure to remain rooted long enough for the greatest growth to occur.

When I started this project, I was hopeful that I'd see evidences of the book of Acts in action today. Now, after seeing the proof in living color, I can hardly keep quiet! Seeing this holy temple being rebuilt in the twenty-first century has changed my life in a profound way.

THE COST OF COMMUNITY

At this moment, I'm thinking of Dietrich Bonheoffer's book entitled *The Cost of Discipleship*. Bonhoeffer, a German theologian, was living in New York City when Hitler was rising to power. While other Christians of conscience were fleeing Germany, Bonhoeffer followed *his* conscience right back home to his native Germany. He knew that his biblical convictions would bring him into potentially lethal conflict with the Nazis, and in fact, he was eventually executed in a Nazi prison camp in 1945.

Bonhoeffer wasn't ignorant of the implications of returning to Germany, and yet he went back.

Why?

Because he was a German Christian with deep compassion, and he knew he needed to be with his people. He felt he was doing what Jesus would do.

To Dietrich Bonhoeffer, *we* was more important than *me*.

This is a sobering thought for this discussion about intentional Christian community. And yet his story was told to me by people who are living in community. These people pointed me to many of the Bonhoeffer quotes that are included in this book. Therefore, I have to conclude that there is a relevant message for us here.

One of the final things that I discovered about community is perhaps a twist on the title of Bonheoffer's preeminent work.

Count *the cost of community* before plunging into it.

For me, that means not viewing community simply as a fun way to meet my needs, like joining a club of like-minded people. The move toward community should be as much for others as it is for self. But don't let anything hold you back from community. We are like starving people, and the food we need cannot be found alone.

Just remember the lesson of Dietrich Bonhoeffer, that *we* is more important than *me*.

THIS IS OUR DESTINY

While out walking this morning, it finally hit me that this is not just a book about intentional Christian communities.

I may be slow, but I finally understand what a number of community members are saying. They make it clear that you can't live without community.

Well, as I was trying to figure out the bottom line of this message, words like "happiness," "fulfillment," "connectedness," "life purpose," and "destiny" came to mind.

And I said to myself, *Christian community takes you to the deepest level of joy and fulfillment that is humanly possible. This book is not about a narrow, special interest topic. This is huge. The attraction to God and community is hardwired into every human heart. This is our life purpose and destiny!*

Therefore, living in community with others who pursue God's ultimate purpose is not optional. God himself *is* community, and he draws us to himself through others.

We are talking about *LIFE* here, not some optional country club membership. This is the path to our *life purpose*. This is our *destiny*. We were created for this. It is just that huge!

This was my final revelation. It encourages me to walk this reality out in faith, love, and childlikeness, and I hope it encourages you as well.

Surprising Discoveries about Intentional Communities

Wow! That turned out to be a longer list than I expected! These are the surprising things that I discovered while researching intentional Christian communities!

Chapter 7

Down in the Dirt

In this final chapter, I hope to leave with you a small treasure that has spilled over from all the previous pages. Each community member we've heard from has priceless truths to share. These humble, childlike heroes have spoken riches into our lives. It has been a joy to walk alongside them and learn from them.

You might say that we've been digging in the dirt, mining these gems, and now we're ready to tidy up a little. We want to roll out the sod, plant some flowers, plant a few trees, put up a white picket fence, and call it done. That's how the book is supposed to end, right? Wrap a neat little ribbon around it. Lay it aside with a contented sigh.

But how can we even do that?

Which one of these communities has discovered a magic formula that we can follow? These are broken people, and so are we. How can you and I assimilate the things we have learned when we have years of habitual ruts and ruins that defy and oppose healthy community? Old patterns are hard to break. We might think our ground is fertile for new seeds, but then we see all this rubble scattered around.

What's more, the path to community is so individualistic that one triumphant concluding summary here will hardly apply to all. The best advice I can give you is to humble yourself and receive the riches that come from low places. The dirt around this old mine is a mess, but you will find room to kneel here. I have a strong impression that the answer lies at your feet. You will find treasure there, down in the dirt. Don't give up until you find it. Follow your heart and you won't be disappointed.

Down in the Dirt

What are you looking for? Heck if I know! Nobody can tell you that, but you will know when you see it. If your treasure is a seed, then get some soil for it to grow. If your treasure is a diamond, then find a place for it to glow.

That's all very nebulous and artsy, but stick with me and I'll tell you a story that will bring form to these misty concepts. You'll understand a lot better, once you see what I found down in the dirt.

Here's a quick update on my personal journey, because it relates to what follows. In case you're wondering, Joan and I aren't moving into any of these wonderful communities that I've written about here.

Why not?

Because they are not on our street.

My wife and I have been impacted so profoundly by the concept of stability that we will not move again so easily. Although I loved each one of the communities in this book, we are staying put to grow into the community around us. Although we didn't hand-pick these neighbors and friends, nothing is random or trivial in God's economy. So we are at this time committed to this place and these people.

Community is also growing right here in our own home. When some college students moved out of our downstairs apartment, we were thrilled to have a fabulous Christian couple who we've known for years move in. We enjoy sharing the gardens and chickens, with occasional shared meals and backyard campfires. Our friendship deepens as we walk this out one step at a time.

I thank God for Joan, who has been such a faithful companion in this journey. I still grieve about the relationships I have broken. The seeds of instability that I have sown continue a painful cycle that I thought I'd left behind over twenty years ago. We had hoped to give our offspring some of the precious gifts that we had missed, like siblings, cousins, aunts, and uncles whose lives are intertwined with theirs, but mercy abounds and God works all things out for good in the end.

Moving forward, I try to set aside the motivations that have so frequently put my own needs first. I can't say that I have torn down the walls protecting my stuff and time, but I am moving in that direction. God is strengthening tribal bonds and developing our core community. This all takes time, of course, because a forest of oak trees does not grow in a year or two.

I am challenged and encouraged by the commitments of so many community members. Someday, I would hope to say words like these to the friends and family who join Joan and me in this journey:

> I have given my life to Jesus. I also give it to you. I commit to do whatever it takes to assure your well-being, even to lay down my life for you. I'm sorry I have failed you in the past, but now I finally understand that this is the essence of Jesus's example, to love my neighbor as myself. God help me to love you and serve you well.

So we have a little community, and little is enough. This is our pot of gold at the end of the rainbow. We have arrived.

Big fanfare.

Orchestral *kabooms* and choirs of angels.

Not really.

There is no big fanfare. I won't sell you slick marketing slogans about a well-marked road into community, because that road doesn't exist. Truthfully, you may stumble there with dirt and blisters on your feet, with sweat and gnats in your eyes. I honestly believe that you will find it—you will be successful—if you persist, and if you walk it out like a child, because it's all very humble and childish.

As it should be.

Walk with me, now, through one last encounter, as we see each other home. Let's be team members in this last part of the story. I hope you don't mind, but I'm going to put you on the spot. You'll play the part of the interviewer, and I'll answer the questions.

Just don't be too hard on me, okay?

Okay.

While you prepare a few questions, I'll get comfortable and take a sip of coffee. You flip on your little hand-held recording device to help you take notes.

You begin the questioning:

> So, here we are at the very end of this book. What's the bottom line for this topic of intentional Christian communities?

Well, I'd have to say that there's not *one* bottom line. I can actually see readers having a number of different reactions to this book. Some readers may have gotten really excited about the communities featured here, and they're eager to go visit a few and do some more research. I'd guess that these folks are a minority, though. Another minority—hopefully—are those who tossed this book into the cat litter and fire-starter material, but I do need to acknowledge that potential response.

My gut feeling is that *most* readers who made it this far in the book are, like me, still trying to figure out what it all means. I'd hope that a lot of them are looking at the friends and family and neighbors around them with a new set of lenses, being a little more optimistic about encouraging the growth of intentional community right where they are.

And do you know what? That wasn't my main focus when I first started writing this book, although it makes me very happy. My main goal was initially to lead people to join an existing community, but now I see why that's often not the best choice.

> How has your perception or working definition of "intentional Christian community" changed or evolved over the past year?

Finding Intentional Community

Mainly, I now see how authentic community is much more *accessible* than I once imagined it to be. I used to think that the search for community would be a lot like finding a retirement home or a gated community, or even a church. You shop around for months or years with a narrow set of criteria until you find one that you like. Now, I perceive that intentional Christian community is more like *family*. Is there anywhere you can *not* find or create family? Of course not! It is accessible everywhere. So now my definition is much more organic, simple, alive, and childlike. Finding community is as simple as planting a seed, and that's extremely accessible for everyone, everywhere.

> Simplicity is so important here, especially as readers process this wealth of collective wisdom about intentional communities. For you, what specific topics or themes rise to the top?

I've mentioned a number of those themes in the previous chapter, but the most poignant idea is also one of the most childlike and simple. It's not complicated! In my interviews, I tried to ask each person to tell me one of their absolute favorite moments of living in community. Without exception, their answers recalled un-extraordinary, commonplace events like being snowed in with housemates, having a music night, playing games or working in the garden together, having handstand competitions, or just being together with no plan or agenda at all. Across the board, the favorite times in community were simply enjoying each other's company. This confirms the fact that Christian community is God's universal design for everyone, since people find their greatest joy and fulfillment in these simple, communal moments of life.

> Were you surprised at those answers?

Yes and no. In a careless moment, I might have imagined that some extreme sport or pleasure cruise might have been the setting for those best times. Think travel commercials: attractive people, blue sea, yellow sun, cool drink, warm sand. In contrast, imagine a primetime advertisement for the lovely Lotus House, inviting you to a depressed neighborhood of St. Louis, where you can join in handstand competitions with community members after evening prayer.

Woo hoo.

Framed in this way, Tahiti will win every time. Who in their right mind would choose handstands in St. Louis over margaritas and palm trees? And yet, people *in their right minds* are telling us that the commercials are wrong. Life *at its best* is much simpler and closer to home than fake and alluring, commercialized promises. Handstands are the real deal! So in the end, I was not surprised to hear these people say that the best things in life are free, simple, and close to home, because that has been my experience as well.

> How has that been your experience?

Gosh, that's been the story of my life! But I haven't always thought that way. When I was young, I believed the greatest fulfillment in life would come from extreme experiences and achievements, and I was knocking them down pretty hard. After I got married, unfortunately I was also knocking Joan down, while pushing hard in Southern California to make a name for myself. But it's a dog-eat-dog world, and people were pushing me down as well. My "salvation experience" occurred less than a year after our first daughter was born. It happened one particularly difficult day when I dragged myself into our apartment, feeling absolutely beat up by the world. My little girl was playing on the carpet across the room, and the moment she saw me, her face lit up and her brown eyes widened. She wasn't speaking yet, but what her face said was, "It's Daddy! My hero is home!" She crawled across the floor as fast as her little legs would carry her and she just wrapped her arms around my ankle. I picked her up and held her tight with tears in my eyes, thinking, *What have I done to deserve this? I expend all my energy on the world, and it gives me nothing. I give this child so little, and she gives me everything.* After that, I gave all I could to my wife and (soon to be) four children. Yes, I still made mistakes, but I have never forgotten that the simple things like the hug of a child are the most valuable.

Jesus said that we cannot enter the Kingdom of Heaven unless we become like children (Matthew 18:3). Isaiah the prophet said, "And a little child shall lead them" (Isaiah 11:6). I can validate this concept with many more stories of building forts and rafts and camping or just sitting around the fireplace reading storybooks together. These very ordinary events have been the absolute *best-best-best* times in life for me and my family, and they never happened alone, but always in community with the ones I love.

> You aren't saying that everyone has to have a similar experience as you, in order to come to that place of fulfillment and happiness, are you?

Of course not! That's my personal story, so don't confuse it with yours. There are, however, some universal concepts that apply to everyone. Every individual has to get out of himself or herself in order to find true happiness. That means moving away from self-centeredness, toward other-centeredness. Also, that concept of childlikeness is so strong and so relevant here. It is profoundly simple. A child led me out of myself and into community. Adults can learn so much from children who are more honest, more inquisitive, more spontaneous, more fun-loving, quicker to make friends, and quicker to forgive. Children completely understand their dependence on others. They are so much more accepting of others. I'm not saying that we should be stupid-vulnerable and let people run right over us. Jesus said that we should be as wise as serpents, and serpents are careful to protect themselves. But at the same time, he said we should be as harmless as doves (Matthew 10:16). Christians living communally model dove-like simplicity, beauty, peace, and enthusiasm for life. It's childishness that makes handstand competitions more valuable than Hollywood bonanzas. If that disappoints anybody who was looking for communities with Disney fireworks, okay. Be disappointed.

> So the big, fireworks ending of this book is, instead, fizzling out with a damp splutter and puff. Is that what you're saying?

Uh . . . Okay. If someone is looking for the Hollywood pizazz and a big Olympic finish, go turn on the telly. What you'll find here is more like child's play. Yeah. This path is more playful than polished.

> How does this relate to what you said earlier about helping your readers discover one last treasure on their journey home?

Well, for one thing, that treasure is not marked with fireworks and Las Vegas signage. To discover it, you'll need a little childish curiosity. You see, all kinds of *perfect-life* and *perfect-body* and *perfect-day-at-the-beach* lies are thrown at us by the culture, every single day. These lies set a false standard for happiness and self-worth. They stamp their price tag on people and things, giving value to some and taking value from others. So when I talk about discovering treasure in the context of community, we first of all have to strip away all the shimmering façades and misconceptions about community.

> These misconceptions have been discussed earlier, but could you remind us of them?

That community is a place where all of our dreams come true. That it will fix everything that is wrong in our lives. That we need the perfect location, the perfect people, the perfect weather, the perfect health, and the perfect budget for community to work. The culture teaches us to be very self-centered about these things, when in fact, we need to think more about *others* if we want healthy community to work.

> So you remove the self-centered misconceptions about the perfect community. What remains after you strip all that away?

Authentic love remains.

Actually, that's not my answer. I only said that because it sounds really smart. But instead of being smart, let me be honest. Whenever I've stripped away all the crap, do you know what remains? This will be different for everyone, but for me, what remains is something like a cardboard box.

Give me a kid and a cardboard box, and I'll be the richest man in the world! Not just any box, mind you, but a big ol' washing machine or refrigerator box. When I have that, I get a big grin on my face and I tell that child, *Boy! Are we gonna have some fun!*

Then I cut a door and some windows in the box and we play house or store. We write graffiti on the walls. I deliver mail and then we fix the leaky plumbing. We make up new games until we get bored. Then one of us gets the idea to take the box outside and roll it down the hill. First, we roll it down the hill with one of us inside; then with the other. The box is all beat up now, not to mention we're hot and sweaty and I'm starting to get a headache. So we set the box upright, get inside, and bash the walls out.

Now we have a dance floor out in the middle of a green, grassy lawn, which is the perfect place to celebrate life.[1] Then we dance a while, finally collapsing on the crumpled cardboard.

"Do you see the elephant?' I say, pointing to a cotton-white cloud drifting across the sky.

"That's not an elephant," my little friend says. "That's an ele-*fart*!"

We laugh and laugh, celebrating life in all its craziness and beauty, while time and everything grown-up and serious ceases to exist.

Then my wife arrives, bringing popsicles and more kids. A lady who is walking her dog stops by to chat. I find myself sprawled on the dirty cardboard with two kids sitting on my chest. Someone or something is licking melted popsicle off my leg. I brush an insect from my cheek.

---

1. Thanks to Kenneth Caraway and Maril Parker, as mentioned in the Julian Project chapter.

Listening to a heated debate about who does or doesn't eat boogers, I sink farther into my cardboard pallet with a smile on my face.

Then, as if I am speaking in unison with so many others who have experienced this in community, I say:

This is it.

I have arrived.

This busted up, filthy box with sweaty, sticky kids is a little piece of heaven on earth. I'm crushed down, beaten, and broken, lower than these precious children who will someday learn that they are just as messed up as I am. That woman over there is my beloved wife who I know better than anyone on earth. That other woman . . . I don't have a clue who she is. That mutt . . . I wish it would stop licking my leg.

And together . . . we and God are making heaven come down.

Right here

Right now.

This is my treasure.

It's so humble and holy.

There is no working or doing here.

Only resting and being.

We love . . .

And we are loved.

This is the epic story I have lived out a handful of times, in different ways, and the climax is always the same. Always I have that deep assurance that I have arrived in a sacred place, having done nothing to make it happen . . . apart from getting out of the way and allowing it to happen.

Now you know my story.

Now you have seen my treasure.

This treasure is the journey's end. It is also the journey's beginning. It is the journey's middle. In fact, *this is the journey*. This is the *best* of life.

Ta da.

We have arrived.

Now you see how this book is not, really, about a search for anything "out there." It's about love and life with others, and heaven that grows today like a seed in your heart.

My temptation—and possibly yours—is dissatisfaction. Sure, it's okay to want more than a child and a box. If so, then invite more people into the

Down in the Dirt

picture. Sure, it's okay to ask for healing or restoration or balance for things that don't seem whole in your life. There's nothing wrong with that.

But right here and right now, is there anything better than a child and a box and the presence of God?

Absolutely not.

Life cannot get any better than this precious, sacred moment.

We must believe that's true, because if we cannot receive the most precious experience of life that surrounds us right here and now, will we even be able to receive it anywhere?

Will we?

In conclusion, this is the treasure I discovered on my knees, down in the dirt:

A box and a kid.

Now I wonder, my friend . . . what is *your* treasure?

Only you can answer that.

And if you're not sure what that treasure is, at least you know where to look . . . [2]

---

2. Before you set this book aside, check out the dedication page at the beginning of the book. You might find a special word for you there.

> I think a lot of people have this goal of feeling like you arrive at a certain destination, but really the journey is the destination. We are constantly becoming something. The journey is constantly changing. Beauty is found in the temporal, in the fleeting, in the good, and even in the bad. That is community, the ever-changing, always learning movement of life.
>
> —Brandon Mott,
> Dathouse

> It's actually best to be interdependent, to be in community with other people, to know that we need God together. Maybe that's why Jesus continually pointed towards children who are the most dependent people in the world. He said, 'If you want to enter the Kingdom, you need to enter like a child.' A child is very vulnerable—very in need—and yet that's who we're called to follow, not the princes and presidents. We're called to follow the children, and to know that we need God and other people.
>
> —Shane Claiborne,
> *The Simple Way*

Postscript

HOW TO BUILD COMMUNITY

Text by SyracuseCulturalWorkers.com, SCW copyright 1998[1]

Turn off your TV
Leave your house
Know your neighbors
Look up when you are walking
Greet people
Sit on your stoop
Plant flowers
Use your library
Play together
Buy from local merchants
Share what you have
Help a lost dog
Take children to the park
Garden together
Support neighborhood schools
Fix it even if you didn't break it

1. Syracuse Cultural Workers, "How to Build Community," copyright 1998, used with permission, accessed June 2017, www.syracuseculturalworkers.com/products/notecard-how-to-build-community.

Have potlucks
Honor elders
Pick up litter
Read stories aloud
Dance in the street
Talk to the mail carrier
Listen to the birds
Put up a swing
Help carry something heavy
Barter for your goods
Start a tradition
Ask a question
Hire young people for odd jobs
Organize a block party
Bake extra and share
Ask for help when you need it
Open your shades
Sing together
Share your skills
Take back the night
Turn up the music
Turn down the music
Listen before you react to anger
Mediate a conflict
Seek to understand
Learn from new and uncomfortable angles
Know that no one is silent though many are not heard
Work to change this

SOME THOUGHTS BEFORE JOINING OR STARTING A COMMUNITY

When my wife and kids and I were running our bed and breakfast, we often met people who'd say, "I'd love to have a bed and breakfast. It's something I've always dreamed of."

Postscript

When I asked these folks how they were sharing their home and space with other people *now*, a common answer was, "Oh . . . we don't do that much."

Then I would explain that Joan and I had nearly always shared our home with others. We loved being a gathering place for friends and festivities. Someone was often living in our spare bedroom, and Joan loved reading books on cooking, gardening, and hospitality. For us, starting the Fox and Fiddle bed and breakfast was simply stepping up all the things we were already doing. I would suggest that if hospitality was perhaps new to these people, they might want to start on a small scale before taking their dream to the big leagues. It kind'a seemed obvious to Joan and me.

In the same way, I caution folks against believing that they can seamlessly move into community if it's something they don't know how to cultivate or find in their lives today. People who have trouble connecting with others can move into community and still be isolated.

The first step in coming home to community is to embrace community and stability . . . right here and now. This was the main point of chapter 7, which spoke of childlikeness and creating simple moments of sacred community, on any ordinary day, in common places.

Additionally, these are some thoughts that you might find helpful:

- I'd suggest not making a move until you have found peace where you are.
- Imagine what joy-filled community would look like right where you are. What changes can you make to cultivate community? What is best *not* to change, but to accept?
- Consider having friends over regularly for food, games, arts, crafts, music, gardening, book discussions, projects, and to share other interests and needs you have in common.
- Share a room in your house with family, friends, and people in need.
- Cultivate simplicity and childlikeness. Play with a child!
- Get *real* and wean yourself from too much media and electronic device usage.
- Rearrange or renovate your home and gardens to create spaces that will cultivate community.
- Share more of everything you have with others.

- Seek counseling if you have a long history of repelling friendships. Honestly seek to uncover any unresolved issues that might be working against you.
- Discover contentment, even if your life isn't perfect . . . *especially* if your life isn't perfect.
- Talk with your closest friends about your visions for community.
- Do fewer activities alone. Do more activities with friends.
- Like people who you've considered to be unlikeable.
- Know Jesus better, and study his example of love.

Shane Claiborne of The Simple Way Community gave me this piece of advice: "When I invite people to build community, I think of it like beginning to exercise muscles that have atrophied. You don't run a marathon. You have to learn to move a little bit. So we can start by growing relationships in deeper ways, and beginning to share money and life and accountability and prayer and meals and things like that. Not everybody's gonna move to the streets of New York City. I think there are a lot of creative ways to find and build and create community beginning right where you are."

So take small steps toward community right here and now. Then, when your branches and roots are bumping up against the walls of that box, look into ways of taking down the walls and discovering a deeper experience of community. Consider partnering with others in your town or neighborhood. Visit some of the communities that you find online or in this book. Ask questions and learn from those who are ahead of you on this journey.

And let me know about your journey. You are welcome to contact me through www.foxandfiddle.net with your questions and comments. I would love to hear from you!

Above all, never stop taking small steps toward community. Remember that the God who made you in his image is himself community: Father, Son, and Holy Spirit. Moving toward the community of believers is moving deeper into his image.

Ask yourself:

How much time do I have left on this little green and blue planet?

Am I satisfied with my life as it has been?

Are my friendships deep and enduring?

POSTSCRIPT

Am I regularly spurred on toward love and good works by God's people around me?

Is it time to increase the intensity of sharing, giving, receiving, laughter, and friendship in my life?

Is it time to lesson my attachment to material things, and increase my attachment to people?

Am I ready to release my fears, break the chains, loosen my grip on job, finances, home, and all the material things that have been my security, so that I might receive a higher level of love, contentment, joy, and fulfillment in relationship with others?

Only you can answer these questions.
The next step is yours. I wish you much joy in the journey!

Appendix 1

Intentional Christian Community Associations

THESE UMBRELLA ORGANIZATIONS OR religious associations bring together intentional Christian communities that have similar beliefs and practices. In the chapter featuring intentional Christian communities, I did not write about communities from the largest, denominational or sect-based groups that are mentioned here.

Bruderhof—
www.bruderhof.com

Bruderhof—the "place of brothers"—was birthed from post-World War I Germany as an expression of community, justice, pacifism, and shared financials and possessions. Like other groups with Anabaptist roots or affiliations, members dress simply and women wear head coverings. They have more than twenty-seven hundred members in twenty-three communities on four continents.

Catholic Fraternity of Charismatic Covenant Communities—
www.catholicfraternity.org/

This international association links charismatic Catholic communities together, facilitating dialog between communities, strengthening

Appendix 1

connections with the Catholic Church, and encouraging growth in the gifts of the Spirit.

Catholic Worker Communities—
www.catholicworker.org/communities

Catholic Worker Communities grew out of the poverty and injustices of the Great Depression. They have over 245 communities and farms in eleven different countries. Key values include nonviolence, justice, voluntary poverty, prayer, hospitality, and helping poor and oppressed people.

Christian Community Development Association—
www.ccda.org

Established by Dr. John Perkins in 1989, CCDA exists to bring spiritual, emotional, physical, economic, and social restoration in the context of Christian communities that are planted and rooted in the neighborhoods of greatest need.

Eastern Orthodox Monasticism

There are many different expressions of Eastern Orthodox monasticism, including Greek, Antiochian, Russian, and more. Search online to learn more.

Hutterite Communities—
www.hutterites.org

About fifty thousand Hutterites live in over two hundred communities in northwestern North America. They practice pacifism, shared possessions, simple dress, and head coverings for women, as do many other communities with similar Anabaptist roots.

Intentional Christian Community Associations

Mennonite Communities—
http://mennoniteusa.org

Not all Mennonites live in community, but many intentional Christian communities have aligned themselves with the Mennonite Church because of its Anabaptist foundation and communitarian beliefs.

Missional Wisdom Foundation—
www.missionalwisdom.com

This organization primarily serves the United Methodist Church in developing New Monastic intentional communities. The Susanna Wesley House is under this umbrella organization.

Old Order Amish—
http://amishamerica.com

The Amish are known for plain clothes, simple living, separation from secular society, and avoidance of modern technology. Like many other communal Christians, they grew out of an Anabaptist tradition.

Roman Catholic Monastic Orders—
http://theolibrary.shc.edu/orders.htm

Roman Catholic monastic and missionary orders such as the Benedictines, Franciscans, Dominicans, Jesuits, and more have lived in community since the early centuries after Christ. They represent diverse monastic expressions of Catholicism. These Roman Catholic orders give inspiration to the New Monastic movement, which is a primarily-Protestant expression of monasticism in a post-modern context.

Shalom Mission Communities—
www.shalommissioncommunities.org

Shalom Mission Communities is an association of six Anabaptist communities, including three that are featured in this book. They practice non-violence, justice, prayer, worship, Bible study, and service to others.

Appendix 1

Sword of the Spirit—
www.swordofthespirit.net

Over seventy-five communities and seventeen thousand members worldwide belong to Sword of the Spirit. They describe themselves as a "community of communities," being ecumenical, including both Protestants and Catholics. Each community that belongs to Sword of the Spirit is self-governing, although all communities support each other and are accountable to similar beliefs and practices. Communities typically do not share all possessions in common, but members contribute a portion of their income for community needs. Sword of the Spirit has subgroups which include the charismatic Association of Ecumenical Communities (www.swordofthespirit.net/aec/), a community of single women called Bethany (http://bethany.swordofthespirit.net/), and a Catholic association called Christ the King (http://swordofthespirit.net/cka/).

Appendix 2

Community Covenants

IF YOU ARE INTERESTED in possibly joining an intentional Christian community, ask to see the covenant that binds members together. Some of these covenants are posted online. Community covenants tend to be quite general, using broad language to bind members together in servanthood, other-centeredness, holiness, submission to pastoral care and God's Word, compassion for poor and oppressed people, conformity to community structure and practices, and more.

The Alleluia Community covenant gives us a good picture of some of the typical provisions of a community covenant. Here is an excerpt from that covenant:

> In his joy and peace, therefore, we yield our lives to Jesus; everything past, present and future and we agree to:
>
> Love one another as brothers and sisters in Christ.
>
> Be faithful to our commitments to community prayer, fellowship and service, seeking always the vision and the growth to which the Spirit is calling us.
>
> Accept responsibility for community order.
>
> Foster the growth of the community by accepting responsibility for a program of Christian initiation and formation in community life.
>
> Recognize the headship of the coordinators and agree to obey, correct, and pray for them.

APPENDIX 2

> Accept our financial responsibility to the community.
>
> Be held to this covenant and to hold one another to it.
>
> We promise to love one another and to call each other to holiness. We believe that this is the way God has chosen for our sanctification. We willingly ask him to use it. We regard this as a solemn and serious commitment which we enter in good conscience, freely, and in faith.[1]

Some covenants encourage members to make a lifetime commitment, although all allow for the possibility of people leaving community. For example, Church of the Sojourners members agree to "be together for as long as God allows."[2]

I appreciate how explicit and specific some covenants are, as the Rule of the Lotus House illustrates in these selected excerpts:

> 2. We will call nothing our own, but everything will be ours in common. Our property will be available to whoever is in need, just as the early church *had all things in common* and *distribution was made to each one according to each one's need*. Expenses for the house will be shared, including food, utilities, and rent. We will also share household responsibilities such as cleaning, cooking, and yard work . . .
>
> 4. At least two nights a week we will prepare a meal and gather around the table as a community, recalling that Jesus is encountered in the breaking of bread. Our table will be open to all, but especially to the poor, the crippled, the lame, and the blind . . .
>
> 6. The Lotus House is a house of hospitality. If one of us encounters a stranger in need of shelter for the night, our home is open to them, *for by doing this some have entertained angels without knowing it* . . .
>
> 8. We submit ourselves completely to Christ's Church. We will continue to worship regularly on the Lord's Day with our home congregations, serving them faithfully and submitting to their oversight . . .

---

1. The Alleluia Community, "Our Covenant," accessed June 2017, www.yeslord.com/about-us/our-covenant/.

2. Church of the Sojourners, "Covenant," accessed June 2017, http://churchofthesojourners.org/covenant/.

12. We covenant to imitate the simplicity and humility of Jesus. *Though rich beyond measure he emptied Himself for our sake* and chose poverty in this world. Let us remember that *if we have food and clothes, we will be satisfied with that*. In our speech, our dress, and our home, let us have nothing to attract undue attention; after all, we are not trying to please by our outward appearances, but by our good lives . . .

15. Because *the earth is the Lord's and all that is in it*, we are committed to living in harmony with and lessening our harmful impact upon the earth and the community. Thus, as good stewards of Creation, we will strive to decrease our energy consumption and increase our efficiency in the House in the areas of transportation, heating and cooling, and water usage. We will consume less, discard less, and take care of the gifts we have been given. We will buy necessary clothes and goods second-hand when possible. We will also try to live more sustainably by growing and preserving as much of our own food as possible; what remains to be bought will be organic and local when possible. We will eat less meat, especially beef.[3]

The Epworth Rule of Life is another good covenant that you can find reprinted at the end of the Susanna Wesley House section.

---

3. Lotus House, "The Rule of the Lotus House," accessed June 2017, https://lotushouse.wordpress.com/rule/.

Intentional Christian Community Resources

Alexander, John. *Being Church: Reflections on How to Live as the People of God* (Eugene, OR: Wipf and Stock, 2012).

Arnold, Eberhard et al., *Called to Community: The Life Jesus Wants for His People* (Walden, NY: Plough, 2016).

Belic, Roko. *Happy* movie (New York: Wadi Rum, 2011). This intriguing video shows how interdependence and happiness are directly related. Note also how cohousing arrangements increase happiness.

Boiler Room Network of communities and 24–7 Prayer, "Boiler Rooms website," accessed June 2017, www.24-7prayer.com/boilerrooms. A worldwide family of missional and monastic communities committed to prayer, mission, and justice.

Bonhoeffer, Dietrich. *Life Together: The Classic Exploration of Christian in Community* (New York: Harper Row, 1954).

Cahill, Thomas. *How the Irish Saved Civilization: The Untold Story of Ireland's Heroic Role from the Fall of Rome to the Rise of Medieval Europe*, (New York: Anchor, 1998).

Claiborne, Shane, Jonathan Wilson-Hartgrove, and Enuma Okoro. *Common Prayer; A Liturgy for Ordinary Radicals* (Nashville: Zondervan, 2010).

Claiborne, Shane. *The Irresistible Revolution: Living as an Ordinary Radical* (Grand Rapids: Zondervan, 2016).

Cohousing Association of the United States, "The Cohousing Directory website," accessed June 2017, www.cohousing.org/directory.

Dreher, Rod. *The Benedict Option: A Strategy for Christians in a Post-Christian Nation* (New York: Sentinel, 2017).

Fellowship for Intentional Community, "Map of Intentional Communities website," accessed June 2017, www.ic.org/directory/maps. This resource includes communities of all and no spiritual beliefs. You can search for Christian communities on the Advanced Search page: www.ic.org/directory/search.

Intentional Christian Community Resources

Fellowship for Intentional Community, *Communities Directory: The Guide to Intentional Communities and Cooperative Living* (Rutledge, MO: Fellowship for Intentional Community, 2016).

Grenz, Stanley. *Created for Community: Connecting Christian Belief with Christian Living* (Grand Rapids: Baker Academic, 2015).

Janzen, David. *The Intentional Christian Community Handbook: For Idealists, Hypocrites, and Wannabe Disciples of Jesus* (Brewster, MA: Paraclete, 2012).

Lynn, Monty, Kent Smith, and Brandon Young. "Modeling Intentional Community: Resources website," accessed June 2017, *http://modelingintentionalcommunity.org/resources/*.

Lupton, Robert. *Toxic Charity: How the Church Hurts Those They Help and How to Reverse It* (New York: HarperOne, 2011). This book is not about community, but it describes a wonderful dignity-building approach to helping people in need.

New Creation Christian Community, "Links to Other Christian Communities website," accessed June 2017, http://christiancommunity.org.uk/links-to-other-christian-communities.

Parish Collective, "Parish Collective website," accessed June 2017, http://parishcollective.org. This is also a wonderful resource for networking with others and equipping you to move toward community.

Plough Publishing, *Plough Quarterly* magazine (Walden, NY: Plough). See also articles at their website: www.Plough.com.

Pohl, Christine. *Living Into Community; Cultivating Practices that Sustain Us* (Grand Rapids: Eerdmans, 2012).

The Simple Way Community, "Community of Communities website," accessed June 2017, www.communityofcommunities.info. This is one of the best resources for connecting with specific intentional Christian communities.

Smith, Luther. *Intimacy and Mission; Intentional Community as Crucible for Radical Discipleship* (Eugene, OR: Herald, 1994).

Thresholds, "Thresholds Home Page," accessed June 2017, http://thresholdscommunity.org/. Thresholds is a network of missional leaders and coaches offering counseling and seminars for community support.

Wilson-Hartgrove, Jonathan. *New Monasticism: What It Has to Say to Today's Church* (Grand Rapids: Brazos, 2008).

Wilson-Hartgrove, Jonathan. *The Wisdom of Stability; Rooting Faith in a Mobile Culture* (Brewster, MA: Paraclete, 2010).

www.ingramcontent.com/pod-product-compliance
Lightning Source LLC
Chambersburg PA
CBHW051634230426
43669CB00013B/2295